Preface

Writing this Guide has been both rewarding and challenging. It has been rewarding to deal with an area of such potential importance to the lives of so many people, young and old and in-between. There are very few of us who do not feel, at some stage or other of our lives, that we have been discriminated against because we are too young or too old. We have felt that it was unfair, and that 'someone ought to do something about it'. Well, someone has. And it is a rewarding experience to explore how the effort to do something about it is likely to work out. At the same time, it is in some ways much more difficult than dealing with established legislation, familiar with the passage of time, and illuminated by the interpretation of the appellate courts.

There is another feature which has proved challenging in relation to this Guide. The interest generated by the Regulations has been enormous. In its consultation process on the draft regulations, the Department of Trade and Industry received nearly 400 responses, from interested parties who included professional organisations, trade unions, companies, local authorities and specialist campaigning bodies. It is likely that the implementation of the Regulations themselves will foster even more interest. That means that any Guide should make the subject of age discrimination as accessible as possible to a wide audience The concepts involved are legal ones, and will be interpreted by the courts and the tribunals. That means that there are points where a legal discussion is necessary, and the Regulations (Appendix 1) and the Directive upon which they are based (Appendix 2) are available within these covers for readers to follow the precise wording. At the same time, I have tried in the commentary which forms the main part of the book to address a wider audience – including employers and employees and those who advise them. This task is helped by the inclusion (Appendix 3) of the helpful and user-friendly guidance issued by ACAS.

I would welcome feedback and the correction of any errors, and can be reached by e-mail: j.m.sprack@btinternet.com

My sincere thanks are due to my publishers at Tottel, who have made efforts above and beyond the call of duty to ensure that the book gets into the hands of those who need it as soon as possible. In particular, I am grateful to Sarah Thomas for her enthusiastic adoption of the project, and to Heather Saward for her professional expertise and wise counsel.

John Sprack

Guide to the
Age Discrimination
Regulations 2006

Guide to the Age Discrimination Regulations 2006

By

John Sprack, BA LLB, Barrister

Tottel

publishing

Tottel Publishing, Maxwelton House, 41–43 Boltro Road, Haywards Heath, West Sussex, RH16 1BJ

A CIP Catalogue record for this book is available from the British Library.

ISBN 13 978 1 84592 307 5

ISBN 10 1 84592 307 3

Typeset by Kerrypress Ltd, Luton, Beds

Printed and bound in Great Britain by Antony Rowe, Chippenham, Wilts

Contents

Chapter 1   Introduction

Historically, there has been no legislation in the United Kingdom dealing with age discrimination. Discrimination on grounds of age, in its various forms, is endemic throughout the British economy, and dealing with it will inevitably involve a seismic shift in employment practices. In recent years, it has become apparent that (quite apart from the human impact upon individuals concerned), age discrimination is a source of economic inefficiency. The age profile of the population has undergone a dramatic shift, due to higher rates of life expectancy, while the birth rate remains static. For a buoyant economy, it is necessary to encourage the employment of older people, as well as ensuring that there are no discriminatory barriers in the way of young entrants to the labour market. As the Department of Trade and Industry put it in their *Regulatory Impact Assessment for the Employment Equality (Age) Regulations* in March 2006:

> 'Discrimination results in poorer quality matches in labour markets, which leads to lower national output ... Older workers may find it difficult to re-enter the labour market after a period of absence because of negative stereotypes, even though they are still productive. Young workers may also find it difficult to enter the labour market initially.'

In April 2000, a Cabinet Office Report *Winning the Generation Game: Improving Opportunities for People aged 50–65* estimated that low employment rates among older workers reduced Gross Domestic Product by around £16 billion per annum.

Although the United Kingdom government has been aware of this situation for a number of years, the impetus to grapple with the problem through legislation has come from the European Union. In 2000, the Member States agreed a Directive that required them to outlaw discrimination on grounds of religion or belief, disability, age and sexual orientation in the areas of employment and vocational training – 'Council Directive 2000/78/EC of 27 November 2000 establishing a general framework for equal treatment in employment and occupation' (the Directive). As far as the United Kingdom is concerned, there was already in place legislation against discrimination on grounds of disability (the Disability Discrimination Act 1995), although a number of changes were made as a result of the requirements of the Directive. In 2003, regulations were introduced to outlaw discrimination on grounds of religion or belief and sexual orientation.

1

As far as age is concerned, however, the process was more lengthy. Member States had until 2 December 2003 to implement most of the provisions in the Directive. But an additional period of three years was permitted for the implementation of the provisions on age discrimination. The United Kingdom government made use of this period of grace, and embarked on a lengthy process of consultation. The first stage of this consultation (*Towards Equality and Diversity: Implementing the Employment and Race Directives*) was undertaken in December 2001 in respect of several of the strands of anti-discrimination law, but that relating to age provoked a large number of responses. In July 2003, the consultation *Equality and Diversity: Age Matters* was devoted exclusively to the subject of legislation relating to age discrimination. Again, a large number of responses were received, and the government formed the view, largely as a result of those received from business, that there ought to be a 'default retirement age' (at which employers could compulsorily retire employees without any need for justification).

The draft Regulations were published in July 2005, and were accompanied by a further consultation process – *Equality and Diversity: Coming of Age*. The draft Regulations contained the default retirement age of 65, and also embodied a number of other features which have found their way into the Regulations as enacted. The consultation process upon the draft ended in October 2005, and the Department of Trade and Industry (DTI) began work upon the final draft Regulations, which were laid before Parliament early in March 2006. That final draft was approved by both Houses of Parliament by the end of March, with a commencement date of 1 October 2006. The implementation of the Directive therefore takes place some two months before the extended deadline. The date of commencement was apparently chosen because of the DTI's policy of introducing new employment legislation on only two dates each year – 1 October being one of them.

The Employment Equality (Age) Regulations 2006 (the Regulations) are structured as follows:

(a) Part 1 covers interpretation and sets out what constitutes the different forms of discrimination, including victimisation, harassment and instructions to discriminate.

(b) Part 2 deals with discrimination in the field of employment and vocational training. It defines the ambit of the protection, setting out in different regulations the provisions covering such groups as contract workers, office-holders and partners. It contains regulations which specifically deal with such bodies as institutions of further and higher education, employment agencies and trade organisations.

(c) Part 3 provides for the liability of employers for their employees and principals for their agents, as well as those who aid unlawful acts.

(d) Part 4 sets out a series of exceptions from the operation of Parts 2 and 3, such as those for statutory authority, for retirement and for positive action.

(e) Part 5 deals with enforcement, granting jurisdiction generally to the employment tribunals (except in relation to institutions of further and higher education where the county and sheriff courts have jurisdiction). It also covers matters such as the burden of proof, questionnaires, time limits and remedies.

(f) Part 6 deals with supplemental matters, including the application of the Regulations to the Crown and to Parliamentary staff.

(g) Various schedules flesh out the detail of the Regulations. The most important are Schedule 2 (pension schemes) and Schedules 6 and 7 (which deal with the new duty on employers to consider any request by an employee to work on after his retirement date). In addition, there are a number of important changes to other legislation, which are mainly contained in Schedule 8. Of particular note are the amendments to the Employment Relations Act 1996, which recast the law on unfair dismissal.

The text of the Regulations is set out in Appendix 1 to this book. Appendix 2 contains the text of the Directive. Appendix 3 consists of the Guidance issued by the Arbitration, Conciliation and Advisory Service (ACAS) to accompany the Regulations. It does not have the force of law, but contains useful explanation, concentrating on the practical application of the Regulations for employers in particular, although there is also guidance for employees. There is a detailed flowchart which appears as Annex 5 to the ACAS Guidance, and which sets out the stages to consider in deciding whether a retirement is fair, in the light of the amended unfair dismissal provisions.

When the Regulations were finalised, the DTI published extensive Explanatory Notes to accompany them. For the most part, these set out in summary form the provisions contained within the Regulations. On occasion, they put forward the reasons why the government believes that the Regulations implement the Directive, and provide some assistance in interpretation. Where relevant, the text of this book cites the Explanatory Notes as part of its commentary.

As far as the layout of this book is concerned:

(a) Chapter 1 (this chapter) gives a very brief historical and legal context of the Regulations.

(b) Chapter 2 deals with the definitions of discrimination (direct and indirect), harassment, victimisation and instructions to discriminate, and gives examples of what is likely to be unlawful. It also covers the liability of employers and principals, and those aiding unlawful acts. Flowcharts are provided to show the way in which direct and indirect discrimination operate.

(c)   Chapter 3 indicates the scope of the protection afforded by the Regulations – the groups of people whom it covers. It makes it clear that the ambit of the protection varies significantly from one group to another – those who are employees in the strict sense of the word, employees in an extended sense to include those on a contract for services, office-holders and partners are all covered, together with other groups, but the nature of the coverage differs depending on the regulation which one examines.

(d)   Chapter 4 deals with the central concept of justification. The legislation on age-related treatment is unique in that it allows justification for direct, as well as indirect, discrimination. The components of justification – legitimate aims and proportionate means – are explored. Examples are put forward as to the way in which the defence is likely to operate.

(e)   Chapter 5 describes the exceptions to the operation of the legislation. It covers genuine occupational requirements, statutory authority, national security and positive action. Other exceptions are left to be described in their appropriate context.

(f)   In Chapter 6, the process of recruitment and selection is dealt with in some detail. 'Danger points' are identified, where the employer in selecting staff is likely to fall foul of the Regulations. Each stage of the recruitment process is looked at in turn. The chapter ends with a checklist setting out the points which an employer ought to bear in mind during the selection and recruitment process – to avoid discrimination generally, as well as age discrimination in particular.

(g)   Chapter 7 looks at the Regulations as they affect the terms and conditions of workers. It examines some of the important exemptions, particularly that enabling employers to give preferential treatment on the basis of length of service. Examples are given of the way in which such exemptions might operate in practice.

(h)   The most complex (and potentially most significant) part of the Regulations relates to retirement and dismissal, and this aspect is covered in Chapter 8. The controversy surrounding the default retirement age is explored – do the Regulations fail to implement the Directive by allowing employers to retire employees compulsorily at age 65? The important new 'duty to consider procedure' contained in Schedules 6 and 7, is dealt with. Checklists are provided for both the employer and the employee in relation to this procedure. The major changes to the law on unfair dismissal are examined in some detail. A table and a flowchart are provided to assist understanding of the way in which the concepts operate.

(i) Chapter 9 deals with the provisions related to pension schemes, contained within Schedule 2.

(j) Chapter 10 covers the amendments which have been made to other legislation by Schedules 8 and 9, although some of the amendments are considered elsewhere in their natural context, such as the provisions relating to unfair dismissal, which fall naturally into Chapter 8.

(k) Chapter 11 is devoted to enforcement in the tribunals and the courts, covering matters such as the burden of proof, questionnaires and time limits. There is also a discussion of the implications where it is asserted that the Regulations do not implement the Directive.

(l) Chapter 12 deals with remedies. Some of the text relates specifically to remedies under the Regulations, but there are also summaries of the general law relating to remedies for discrimination and unfair dismissal, which will apply equally to claims under the Regulations.

2 What Constitutes Age Discrimination?

The ways in which the Age Discrimination Regulations can be contravened are set out in regs 3, 4, 5 and 6. They set out the following categories of unlawful act:

(a)   direct discrimination;

(b)   indirect discrimination;

(c)   victimisation;

(d)   instructions to discriminate;

(e)   harassment.

This chapter deals with each of these five forms of unlawful conduct. It also covers vicarious liability on the part of employers and principals, and liability for those who aid unlawful acts. The topic of justification (which has relevance to direct and indirect discrimination) is covered in Chapter 4. In brief, an act which on the face of it is discriminatory may be lawful if it is justified – shown to be 'a proportionate means of achieving a legitimate aim'.

Direct discrimination

Regulation 3(1) states in part:

> 'For the purposes of these Regulations, a person ("A") discriminates against another person ("B") if:
>
> (a)   on grounds of B's age, A treats B less favourably than he treats or would treat other persons ... and A cannot show the treatment ... to be a proportionate means of achieving a legitimate aim.'

The feature of this definition of direct discrimination, which is unique in discrimination law, is that justification provides a defence. In the case of any other prohibited form of direct discrimination (race, sex, disability, sexual orientation, religion or belief), justification cannot be put forward in order to escape liability. This aspect of direct age discrimination will be dealt with in more detail in Chapter 4. The reasoning process involved is illustrated in the flowchart on direct discrimination which appears at the end of this chapter.

B's age

The way in which reg 3(1)(a) is worded ('on grounds of B's age') means that there is no coverage of discrimination by reason of the age of someone with whom B associates. This differs, for example, from the Race Relations Act 1976, where the relevant wording is 'on grounds of race' and the case law has established that there can be discrimination based on the association of the complainant. For example, a racist employer who subjected a white employee to a detriment on the grounds that he was married to an Asian would be liable for a claim of racial discrimination. This principle does not apply to direct age discrimination, as the following example illustrates:

> B's partner is much younger than her, and her line manager finds this unacceptable. He refuses to allow B to do voluntary overtime, saying 'You will only use the money on your toy boy'. He has treated her less favourably on grounds of age (her *partner's* age) but the treatment is not on grounds of *her* age. There is no apparent basis for a claim of direct discrimination, although there may be a valid claim for harassment (see later in this chapter).

Comparators

In order to establish that he has been directly discriminated against, B has to show that he has been treated 'less favourably' than other persons. This brings in the need for a comparator – someone with whom B can be compared to determine whether there is a possibility that he has been discriminated against. The comparator's characteristics are defined by reg 3(2):

> 'A comparison of B's case with that of another person under paragraph (1) must be such that the relevant circumstances in the one case are the same, or not materially different, in the other.'

The terms of the definition of the comparator are similar to those in other discrimination legislation. As is the case with regard to those provisions, the comparator may be a real one, or a hypothetical one. When one looks for a comparator, it is necessary to identify an individual of a different age, who has all the other characteristics of the complainant which have relevance to the way in which he was treated. It is apparent, however, that there are differences (and difficulties) in selecting a comparator by contrast to the position in other types of discrimination. There is usually a clear boundary, in respect of other allegations of discrimination, between the complainant and his comparator: the comparator is male, the complainant is female; the comparator from one ethnic group, the complainant is not from that group. Where the allegation is of age discrimination, however, the position is not so clear-cut. Age can be viewed as a spectrum, and the comparator could theoretically be taken from any point on that spectrum – close to the complainant, or distant from him. An example illustrates the point:

> B (aged 25) alleges that he was chosen for compulsory transfer to a distant depot because of his youth. It is his case that management wanted to avoid sending older workers to the depot in question because of favouritism towards them on account of their age. He chooses as his comparator C (aged 31) who was not sent to the depot. He avoids choosing D (aged 35) who was. Clearly, the employer will have a powerful argument (in the person of D) for showing that their decision was not 'on grounds of age'. But that does not prevent B from choosing C as his comparator, which may have important consequences in relation to the burden of proof (see Chapter 11).

'On grounds of'

In order to constitute direct age discrimination, it is not enough that the complainant should have been treated less favourably than his comparator. The treatment must have been *on grounds of* his age. The unlawful reason (age) must have been an effective cause of the detrimental treatment. It need not be the only or even the main cause, as long as it is an effective cause: *Owen & Briggs v James* [1982] IRLR 502, CA (dealing with race discrimination, but the same principles apply). In deciding whether the unlawful reason (e.g. race or age) caused the less favourable treatment, the tribunal will have regard to 'the surrounding circumstances and the previous history' as well as to the act of alleged discrimination itself: *Anya v University of Oxford* [2001] IRLR 377, CA. The reasoning process of the tribunal is considered further when the burden of proof is examined in Chapter 11.

Apparent age

It is made clear in reg 3(3)(b) that the reference to 'age' in the prohibition against direct discrimination 'includes B's apparent age'. For example:

> A company interviews internally for a management position. It is well aware from its records that one of the applicants, B, is aged 37. However, B is of a somewhat careworn appearance, and the interviewers are anxious that the appointee should look young and (as they put it in their notes of interview) dynamic. As a result, they decide not to

appoint B, and appoint someone also aged 37, but of a more youthful appearance. In preparation for the tribunal case brought by B, the notes of interview are disclosed to his representatives. The fact that they decided not to appoint him constitutes less favourable treatment. Is it on grounds of his age? It is, in view of the definition of age so as to include apparent age. The employer will be liable unless it can justify its decision objectively (see Chapter 4).

Indirect discrimination

The prohibition against indirect age discrimination is contained in reg 3(1)(b). It will take place where:

(a)   A applies to B a provision, criterion or practice (PCP);

(b)   the PCP applies equally to other persons;

(c)   the PCP puts persons of B's age group at a particular disadvantage; and

(d)   B suffers that disadvantage.

The concepts involved are similar to those in the legislation on discrimination related to sex, race, sexual orientation, religion or belief. At the end of this chapter there is a flowchart illustrating the concepts involved in indirect discrimination.

Provision, criterion or practice

The need to establish a provision, criterion or practice is relatively undemanding, as is illustrated by the sex discrimination case of *British Airways plc v Starmer* [2005] IRLR 862. Mrs Starmer was employed by BA as a pilot. She applied to work on a part-time basis, seeking to work 50 per cent of full time, so as to accommodate her childcare arrangements. This was refused and she was told she must work 75 per cent of full time. She claimed indirect sex discrimination. The EAT held that the tribunal (which found in her favour) was entitled to find that the employer's decision was a 'provision' notwithstanding that it was a discretionary management decision. A provision did not have to be an absolute bar. It could allow for exceptions to be made.

Applying equally to others

If the employer did not apply the provision, criterion or practice (PCP) equally to others, then it is likely that the situation would constitute direct discrimination. However, the wording of the Regulations (and the equivalent legislation in relation to indirect sex discrimination, etc) does require that the employer 'applies or would apply [the PCP] equally to others'. In the *Starmer* case, the EAT emphasised that there was no necessity for the PCP actually to apply to others. What was required in order to test whether the PCP was discriminatory was to extrapolate it to others. This gives force to the phrase 'which he applies or would apply' which appears in the age discrimination regulations as it does in the sex discrimination legislation.

Places his age group at a particular disadvantage

For a claim for indirect discrimination to succeed, it is necessary for the complainant to show that those in his age group were put at a particular disadvantage. The words bear their common-sense meaning, and there is no need to show financial loss, as has been held at various times in relation to other sorts of discrimination.

The concept of an 'age group' is, however, unique to age discrimination. It is necessary to identify the right 'pools' for comparison. First: what is the pool to which B (the complainant) belongs? Second: what is the pool of comparators in relation to whom B's pool has been put at a disadvantage? In each case, one needs to identify the 'relevant population' (see *Jones v Chief Adjudication Officer* [1990] IRLR 533, CA), and then divide it into groups representing those who satisfy the provision, criterion or practice and those who do not. In a sex discrimination case, one then needs to determine how many in each of the groups are women, and look at the overall figures in order to see whether women are under- or over-represented in each of the groups.

These tasks have proved difficult and controversial in relation to other forms of discrimination (see for example *Rutherford v Secretary of State for Trade and Industry* (*No 2*) [2004] IRLR 892, CA). But these problems pale into insignificance when one looks at indirect age discrimination. The reason is that, in performing these tasks, the 'age group' concept comes into play. It is defined in reg 3(3)(a) as meaning 'a group of persons defined by reference to age, whether by reference to a particular age or a range of ages'. It seems that this definition is only of relevance to indirect discrimination, as the phrase 'age group' appears in reg 3(1)(b) but not 3(1)(a).

The problems associated with the notion of 'age group' can be illustrated by the following example:

> Company A carries out a series of redundancies. In the process, they take seniority into account as one of the criteria: each year with the company entitles the employee to one point. There are other criteria involved, such as attendance record and appraisal history. At the end

of the process, the 100 employees with the most points are retained, and the remaining 60 are made redundant. Employee B (aged 35 and with the company three years) is among those declared redundant. He alleges that the selection process was indirectly discriminatory in relation to age. It is not directly discriminatory, since age itself was not the basis upon which selection took place. In deciding whether the employer has acted unlawfully, it will be necessary to determine the relevant pools. Assume that B selects 50 as the dividing line. He may then be able to show adverse impact ('particular disadvantage') for those aged under 50, who have been disproportionately selected for redundancy. The company for its part, however, argues that, if one takes 40 as the dividing line, an equal percentage of workers aged below 40 were selected for redundancy as those over 40. The tribunal will be faced with the Herculean task of determining which is the proper dividing line, and hence which are the proper 'pools' for comparison. In these circumstances, the cautious employer with hindsight will no doubt wish that it had avoided any such potentially indirectly discriminatory criteria! (Note that the company will be entitled to advance a defence of objective justification, even if the selection criteria are shown to have disadvantaged B's group.)

'Puts B at that disadvantage'

It is not sufficient for the complainant to show that the group to which he belongs is disadvantaged. He must himself be put at that disadvantage in order to satisfy the requirements of indirect discrimination. In the example above, if B was not himself found redundant, he would not be able to satisfy this limb of the test.

Examples of indirect discrimination

Some illustrations are given of what might constitute indirect discrimination, and how it differs from direct discrimination. In relation to all these scenarios, it needs to be remembered that it will still be open to the employer to provide objective justification (see Chapter 4), and thus show that the act in question was not unlawful.

Company A imposes a health test upon all its employees, and makes it clear that those who fail will be candidates for dismissal. This is likely to be held to be indirectly discriminatory (although it may be justified and hence lawful). Those who are older will be more likely to fail the health test. If the company laid down that only those over 50 were to be tested, then it would be direct discrimination 'on grounds of age'.

Company B seeks applicants for a position as a driver, stating that those who apply must have held a clean driving licence for four years or more. This would be indirectly discriminatory (subject to arguments as to justification). Those under the age of 21 would be unable to fulfil the criterion. If the company refused to entertain applications from those under the age of 21, that would constitute direct discrimination (again, subject to any possible defence of justification).

In Company C, it is a long-standing custom and practice that the longest serving members of staff are entitled to first refusal on any voluntary overtime available. Those who are longest serving are likely to be older. As a result, the practice is indirectly discriminatory. This is subject to the establishment of any exception under reg 32 (see Chapter 7) or a defence of justification (see Chapter 4).

Victimisation

Within the sphere of discrimination legislation, 'victimisation' has a somewhat specialised meaning. In everyday speech, a person might claim to have been 'victimised because of my age (or race, sexual orientation, etc)'. But the concept of victimisation within the legislation is built around the need to protect those who bring complaints, or assist those who bring complaints, of discrimination.

With respect to age discrimination, victimisation is dealt with in reg 4, which requires that:

(a)   A treats B (the complainant) less favourably than he treats or would treat someone in the same circumstances;

(b)   by reason that B has committed a protected act.

In this context, a protected act is one which provides the person carrying it out with a shield against victimisation. The various acts which are protected are set out in reg 4(1), which may be paraphrased as follows:

(a)   bringing proceedings under or by virtue of the regulations;

(b)   giving evidence or information in connection with proceedings under or by virtue of the regulations;

(c)   doing anything under or by reference to the regulations;

(d)   alleging that anyone has committed an act which would contravene the regulations (whether or not the allegation so states).

In each case, A must know or suspect that B has done or intends to do the act in question. In the usual course of events, it will be A against whom the proceedings were brought, the allegation made, etc. In each case, the act will be protected even if the proceedings, etc were against someone other than A.

B will fail, however, if any allegation, evidence or information by him was false and not in good faith. Two examples will show the way in which the provision operates:

> Employee B claims that the Company has discriminated against him by refusing him a pay increment because of his lack of seniority. His case is that the denial of the increment is indirectly discriminatory because the Company's policy disadvantages younger workers. He tells the Managing Director this, and asks for a grievance hearing. The Managing Director is of the view (rightly as it turns out) that the Company's policy is justified under reg 32 in particular (see Chapter 7). He decides that B's claim is so outrageous that he ought to be disciplined, and refuses to shortlist him for a forthcoming promotion. On the assumption that B has acted in good faith, this will constitute victimisation. B has committed a protected act (see (d) above). The Company has treated him less favourably than other persons in the same circumstances. It has done so by reason that he committed the protected act. B acted in good faith, even if the allegation was false (for him to lose protection, the allegation, etc must be *both* false *and* not made in good faith: reg 4(2)).

> Employee C makes a claim that Company A discriminated against him on grounds of age by subjecting him to compulsory retirement at the age of 60. At his tribunal hearing, he calls as a witness his line manager B, who gives evidence that C is a good worker, and the Company should be pleased to have him continue in its employment. B is giving his honest opinion, because he has lost the continued services of a valued employee. The Company takes the view that B's evidence (although no doubt well meant) is too favourable to C. It decides that B's judgement is faulty, and demotes him from his managerial position. In this situation, B will have been victimised by the employer. He committed a protected act (see (b) above). He did so in good faith (even if his evidence was inaccurate). The Company has treated him less favourably than it would have treated someone in the same circumstances (by demoting him). And it did so by reason that he gave evidence in connection with proceedings brought by B against A.

There is no justification defence available for an act of victimisation.

Instructions to discriminate

Article 2.4 of the Equal Treatment Directive states:

> 'An instruction to discriminate against persons on any of the grounds referred to in Article 1 [including age] shall be deemed to be discrimination within the meaning of paragraph 1 [which refers to direct or indirect discrimination].'

In the case of the sexual orientation regulations, and the religion or belief regulations, the definition of discrimination is wide enough to cover discrimination against a person by reason of a refusal to follow an instruction to discriminate. For example, the sexual orientation regulations refer to less favourable treatment 'on grounds of sexual orientation'. If A instructs B to discriminate against C on grounds of C's sexual orientation, B refuses and A sacks him, then B has been less favourably treated 'on grounds of sexual orientation'. However, in the case of the Age Equality Regulations, the definition of direct discrimination refers to 'on grounds of B's age'. That particular regulation does not therefore prohibit instructions to discriminate, with the result that, if it were to stand alone, the Directive would not be properly implemented.

As a result, reg 5 makes it unlawful for A to:

(a)   treat B less favourably than he treats or would treat someone in the same circumstances;

(b)   by reason that B has either:

  (i)   not carried out (in whole or in part) an instruction to do an act which is unlawful under the regulations; or

  (ii)   having been given an instruction, has complained to A or anyone else about it.

To take an example:

> Company A's Managing Director tells its Human Resources Manager, B, to compile a list of employees, select those who are oldest, and serve them with notices of redundancy. The HR Manager compiles the list reluctantly, but complains to one of the non-executive directors of the company about the instruction. When the Managing Director hears of this, he institutes disciplinary proceedings against B, as a result of which B resigns. B has an action for age discrimination (in addition to any possible action for constructive dismissal). He

has been given an instruction which is unlawful under the Regulations, and has complained about it. By reason of his complaint, he has been less favourably treated than those who did not complain. The company has contravened reg 5. (Depending upon the terms of the complaint, it is also possible that B has been victimised contrary to reg 4.) To take an alternative scenario, if B refused to issue the notices of redundancy in line with his instructions, and was subjected to detriment as a result, that might not meet the requirements for a protected act under reg 4, but it would fit the conditions for reg 5.

There is no justification defence for discriminating contrary to reg 5. If the original act (e.g. the drawing up of the list in the above example) was justified, however, it would not be unlawful, with the result that the conditions in reg 5 would not be met.

Harassment

The Equal Treatment Directive deals with harassment in Article 2.3 as follows:

'Harassment shall be deemed to be a form of discrimination within the meaning of paragraph 1, when unwanted conduct related to any of the grounds referred to in Article 1 [which include age] takes place with the purpose or effect of violating the dignity of a person and of creating an intimidating, hostile, degrading, humiliating or offensive environment. In this context, the concept of harassment may be defined in accordance with the national laws and practice of Member States.'

Although reg 6 replicates Article 2.3 of the Directive in most respects, there are significant differences. Regulation 6 defines it as harassment by A of B where:

(a)   A engages in unwanted conduct;

(b)   that conduct has the purpose or effect of:

    (i)   violating B's dignity; or

    (ii)   creating an intimidating, hostile, degrading, humiliating or offensive environment for B.

There is an important rider in reg 6(2). Conduct shall only be regarded as having the effect described in (i) or (ii) above if 'having regard to all the circumstances, including in particular the perception of B [the complainant], it should reasonably be considered as having that effect'.

There are a couple of clear differences between the formulation in the regulation and that in the Directive. The Directive defines harassment as conduct which violates a person's dignity and creates an offensive, etc environment. The regulation prohibits these two results in the alternative. It is difficult in practice to envisage an example of harassment which violates a person's dignity and does *not* create an offensive environment (or vice versa). As a result of this overlap, the formulation in the Regulations is unlikely to result in any difference in practice.

A more important difference between the Directive and the Regulations is that the Directive has no rider such as that contained in reg 6(2). This is addressed later in this section under the heading 'Regulation 6(2)'.

On ground of age

An important point to note about the definition of harassment is that it refers to conduct 'on ground of age'. The harassment need not be based upon the age of the person being harassed. It could just as well be based on the age of someone with whom they are associated. For example:

B is subject to a series of derogatory remarks about her partner, who is considerably older than she is, including references to her 'sugar daddy' and 'how can you see anything in that old git'. The remarks are made by her line manager, during the course of the working day. B has a potential claim for harassment. Although the remarks are not on the grounds of *her* age, they are 'on grounds of age' and hence fit the definition in reg 6.

C is considerably older than his colleagues. He is subject to constant abuse for his untidiness and lack of personal hygiene. He does not (unless there are other factors involved) have a claim for harassment, because the abuse to which he is subjected does not appear to be 'on grounds of age'.

Unwanted conduct

The conduct in question could consist either of words or actions, and this is likely to be widely construed. In its advisory booklet, *Tackling discrimination and promoting equality – good practice guide for employers*, the Arbitration Conciliation and Advisory Service (ACAS) sets out some examples of conduct which might, in appropriate circumstances, be considered harassment. Although the booklet is directed at harassment in the context of discrimination generally, the following examples might be of relevance in respect of age:

(a)   Any physical contact which is unwanted.

(b)   Coercion, isolation or 'freezing out'.

(c)   Display of offensive material.

(d)   Offensive jokes.

(e)   Unwelcome remarks about a person's dress or appearance.

(f)   Shouting at staff.

(g)   Personal insults.

(h)   Persistent criticism.

(i)   Setting impossible deadlines.

As to the content of the 'offensive jokes' or 'personal insults', clearly remarks which ridicule older employees as lacking in verve or out of touch, suggestions that they are past their prime and should pass the baton to someone younger would have the potential to constitute harassment.

Equally, it is possible that someone could be subjected to harassment on the grounds of their youth. In a case brought under the Employment Equality Act in Ireland, a young manager won a claim for harassment after being systematically humiliated in front of other staff by a manager in his sixties. He frequently belittled her, one typical comment being that she was 'only a foolish young girl'. More senior managers failed to intervene, despite the claimant's requests, and she eventually resigned and won a harassment action based upon age (as well as sex-based harassment.

The conduct in question must also be 'unwanted'. This does not mean that the complainant must have explicitly said that the conduct was unwelcome. If that were the case, then it would give a licence to the harasser to say or do something which was deeply offensive, provided that it was only done on one occasion. In the case of *Insitu Cleaning Co Ltd v Heads* [1995] IRLR 4, the EAT was dealing with the way in which 'unwanted conduct' should be interpreted in a sex discrimination case, where the Code of Practice of the European Community was in point, and put it like this:

> 'That the EC Code of Practice refers to "unwanted conduct" does not mean that a single act can never amount to harassment in that it cannot be said to be "unwanted" until it is done and rejected. The word "unwanted" is essentially the same as "unwelcome" or "uninvited".'

So there does not need to be explicit rejection of the conduct in question for it to constitute harassment. Nevertheless, it would no doubt be sensible for the recipient of such unwelcome conduct to make it clear that it is not wanted.

Purpose or effect

The Regulations (and the Directive) speak of conduct which has 'purpose or effect' of violating the complainant's dignity or creating an offensive, etc environment. It is clear from this formula that the conduct does not have to be intended to have the effect in question. In this context, 'light-hearted banter' should be viewed with care. The intention may be to lighten the working day with a few jokes which happen to be at the expense of the oldest (or youngest) employee. But the effect of the jokes must be borne in mind. Do they violate the dignity of the butt of the jokes? Or create a hostile working environment for her? That will be a question of fact and degree. One pointer may be the extent to which someone cracks jokes about their own age. But care needs to be exercised when someone else is the source of the joke.

Regulation 6(2)

One important difference between the Directive and the Regulations is that the Directive has no rider such as that contained in reg 6(2) which states that:

> 'Conduct shall be regarded as having the effect specified in paragraph (1) (a) or (b) only if, having regard to all the circumstances, including in particular the perception of B [the complainant] it should reasonably be considered as having that effect.'

It should be emphasised that the limitation relates only to the case where it is the *effect* of the conduct which is relied upon. Where the *purpose* of the conduct is relied upon, then the limitation does not apply. Nevertheless, the Directive makes no reference at all to the reasonableness of the complainant's perception. It might be argued that, to that extent, the regulation fails to implement the Directive. However, the Directive does clearly state at the end of Article 2.3 that:

> 'In this context, the concept of harassment may be defined in accordance with the national laws and practice of the Member States.'

Regulation 6(2) appears to adopt the approach in *Driskel Peninsula Services Ltd v Holland* [2000] IRLR 151, in which the EAT suggested that the Employment Tribunal should make an objective assessment of all the facts, and should consider the subjective perception of the complainant and the understanding, motive and intention of the alleged harasser. It is clear, however, that the alleged harasser is not entitled to rely on an absence of intention as a defence. The regulation uses 'purpose or effect' in the alternative, so if the complainant establishes that the effect of the unwanted conduct was that his dignity was violated, he succeeds in the harassment claim, regardless of the intention behind the offensive conduct. It is also worth noting that the rider does single out the perception of B (the complainant) as a particular factor in considering the effect of the conduct. No such special mention is made of the perception of A (the alleged harasser).

Liability of employer

Regulation 25(1) deals with what is sometimes (possibly erroneously) called vicarious liability. It fixes an employer with liability for any acts of age discrimination committed by his employee in the course of his employment. Such liability will attach to the employer whether or not the act in question was done with his knowledge or approval. In this respect, the Age Regulations reflect those in respect of discrimination on grounds of sex, race, disability, sexual orientation and religion or belief.

In the course of his employment

It is clear from the case law in respect of race and sex discrimination that 'in the course of his employment' is to be broadly interpreted. As it was put by the Court of Appeal in *Jones v Tower Boot Co Ltd* [1997] IRLR 168:

> 'The words "in the course of employment" should be interpreted in the sense in which they are employed in everyday speech and not restrictively by reference to the principles laid down by case law for establishing an employer's vicarious liability for the torts committed by an employee. The application of the phrase is a question of fact for each employment tribunal to resolve.'

In *Chief Constable of the Lincolnshire Police v Stubbs* [1999] IRLR 81, a police officer was held to be acting in the course of his employment when he subjected a female colleague to inappropriate sexual behaviour. This was despite the fact that the incidents occurred at social events away from the police station. The incidents were at social gatherings involving officers from work. To take analogous examples in the field of age discrimination:

B is subjected to derisory comments about her age, amounting to harassment, while she is at a picnic organised by her employers and largely attended by fellow employees. The conduct is likely to be held to be 'in the course of employment' of the colleagues in question.

C goes to the pub for a drink after work with some colleagues, members of their families, and friends. The employers and C's managers play no part in the session or its organisation. During the evening, he is the subject of abusive comments directed at his youth, to an extent which is clearly offensive. The conduct in question will not be in the course of employment of the colleagues in question, such as to fix the employers with liability.

The employer's defence

There is a defence available to an employer whose employee commits an unlawful act of age discrimination. It is set out in reg 25(3), which lays down that, in order to avoid liability, the employer must 'prove that he took such steps as were reasonably practicable to prevent the employee from doing that act, or from doing in the course of his employment acts of that description'.

The purpose of the defence was set out by the Court of Appeal in *Jones v Tower Boot Co Ltd* [1997] IRLR 168. It is to:

'exonerate the conscientious employer who has used his best endeavours to prevent such harassment, and ... encourage all employers who have not yet undertaken such endeavours to take the steps necessary to make the same defence available in their own workplace.'

The key phrase in the defence is 'reasonably practicable', and some guidance as to its interpretation was provided in *Croft v Royal Mail Group plc* [2003] IRLR 592, CA. In deciding whether an action is reasonably practicable, the Court of Appeal stated that it is permissible to take account of the extent of the difference which the action is likely to make. The employer is entitled to consider whether the time, effort and expense of the suggested measures are disproportionate to the result likely to be achieved. However, an employer will not be exculpated from taking reasonably practicable steps simply because, if it had taken those steps, they would not have prevented the unlawful act from occurring: *Canniffe v East Riding of Yorkshire Council* [2000] IRLR 555, EAT. *Canniffe* is explicable on the basis that the statutory defence involves a carrot and stick approach, and is partly there to encourage employers to take reasonably practicable steps so as to escape liability, as emphasised in the *Tower Boot* case.

What, then, are the steps which are likely to aid an employer in setting up the reg 25(3) defence? It is impossible to provide a watertight formula, or even an exhaustive list. The steps will depend on the situation of the employer, and the likely hazards, as far as age discrimination is concerned, within the work situation. For example, a tribunal is likely to scrutinise much more carefully the measures taken by a large employer with considerable resources than a small family business. However, the following measures are likely to be of relevance, and should form part of the thinking of any enterprise:

(a) Putting an Equal Opportunities Policy in place which covers age discrimination.

(b) Ensuring that there is a policy to deal with bullying and harassment, and that it covers harassment on grounds of age (obviously it could be part of the Equal Opportunities Policy).

(c) Setting up mechanisms to ensure that all employees read the policy and sign to say that they have done so.

(d) Ensuring that there is a grievance procedure in place which can deal with age discrimination and harassment.

(e) Providing training courses to deal with discrimination and harassment on grounds of age.

(f) Keeping copies of materials used for training (e.g. slides), and making sure that those attending sign the register.

(g) Monitoring the policies to ensure that they are carried out.

(h) Setting in place adequate staff supervision, including where appropriate advice from Human Resources professionals.

There is further guidance in Chapter 6 on employer action in relation to 'Recruitment and selection', and in Chapter 7 on 'Terms and conditions'. In addition, ACAS has produced guidance on good practice in relation to discrimination generally, and has produced specific guidance on age discrimination which appears in Appendix 3. Their website can be found at www.acas.org.uk.

Liability of principals

Anyone ('the principal') who gives an agent authority to do something on his behalf is liable for the unlawful discriminatory acts of the agent: reg 25(2). In order to fix the principal with liability, the agent must have the authority, express or implied, before or after the event, of the principal. However, liability is not restricted to situations where the contract of agency in question gives the agent authority to discriminate. The 'authority' referred to in reg 25(2) is the authority to do an act which is capable of being done in a discriminatory manner, just as it is capable of being done in a lawful manner: *Lana v Positive Action Training in Housing (London) Ltd* [2001] IRLR 501, EAT. To take an example:

Company A places its employee B, a trainee quantity surveyor, with Company C, which is in the business of providing training. The placement is based upon two contracts:

(a) a contract between B and Company C, by which Company C agrees to provide B with a work experience placement; and

(b) a contract between Company A and Company C, by which A agrees to pay C £5,000 towards the cost of B's training.

While undergoing training with Company C, B is subjected to harassment on grounds of her age. Company A will be liable because Company C acts as its agent, with authority to do an act which can be done in a discriminatory manner.

The employer's defence of reasonably practicable steps (reg 25(3)) does *not* apply to a principal in respect of the acts of his agent.

Aiding unlawful acts

Someone who knowingly helps someone to do an act which is unlawful under the Regulations is himself treated as having done such an act: reg 26. The rule is applied to employees and agents by reg 26(2). The result is that someone who harasses or discriminates against a fellow employee is treated as aiding his employer to do such an act if the employer would be liable for such acts under reg 25. In this way, both the employer and the employee who actually commits the unlawful act in question will be liable. A similar rule applies in the case of agents and principals.

The question arises: what constitutes 'knowingly aiding' an unlawful act? There are decided cases which deal with the equivalent words in other discrimination legislation. As far as 'aiding' in concerned, the House of Lords in *Anyanwu v South Bank Students' Union* [2001] IRLR 305 said that it was a familiar word in everyday use, bearing no special or technical meaning in this context. A person aids another if he helps or assists, or co-operates or collaborates with him. He does so whether or not his help is substantial and productive, provided the help is not so insignificant as to be negligible.

The legislation also requires the element of knowledge, as well as aid. In *Sinclair Roche & Temperley v Heard* [2004] IRLR 763, EAT, the point was made that, whereas discrimination can be, and very often is, unconscious, aiding cannot be. It is submitted, however, that whereas knowledge is required for the reg 26 form of liability, benevolent motivation remains irrelevant, just as it is in direct or indirect discrimination.

By reg 26(3) a person does not knowingly aid another in an unlawful act if he reasonably relies on a statement by that other that the act is lawful. It is an offence, punishable by a fine, to knowingly or recklessly make a misleading statement to the effect that the act is lawful: reg 26(4). To take an example:

> Assume that Company A wishes to cut its workforce, and decides to dismiss workers who are over the age of 50. It seeks the services of a Human Resources consultant, C, to assist in the process, but does not tell him of its desire to rid the workforce of 'dead wood' (as the Managing Director puts it in an internal memo to the Finance Director). C's task is to interview all the workers, whatever their age, and to rank them according to a set of criteria which are age-neutral. The Company asks him to include in the resulting schedule the ages of each worker. C asks why this is, and is told that it will not form part of the decision-making material, but is merely 'background' and 'required for monitoring purposes'. In due course the Company declares all workers over 50 redundant, including B, who claims direct age discrimination. The Company is itself liable (subject to any unlikely defence of justification). So is its Managing Director (on the basis of reg 26(2)). However, C is not liable, even though he did aid the Company in its unlawful act. He probably did not act 'knowingly' (although he seems to have suspected something) and hence may not fall within reg 26(1). More clearly, he relied on the statement made by the Company that the information was background and required for monitoring purposes, his reliance was probably reasonable, and he can therefore escape liability by virtue of reg 26(3).

Claims for Direct Age Discrimination

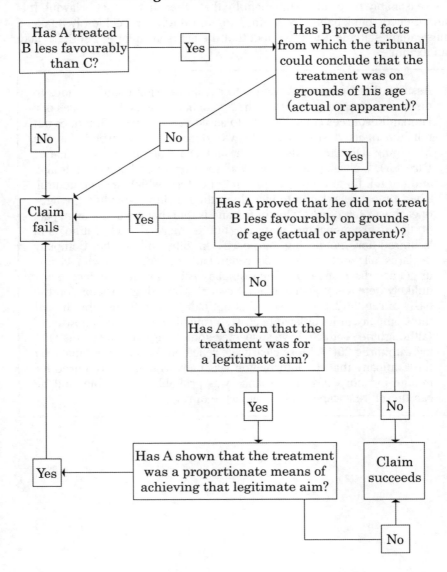

A = the respondent e.g. the employer (actual or prospective)
B = the claimant e.g. the employer or applicant
C = the comparator (actual or hypothetical) whose relevant
circumstances must be the same as, or not materially
different from B's

Claims for Indirect Age Discrimination

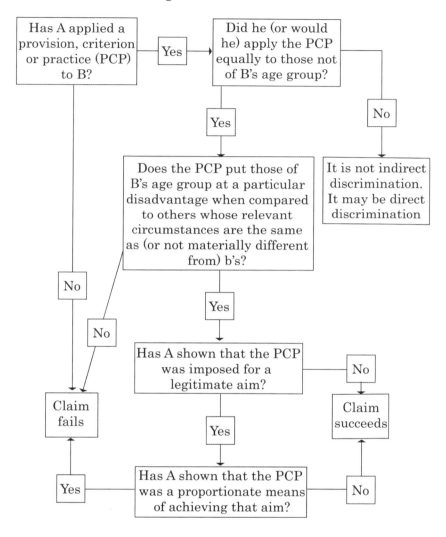

A	= respondent e.g. employer (actual or prospective)
B	= claimant e.g. employee or applicant
PCP	= provision, criterion or practice

3 Scope of the Protection

Introduction

The scope of the Age Regulations has primarily been determined by the terms of the Equal Treatment Directive upon which it is based. The purpose of the Directive is to combat discrimination on the prohibited grounds (including age) and to promote equality in the sphere of employment (Article 1). Like the Regulations dealing with sexual orientation, and those dealing with religion and belief, the focus is upon employment. Unlike the legislation aimed at discrimination on grounds of sex, race and disability, there is no protection under the Employment Equality (Age) Regulations in the field of goods and services provided to the public. The technical reason for this limited coverage appears to be that legislation within the scope of the Directive could be passed by statutory instrument, since regulations can be made under the European Communities Act 1972. If goods and services were to be covered, that would have taken the project outside the ambit of the Directive, and required an Act of Parliament.

The limited scope of the Regulations means in practice that a business can discriminate against its customers, but not against those who are employed by it. As will be seen in the next section, however, 'employment' in the context of the Age Regulations is widely defined for most purposes. As a result, if the owner of a property instructs an architect on the basis that the architect must personally design the building which the owner is commissioning, then the owner must be careful not to discriminate in the process of hiring the architect, or the way in which he requires him to carry out his contract. However, either the owner or the architect can discriminate in relation to actual or potential clients or customers – for whom they provide goods or services, rather than employment.

Employees

Regulation 7 makes it unlawful to discriminate against 'applicants and employees'. The word 'applicant' comes from the heading and does not appear in the regulation itself. Regulation 7(1) makes it unlawful for an employer to discriminate in relation to offers of employment and the arrangements and terms to which they are subject (hence it protects 'applicants'). Regulation 7(2) imposes a similar prohibition upon discrimination once the subject of the discrimination is employed (thus protecting 'employees'). Central to both of these provisions is the concept of 'employment', which is defined in reg 2 as 'employment under a contract of service or of apprenticeship or a contract personally to do any work'. Related expressions such as 'employee' are to be interpreted accordingly. The definition does not apply to the exception for retirement, however (see Chapter 8 for a discussion of this issue in the context of retirement and dismissal).

It follows that the definition of 'employee' is a relatively wide one. It is not confined to those with a contract of employment (as the unfair dismissal legislation is). The definition is similar to (although not identical with) that contained in the Sex Discrimination Act 1975, s 82(1) and the Race Relations Act 1976, s 78(1). As a result, it covers many people who are self-employed, provided that their contract for services is 'a contract personally to do any work' and cannot, for example, be delegated at will by the employee.

In *Percy v Church of Scotland Board of National Mission* [2006] IRLR 195, the House of Lords made it clear that the similar definition in s 82(1) of the Sex Discrimination Act 1975 was wide-reaching, so as to include an associate minister's relationship with the Church of Scotland. She was employed under a contract 'personally to execute' work as an associate minister, and was therefore entitled to bring her claim of sex discrimination against the church in an employment tribunal. As Lady Hale put it (paragraph 146):

> 'The fact that the worker has very considerable freedom and independence in how she performs the duties of her office does not take her outside the definition. Judges are servants of the law, in the sense that the law governs all that they do and decide, just as clergy are servants of God, in the sense that God's word, as interpreted in the doctrines of their faith, governs all that they practise, preach and teach. That does not mean that they cannot be 'workers' or in the 'employment' of those who decide how their Ministry should be put to the service of the church.'

Although reg 7 covers applicants and employees in this relatively broad sense, there are certain exceptions to the protection which it affords. There is no protection for job applicants aged 65 and over (see reg 7(4) and Chapter 6). In certain circumstances benefits provided by an employer are excluded where they are equivalent to goods and services provided to the public (see reg 7(6) and Chapter 7).

Contract workers

Agency workers (whether 'temp' or 'perm') are covered by reg 9. This regulation covers 'contract workers' as defined in reg 9(5). A 'principal' is

27

defined for the purposes of this regulation as a person ('A') who makes work available for individuals who are employed by another person who supplies them under a contract made with A. The contract worker is anyone who is supplied to the principal under such a contract, and he can make use of reg 9 to bring a claim against A, i.e. the company to which he is sent by the supplier. He could in any event bring a claim for any unlawful act of discrimination against the supplying company under reg 7 (if it is his employer) or under reg 21 (if it is acting as an employment agency, see the section on this topic below).

Territorial jurisdiction

The operation of regs 7 and 9 (dealing with employees, applicants and contract workers) is limited geographically by reg 10. The employment in question in reg 7 must be 'at an establishment in Great Britain', and the 'contract work' in reg 9 is similarly confined. Help is provided by reg 10 in determining whether employment is to be regarded as 'being at an establishment in Great Britain'. It will be if the employee does his work wholly or partly in Great Britain. It will also be so regarded if his work is wholly outside Great Britain, provided that:

(a)   the employer has a place of business at an establishment in Great Britain;

(b)   the work is for the purposes of a business carried on at that establishment; and

(c)   the employee is ordinarily resident in Great Britain when he applies for or is offered the employment or during the course of it.

Two examples will illustrate the operation of the rules:

> A company is based and registered in Australia, with an office in London. Their employee, who is an Australian citizen, spends a fortnight a year at the London office, where the alleged discriminatory act takes place. He can claim against the company under the Regulations.

> C, who lives in London, applies for a job with a South African company which has an office in Manchester. He is invited for interview in Johannesburg, and gets the job. He works throughout in Botswana, on a project which is to be used by the Manchester office. He can claim under the Regulations against the South African company.

Members of pension schemes

The trustees and managers of occupational pension schemes are prohibited from discriminating or harassing members (or prospective members) of their scheme (reg 11). There are, however, wide-ranging exemptions from this particular protection, which are detailed in Schedule 2 of the Regulations (see Chapter 9).

Office-holders

Office-holders are specifically given protection by reg 12. This makes discrimination and harassment of office-holders unlawful on a similar basis to that which has been described in relation to employees and contract workers. Typical office-holders are company directors (if without a contract of employment), the chairmen and members of some public bodies, judges, chairmen and members of tribunals, and ministers of religion. In fact, many office-holders (including some in the list just given) may in any event fall within the definition of 'employee', and obtain protection in that way. In the *Percy* case (see above), Lord Nicholls pointed out that 'holding an office and being an employee are not inconsistent. A person may hold an "office" in the terms of, and pursuant to, a contract of employment' (paragraph 20). In so far as any office-holder is not an employee, however, he is given protection by reg 12. It is unlawful to discriminate against office-holders, and those who apply for office. In respect of applicants for office, the discriminator may be the person who recommends or approves the applicants for office (or, rather, fails to do so). The protection extends to any appointment or post where the office-holder is:

(a)   paid (other than expenses and loss of earnings); and

(b)   subject to direction as to where and when he performs his functions.

However, elected posts and political offices are excluded from protection, as they are from the operation of the Directive, which applies only to those supplying a service of economic value under the direction of another: *Lawrie-Blum* [1986] ECR 2121.

One interesting feature of the position of office-holders under the Age Regulations is that the default retirement age set out in reg 30 will not apply to them. There is not, therefore, a blanket exemption making the fixing of a retirement age of 65 or above legal, as the Regulations do in relation to employees (see Chapter 8). The position will rather be that any retirement age for an office-holder will have to be objectively justified (see Chapter 4). This could lead to a complex situation where the individual claiming discrimination is both an employee and an office-holder (as in the *Percy* case). However, reg 12(8) specifically excludes cases where regs 7 (applicants or employees), 9 (contract workers), 15 (barristers), 16 (advocates) or 17 (partnerships) apply, 'or would apply but for the operation of any other provision of these Regulations'. It would seem, therefore, that where an office-holder is also an employee, he can be subject to compulsory retirement at 65 even if that retirement age cannot be objectively justified. The protection is, strangely, more effective for office-holders who are not employees than for those who are – in this respect at any rate.

Police

The position of the police, including those seconded to the Serious Organised Crime Agency, is dealt with in regs 13 and 14. They are given protection from discrimination and harassment in much the same way as employees and applicants for employment. The chief officer is treated as their employer, except in relation to acts done by the police authority, where the authority itself is treated as the employer. Police constables are of course office-holders, and it is arguable that protection has also been extended to them under reg 12.

Barristers and advocates

Barristers and their clerks are prohibited from discriminating against, or harassing, pupils and tenants (reg 15). The same protection is extended to those who apply for pupillage or tenancy. In addition, those who instruct a barrister are forbidden to subject him to a detriment or harass him within the meaning of the Age Regulations. Similar prohibitions in relation to advocates in Scotland are laid down in reg 16.

Partnerships

Partnerships are dealt with in reg 17. It is unlawful for a firm to discriminate against, or harass, a partner or an applicant for partnership in the firm in circumstances which are similar to those applying to employees. The provisions apply equally to limited liability partnerships. However, there is an exemption in relation to the *offer* of a partnership, if a particular characteristic relating to age is a general occupational requirement (see reg 8 and Chapter 5). In addition it is worth noting that the default retirement age of 65 set out in reg 30 does not apply to partners; nor does the 'duty to consider' procedure in Schedule 6 (see Chapter 8).

Trade organisations

Protection for the members of trade organisations is provided by reg 18. The definition includes trade unions, professional bodies and employers' associations. It is unlawful for the organisation in question to discriminate against or harass a member in a variety of circumstances ranging from admission to membership to expulsion, and including the provision of benefits.

Qualifications bodies

A body which confers professional or trade qualifications (or refuses to do so) can obviously affect an individual's access to work, or to vocational training. It follows that the Directive (Article 3.1) requires that discrimination and harassment by such bodies be made unlawful. This is put into effect by reg 19, which covers circumstances ranging from refusing to confer a qualification to withdrawing a qualification which he already holds.

Vocational training

Clearly, some vocational training is provided by employers for those whom they employ, and any discrimination or harassment in respect of such training is covered by reg 7. In addition, some vocational training is provided by institutions of further and higher education, and that area is dealt with in reg 23. Protection is extended to other forms of vocational training by reg 20. There is an exclusion where the vocational training in question would only fit a person for employment which would be covered by a genuine occupational requirement (see reg 8 and Chapter 5). However, the definition of vocational training is an extremely wide one, which covers:

(a)   all types and levels of training which would help fit a person for any employment;

(b)   vocational guidance;

(c)   facilities for training;

(d)   practical work experience provided by an employer to a person whom he does not employ; and

(e)   any assessment related to the award of any professional or trade qualification.

To take an example:

C is a student at university. She is training to be a teacher, and the university arranges with a school that she should do teaching practice with them. When C arrives at the school, the head is concerned to find that she is a mature student who is older than any of the teachers with whom she could be placed. The head decides that C, in her own interests, ought to go to another school where she could be placed with an older teacher. C could bring a claim against the school for age discrimination (although they do not employ her), and the school (and the head) would have to provide justification for their actions.

Employment agencies

Age discrimination and harassment by employment agencies are made unlawful by reg 21. There is an exemption where the employment in relation to which the agency's services are provided is employment for which a characteristic relating to age is a genuine occupational requirement (GOR: see reg 8 and Chapter 5). In addition, an employment agency will not be liable if it reasonably relies upon a statement made by the employer that the employment is one to which a GOR applies. Knowingly or recklessly making a false or misleading statement that employment is one to which a GOR applies is a criminal offence (reg 21(5)).

Further and higher education

Regulation 23 brings institutions of further and higher education within the reach of the prohibition against age discrimination. It makes it unlawful to discriminate against or harass a student, whether in the terms on which he is admitted to the institution, in refusing admission, in respect of access to benefits, or by excluding him or subjecting him to any other detriment. The regulation applies to universities, other institutions within higher education, and institutions within further education. The protection is extended more widely than the Directive required. The Directive covers vocational training, which has been held by the European Court of Justice (ECJ) to include most higher education and many further education courses. As it was put in *Gravier v City of Liege* [1985] ECR 606, this incorporates:

'any form of education which prepares for a qualification for a particular profession, trade or employment, or which provides the necessary skills for such a profession, trade or employment.'

The terms of the Directive, as interpreted by the ECJ, would therefore cover a course in veterinary science, or the legal practice course to become a solicitor. Regulation 23, however, gives protection to students and potential students at the designated institutions, whether the course they apply for or are enrolled upon has any vocational use or not. There is an exception if the discrimination concerns training which would only fit a person for employment for which a characteristic related to age is a genuine occupational requirement in terms of reg 8, but it is difficult to think of any circumstances where this exemption could actually apply in practice. It seems then, that the prohibition on age discrimination will apply comprehensively to institutions of further and higher education which fit the relevant statutory definition. To take an example:

> A wishes to take a course in flower arranging at the local further education college. He is 58 and must pay for the course, whereas the college has determined that those who are over 65 will pay reduced fees. The college will have to provide objective justification for its policy if A brings a claim.

> B obtains his A-levels at the age of 16 and applies to university to do a course in philosophy. The university in question refuses him admission on the grounds that he is too young, and it does not have the support services necessary to deal with students of that age. It will have to provide objective justification if B claims.

In each of the above cases, the claim would be brought in the county court, since that is the forum which is granted jurisdiction in respect of reg 23 (see Chapter 11).

Relationships which have ended

Regulation 24 deals with the position where an act of discrimination or harassment occurs after the employment relationship has come to an end. In such a case, it is unlawful for the employer to discriminate against or harass the former employee if the discrimination or harassment 'arises out of or is connected to that [employment] relationship'. In fact, the ambit of the regulation is broader than that, in that it covers any 'relevant relationship', and is not confined to employment. Hence it will make unlawful an act of discrimination against a former student by her university, for example.

In these cases, the question of time limits may assume particular importance. As discussed in Chapter 11, the claim must be brought within three months of the act complained of where the employment tribunal has jurisdiction or six months in the case of a county court claim (subject to the discretion of the tribunal or court). Time begins to run when the act complained of is committed, and not when the relationship is terminated.

An example may help to illustrate the operation of reg 24:

> A works for a company for 18 months, after which she leaves on good terms and with an exemplary record at the age of 19. She seeks a reference from the company, which is refused on the grounds that

they do not provide references for anyone who is under the age of 21, and in any event, 18 months is an insufficient period for a judgement to be formed as to whether a reference should be provided. The company would have to provide objective justification for its policy of refusing references to those under 21 (direct discrimination) and (possibly) for its decision that 18 months was too short a period (arguably indirect discrimination, but easier to justify).

Civil servants and members of the armed forces

The regulations protect civil servants (reg 44) and members of the staff of the Houses of Parliament (regs 45 and 46). They do not, however, apply to service personnel, whether navy, army or air force, regular forces or reservists (reg 44(4)). This latter exemption does not extend to civilians working for the Ministry of Defence, the MoD Police and Guarding Agency or the MoD Fire Service, all of whom are within the scope of the regulations. The general exclusion of the armed forces differs from the position under the legislation on discrimination on grounds of sex, race, sexual orientation and religion and belief. It is similar to the position under the Disability Discrimination Act 1995, and is permitted under Article 3.4 of the Directive.

4 Justification

Justification is an important concept in the context of discrimination generally. It is available as a defence for indirect discrimination in respect of sex, race, sexual orientation and religion or belief. It is also a defence where discrimination on grounds related to disability is in issue. The regulations in relation to age discrimination are unique, however, in that they allow a defence of justification in relation to direct (as well as indirect) discrimination – but not in relation to victimisation, harassment, or instructions to discriminate.

Regulation 3 is the relevant regulation, describing both direct and indirect discrimination and then including as a necessary element that A (the potential discriminator) 'cannot show the treatment or, as the case may be, provision, criterion or practice to be a proportionate means of achieving a legitimate aim'. As can be seen, the regulation does not use the word 'justification' but speaks rather of 'a proportionate means of achieving a legitimate aim'.

Directive and Regulations compared

To what extent is this approach compatible with the provisions of the Equal Treatment Directive? The Directive in Article 2.2 states that there shall be no direct discrimination whatsoever on any of the grounds referred to in Article 1 (which includes age). It goes on to define in Article 2.2 direct discrimination and indirect discrimination, and sets out a defence in relation to all forms of indirect discrimination covered by the Directive where the indirectly discriminatory 'provision, criterion or practice is objectively justified by a legitimate aim and the means of achieving that aim are appropriate and necessary.'

Article 6 of the Directive singles age out for special treatment by comparison with other forms of discrimination, stating:

'1. Notwithstanding Article 2.2, Member States may provide that differences of treatment on grounds of age shall not constitute discrimination if, within the context of national law, they are objectively and reasonably justified by a legitimate aim, including legitimate employment policy, labour market and vocational training objectives, and if the means of achieving that aim are appropriate and necessary.'

Justification

Article 6 then goes on to set out examples of such 'differences of treatment' which will be discussed later.

It is apparent that the phrase 'objectively justified' in the Directive does not appear in the Regulations. The Explanatory Notes issued by the Department of Trade and Industry to accompany the Regulations (paragraph 13) suggest that the reason is that the addition of these words would not add anything to the requirement in reg 3(1). That would seem to be correct.

Possibly more controversial is the difference between the formula in the regulations about the means of achieving a legitimate aim. The Directive and the Regulations are at one in requiring there to be a 'legitimate aim'. However, the Directive requires that the means of achieving that aim should be 'appropriate and necessary'. The Regulations state that the means should be 'proportionate'.

The leading case from the European Court of Justice on justification is *Bilka-Kaufhaus GmbH v Weber von Hartz* [1986] IRLR 317, ECJ. The court held that, in order to justify a pay practice which discriminated indirectly against women workers, the employer must put forward objective economic grounds relating to the management of the undertaking. This required a finding by the national court that the measures chosen by the employer corresponded to a real need on the part of the undertaking, were appropriate with a view to achieving the objectives pursued and were necessary to that end. They had to be 'necessary and in proportion to the objectives pursued by the employer'. The terms of the Directive, as has been seen, closely reflect the judgment in *Bilka-Kaufhaus*.

What about the differences which are to be found in the Regulations? The Explanatory Notes (paragraph 14) deal with this important point and are worth quoting at some length:

> 'The Directive appears to use the two terms "proportionate" and "appropriate and necessary" interchangeably – compare Articles 2.2(b) and 6.1 with Article 4.1. Similarly, the European Court of Justice (ECJ) has used the two terms interchangeably, explaining that proportionality requires that the means used to achieve an aim must not exceed the limits of what is appropriate and necessary to achieve that aim – (see, for example ... *R v MAFF, ex parte NFU* [1998] ECR I-1211 and ... *Johnston v RUC* [1986] ECR1651). The same formula has been used most recently in Case C-144/04 *Mangold v Helm* ... Since the two terms have the same meaning in light of the case law, the Regulations use the same term ("proportionate") for the sake of consistency throughout.'

The term 'proportionate' is considered to be clearer than 'appropriate and necessary' in implementing the Directive in that it sets the requirement of necessity in its proper context. Were the Directive's formulation to be simply copied out, there might be a risk that this would be interpreted as a very strict requirement (for example, that the legitimate aim pursued was essential to the employer's business), in accordance with the usual English law approach to the concept of necessity. But, as the ECJ case law set out above demonstrates, the term 'appropriate and necessary' in the European context does not set out an absolute test but, rather, one of proportionality involving balance between the discriminatory effects of a measure and the importance of the aim pursued.

It is clear, therefore, that the government consciously rejected an absolute necessity test as part of the test of justification. It aimed to incorporate the test laid down by the European Community, but in terms which would not lead our courts and tribunals to apply an absolute test. The test is meant to be consistent with that applied in respect of other legislation which outlaws discrimination, and should be interpreted in accordance with the decisions of the ECJ (such as *Bilka-Kaufhaus*) and those of our domestic courts. The case of *Mangold v Helm* [2006] IRLR 143 is an important application of the test for justification by the ECJ, and is dealt with in more detail at the end of Chapter 11.

Case law on justification

Case law on the issue of justification refers to indirect discrimination on grounds of sex or race (of course that is the only sort of sex and race discrimination which *can* be justified in terms of the relevant legislative provisions). In *Hampson v Department of Education and Science* [1989] IRLR 69, the Court of Appeal stated that the decision on whether the condition (in our context it would be a provision, criterion or practice) was 'justifiable' required an objective balance to be struck between the discriminatory effect of the condition and the reasonable needs of the person who applies it. It is not sufficient for the employer to establish that *he* considered his reasons adequate.

In *Board of Governors of St Mathias Church of England School v Crizzle* [1993] IRLR 472, the EAT, in a race case, adopted an approach which closely reflects that in the age discrimination regulations. The EAT stated that the approach of the tribunal should be to consider:

(a)   Was the objective legitimate?

(b)   Were the means used to achieve the objective reasonable in themselves?

(c)   Were they justified when balanced on principles of proportionality between the discriminatory effect upon the complainant's racial group and the reasonable needs of those applying the condition?

Taking the test from the wording of reg 3, as reinforced by the European and domestic case law, there are two fundamental questions to pose in determining whether the employer has established justification:

1   Did he have a legitimate aim?

2   Did he carry out that aim by means which were proportionate?

The next sections discuss those two questions in turn.

Legitimate aim

Article 6.1 of the Directive states that certain differences of treatment:

> 'shall not constitute discrimination if, within the context of national law, they are objectively and reasonably justified by a legitimate aim, including legitimate employment policy, labour market and vocational training objectives, and if the means of achieving that aim are appropriate and necessary.

> Such differences of treatment may include, among others:

> (a)   the setting of special conditions on access to employment and vocational training, employment and occupation, including dismissal and remuneration conditions for young people, older workers and persons with caring responsibilities in order to promote their vocational integration or ensure their protection;

> (b)   the fixing of minimum conditions of age, professional experience or seniority in service for access to employment or to certain advantages linked to employment;

> (c)   the fixing of a minimum age for recruitment which is based on the training requirements of the post in question or the need for a reasonable period of employment before retirement.'

When the government published its original draft version of the Regulations for consultation, it replicated the situations set out in (a) to (c) above, suggesting that a tribunal or court might, depending on the circumstances of the case, find them to be a proportionate means of achieving a legitimate aim.

They did not find their way into the final version of the Regulations laid before Parliament and have consequently not been incorporated into the current law.

Nonetheless, the presence of the list in the Directive gives it a certain importance and it is worth drawing some conclusions about it. First, it is clear that the listed practices do not constitute exemptions or exceptions. Each of them would, if adopted by an employer (or by the government in its legislative provisions), have to be individually justified in the particular circumstances of the case. Second, it is equally clear that the practices in question do not constitute an exhaustive list. A variety of other practices could be justified, again depending upon the circumstances. Third, justification of the listed practices, like the various others which do not form part of the list, cannot be done by assertion – evidence will be needed to establish that a particular aim is legitimate, as well as to support the chosen means of furthering it.

That said, the list in Article 6.1 does provide something of an indication of the sort of things which *might* constitute a legitimate aim, and they will no doubt figure in future litigation on whether the practices in question are justified. They also feature in some of the examples set out at the end of this chapter.

In the consultation document *Equality and Diversity: Coming of Age* which accompanied the draft Regulations, the government set out examples of potentially legitimate aims as follows (paragraph 4.1.17 of the consultation document):

(a) health, welfare and safety (including protection of young or older people);

(b) facilitation of employment planning;

(c) particular training requirements;

(d) encouraging and rewarding loyalty;

(e) the need for a reasonable period of employment before retirement; and

(f) recruiting or retaining older people.

Again, the list in question can neither be regarded as exhaustive nor as authoritative (in the sense that presence on it will constitute legitimacy). Further, it does not have the status of the matters listed as (a) to (c) in Article 6.1 of the Directive. Again, some of the aims mentioned will figure in the examples discussed later.

Is minimising cost a legitimate aim?

Clearly a business will have profit in sight as a major goal, and part of the equation in ensuring profitability will be to keep costs to a minimum. To what extent will this constitute a legitimate aim so as to found a case for justification?

The question was dealt with by the EAT in *Cross v British Airways plc* [2005] IRLR 423. In that case, the court was considering whether a provision, criterion or practice (PCP) applied to cabin staff in relation to retirement age was indirectly discriminatory contrary to the Sex Discrimination Act 1975. After reviewing the European jurisprudence, Burton P stated:

'We conclude that the European Court has laid down a perfectly comprehensible structure. A national state cannot rely on budgetary considerations to justify a discriminatory social policy. An employer seeking to justify a discriminatory PCP cannot rely *solely* on considerations of cost. He can however put cost into the balance, together with other justifications if there are any. We do not consider it necessary to make a reference to the European Court.'

In the context of age discrimination, references to a PCP (indirect discrimination) must be taken to include less favourable treatment (direct discrimination). Analysing the general principles laid down in *Cross*, It appears that:

(a)   Where it is the government which is putting forward the treatment or practice as being justified, it cannot rely on cost as a legitimate aim.

(b)   Where the justification defence is being put forward by the employer, it can rely upon cost as a factor, but not as the sole factor.

(c)   It follows that cost cannot be a legitimate aim on its own, but can be put in the balance on the side of justification if there is another aim which can be put forward as legitimate.

Proportionate means

Once it is established that the employer has a legitimate aim, that is not the end of the matter. It must then be considered whether the treatment or the provision, criterion or practice (PCP) is a proportionate means of achieving it. This involves three different questions:

1   Does the treatment or PCP actually contribute to the achievement of the legitimate aim? Say that an employer adopts a PCP (such as a health test) in order to promote safe practices in the workplace. The question here would be whether it actually did promote safety. If it does not, it is not a proportionate means of achieving the legitimate aim of improving safety.

2   The importance of the legitimate aim should be weighed against the discriminatory effects which it produces. It is worth noting that, although direct age discrimination is susceptible to justification, it will usually involve a greater discriminatory effect than indirect age discrimination. The legitimate aim should therefore be a more important one (e.g. protection of health and safety of the workforce and the public) where the discrimination in question is direct.

3   If the legitimate aim can be achieved just as well by a measure which has less discriminatory effects, then the less discriminatory measure should be used. The employer ought to choose the least discriminatory means, or the means will not be proportionate.

It is implicit in these questions that a balancing act is involved between the legitimate aim and its discriminatory effects. The burden of proof is upon the employer.

When the matter is considered by the tribunal, some guidance has been offered by the Court of Appeal in *Hardys and Hansons plc* [2005] IRLR 726, in the context of a sex discrimination claim. Pill LJ stated (paragraph 32):

> 'The employer does not have to demonstrate that no other proposal is possible. The employer has to show that the proposal ... is justified objectively notwithstanding its discriminatory effect. The principle of proportionality requires the tribunal to take into account the reasonable needs of the business. But it has to make its own judgment, upon a fair and detailed analysis of the working practices and business considerations involved, as to whether the proposal is reasonably necessary. I reject the appellants' submission (apparently accepted by the EAT) that, when reaching its conclusion, the employment tribunal needs to consider only whether or not it is satisfied that the employer's views are within the range of views reasonable in the particular circumstances.'

It is clear, then, that the tribunal must make its own judgment as to whether the means adopted were proportionate. There is no room for the 'band of reasonable responses' test, unlike the position in an unfair dismissal case.

Justification in practice

How will the test for justification work in practice? Some examples may serve to illustrate the process:

> An employer has decided to introduce a health test for all employees aged 55 and over. This is directly discriminatory, but is theoretically justifiable. The aim of the test is to reduce accidents in the workplace, where there is a lot of dangerous machinery, by dismissing employees who are more likely to cause accidents. This is, in theory, a legitimate aim. The immediate question, however, would be whether the aim would be furthered by the means proposed. Firm evidence would be needed that employees over the age of 55 were more accident-prone. Further, could the aim be achieved by a less discriminatory means? If the proposal was to have a health test for all

employees, regardless of age, there would be no direct age discrimination. Depending upon precisely what was being tested, there would be likely to be indirect age discrimination (since older employees are less likely to pass a health test). However, that is less discriminatory, and would at least be preferable to the original proposal. Evidence would still be required of the efficacy of a health test in achieving the reduction in accidents. In addition, if the end result is the dismissal of some workers, the draconian effects of the proposal would remain in place. If dismissal was the alleged act of discrimination, the employer (and if necessary the tribunal) would have to examine whether such a result was proportionate in the sense that it was the least discriminatory outcome. Would it not be possible for those concerned to be trained or redeployed?

A bus company wishes to introduce an age limit of 60 for the recruitment of drivers. It argues that the compulsory retirement age for its drivers is 65, and that they take 12 months to train fully. In order to ensure that it obtains value for money from the investment which it has to make in training, it believes that four years as a fully trained driver is necessary. The aim of ensuring a reasonable period of employment before retirement would seem to be a legitimate one (see Article 6.1(c) of the Directive). Does the proposed direct discrimination actually assist in achieving that aim? It is dubious. Evidence would be needed to show that recruits under the age of 60 would be likely to remain in the employment of the bus company for more than five years (e.g. on the basis of statistics within the industry as a whole, and from the records of the company itself). Without such evidence, the proposal may well fail to be regarded as proportionate, with the result that the company may not be able to justify it.

A retailer of trendy fashion items decides to employ young shop assistants in order to contribute to its aim of targeting young buyers. Trying to attract a young target group is an aim which is tainted with age discrimination. As a result it will not be a legitimate aim (see the consultation document *Equality and Diversity: Coming of Age*, p 34 and *Kutz-Bauer v Freie und Hansestadt Hamburg* [2003] IRLR 368 ECJ).

An employer is worried about the composition of its employees who are exclusively white. It wishes to drop its retirement age from 65 to

55 in order to recruit a more ethnically diverse workforce. That would clearly be directly discriminatory on grounds of age. If one of the employees who was compulsorily retired claimed age discrimination, the tribunal would need to consider first whether the aim is legitimate. To begin with, the company would have to convince the tribunal that the introduction of the lower retirement age was genuinely motivated by concern at the composition of its workforce. If it established that this was genuinely the reason, then the recruitment of a workforce which more accurately reflects the composition of the population at large might in general terms be regarded as desirable. As the law stands, of course, that cannot be done by positive discrimination. The company would need to put forward clear evidence of the way in which it intended to handle the recruitment process. It is likely that any aim tainted by racial discrimination (as positive discrimination would be) could not be regarded as legitimate. If the company is able to clear that hurdle, then it would need to show that the means adopted was proportionate. Why did they choose to achieve the aim by lowering the retirement age? Could it not have been done by a process of selection on merit? It is no answer to say that they would have faced unfair dismissal claims if they had – the choice of retirement also lays them open to such claims. And, even if they can show that the choice of retirement as the means of culling the workforce was proportionate, is the selection of the age of 55 proportionate – why not 60?

5 Exceptions

This chapter deals with the exceptions within the Regulations, which exclude particular situations from their operation. In summary, they are:

(a) the genuine occupational requirement (GOR);

(b) statutory authority;

(c) national security;

(d) positive action.

There are other exceptions which are more appropriately dealt with elsewhere, as follows:

(a) the exemption for employers to permit a maximum age for recruitment (reg 7(4), dealt with in Chapter 6);

(b) the default lawful retirement age of 65 (reg 30, dealt with in Chapter-8);

(c) the exception related to the national minimum wage (reg 31, Chapter-7);

(d) the exception for benefits based upon seniority (reg 32, Chapter 7);

(e) the exception for enhanced redundancy payments (reg 33, Chapter-7);

(f) the exception for life assurance cover after retirement (reg 34, Chapter 7).

Genuine occupational requirements

The exception in relation to general occupational requirements (GORs) is set out in reg 8.

What constitutes a GOR?

For the employer to be able to rely on a GOR, the conditions set out in reg 8(2) must be met:

(a) possessing a characteristic related to age must be a genuine and determining occupational requirement;

(b)   it must be proportionate to apply the GOR to the case in question; and

(c)   either:

    (i)   the person to whom the GOR is applied does not meet it; or

    (ii)   the employer is not satisfied, and it is reasonable for him not to be satisfied, that the person meets it.

The provision generally follows that of Article 4.1 of the Directive, with one difference. In the Directive, it is specified that the provision applies only if 'the objective is legitimate'. That condition does not appear in reg 8(2), but its absence would not seem to be significant. If an occupational requirement is established as a genuine one to carry out the job, then it also aims at a legitimate objective (see *R (on the application of Amicus – MSF section) v Secretary of State for Trade and Industry* [2004] IRLR 430 HC at paragraph 70).

The GOR is a 'characteristic related to age' rather than age itself, so that it would cover, for example, the appearance of the person in question.

The example supplied in the consultation document was that of an actor whose appearance (as related to age) did not meet the requirements of the part. That may be true in respect of a part which requires a youthful appearance, but generally actors can be made up to look older so as to fit the part.

Another possibility is a post which requires someone from a particular age group in order to communicate and identify with a group which is being served. Can Help the Aged argue that its workers should be over a specific age in order to deal with the people who will require their help? Can a local authority argue that its youth workers should be below a certain age in order to deal with their clients? It does not seem that these situations throw up *genuine* occupational requirements. Certainly, the age of the appointee might be a factor which those deciding on applications might wish to bear in mind, but that would seem rather to be a situation where the discrimination in question must be justified (in the sense dealt with in detail in Chapter 4).

This last example raises the issue of the distinction between a GOR and justification of discrimination. In neither case will the act of the person treating less favourably (or applying a provision, criterion or practice – PCP) be unlawful. In both cases, there must be a legitimate aim and proportionate means to achieve it. Where the two defences differ, however, is that, in the case of a GOR, the employer can rely on the GOR if he is not satisfied (on reasonable grounds) that the person against whom he is said to be discriminating meets the GOR. It seems unlikely that this distinction will make much difference in practice.

If that is right, then the fact that both direct and indirect discrimination are potentially capable of justification means that the ambit of the GOR is less important than it is in the case of other strands of discrimination (e.g. sex, race). In the case of race discrimination, for example, since direct discrimination cannot be justified in a general way, it will be unlawful unless a GOR applies.

What are the effects of a GOR?

Where a GOR has been established, the results in reg 8(1) follow. In summary, this lays down that:

(a)   an employer can treat the recruitment of job applicants differently on grounds of age;

(b)   an employer can deal with promotion, training and transfer differently on grounds of age;

(c)   an employer can rely on the exception when dismissing an employee.

The GOR defence does not apply to other situations, however:

(a)   it is not available where different terms and conditions are offered to employees;

(b)   nor does it apply where different terms are offered to prospective employees;

(c)   it does not apply to victimisation;

(d)   nor to harassment;

(e)   nor to unfavourable treatment meted out to those who fail to carry out (or complain about) instructions to discriminate.

To what areas do GORs apply?

In the preceding paragraphs, discussion has been on the basis that it is an employer who is seeking to rely on a GOR in respect of a present or prospective employee. However, GORs apply also in respect of contract workers (reg 9(3)), office-holders (reg 12(5)), the provision of vocational training (reg 20(3)), employment agencies (reg 21(3)), and institutions of further and higher education (reg 23(3)).

Statutory authority

Regulation 27 states that:

> 'Nothing in Part 2 or 3 shall render unlawful any act done in order to comply with a requirement of any statutory provision.'

'Statutory provision' is then defined so as to include statutes enacted by Parliament and statutory instruments, as well as the equivalent primary and secondary legislation made by the Scottish Parliament and Ministers.

As a result, where an employer is forced to discriminate against an individual in order to comply with age limits required by legislation, he has a defence by virtue of reg 27. For example:

> The Licensing Act 1964 prohibits the employment of those under 18 in a bar at a time when the bar is open for the sale or consumption of intoxicating liquor. B, who is aged 17, seeks employment as a bar attendant, and is refused on grounds of age. The employer has not committed an act of unlawful discrimination by his refusal to employ him.

> The Department of Trade and Industry has undertaken a trawl of primary and secondary legislation in order to satisfy itself that any statutory provisions which cannot be objectively justified in terms of Article 6.1 of the Directive are repealed, revoked or amended. The resulting amendments have been included in Schedules 8 or 9 (see Chapter 10) or have been undertaken by other government departments.

National security

Regulation 28 provides that the Regulations do not render unlawful any act which is done in order to safeguard national security, provided it is justified. This provision is similar to the exception set out in other discrimination legislation.

Positive action

Regulation 29 permits certain forms of positive action. It is worth emphasising that, while positive action within these bounds is permitted, positive discrimination is generally forbidden in relation to age, as it is with regard to the other strands of discrimination.

Exceptions

Regulation 29(1) states that:

'Nothing in Part 2 or 3 shall render unlawful any act done in or in connection with–

(a)   affording persons of a particular age or age group access to facilities for training which would help to fit them for particular work; or

(b)   encouraging persons of a particular age or age group to take advantage of opportunities for doing particular work;

where it reasonably appears to the person doing the act that it prevents or compensates for disadvantages linked to age suffered by persons of that age or age group doing that work or likely to take up that work.'

As far as the ambit of the exception is concerned, it excludes the operation of Part 2, which deals with discrimination in employment and vocational training, and Part 3, which deals with unlawful acts by employers, principals and aiders and abettors.

Regulation 29(2) gives an exemption to trade organisations (defined in reg 18 to include trade unions, professional associations and employers' organisations). They are allowed to discriminate by offering training facilities solely to members of a certain age or age group, which would help to equip them for holding a post of any kind in the organisation. In addition, they are permitted to offer encouragement exclusively to those of their members who are of a particular age/age group to hold posts in the organisation. In either case, it must reasonably appear to the organisation that the measure prevents or compensates for disadvantages linked to age suffered by post-holders, actual or prospective, from the group in question.

Regulation 29(3) extends the exemption for trade organisations so that it makes lawful encouragement to people of a particular age or age group to become members, where it reasonably appears to the organisation that such action will prevent or compensate for disadvantages suffered by persons of that age/age group who are members or prospective members.

The provisions dealing with positive action (like those in respect of sexual orientation and religion and belief) are based upon Article 7.1 of the Directive:

'With a view to ensuring full equality in practice, the principle of equal treatment shall not prevent any Member State from maintaining or adopting specific measures to prevent or compensate for disadvantages linked to any of the grounds referred to in Article 1 [which include age].'

They are more generous in their attitude towards initiatives for positive action than those contained in the legislation on sex and race discrimination. In the Race Relations Act 1976, ss 37 and 38 provide an objective test in relation to positive action by an employer. In addition, certain conditions must be satisfied before it is regarded as lawful. In brief, what is required is that there should be no persons of the racial group on whose behalf the positive action is introduced doing work at a particular establishment, or that the proportion should be small. The limitations imposed by the Sex Discrimination Act 1975 are even stricter: ss 47 and 48 also require that the exemption must be based upon statistics reflecting the position in the 12 months preceding the decision in question.

Because of the differences between the positive action provisions for age and those for sex and race, the case law on positive action (which derives from the provisions on sex and race) should be treated with caution.

What might the positive action exemption mean in practice? The subject is most likely to crop up in connection with recruitment, so its application is discussed in Chapter 6. An example might be appropriate at this stage, however:

A trade union surveys its full-time officials and finds that the majority are over the age of 50, and none are under the age of 35. The reason which emerges from a survey of its membership is that older members have had the opportunities over the years to acquire skills in negotiation and advocacy, with the result that they are more likely to be elected to full-time posts. It concludes that it should foster applications from the younger generation among its activists. It puts a series of advertisements in the union journal stating that it is seeking 'Development Officers' under the age of 35, whom it will provide with special training. B, who is aged 43, claims that he has been directly discriminated against. The union is likely to succeed in its reg 29(2) defence. It appears to the union that the training which it is providing for those under 35 will compensate for the disadvantages linked to age which those in that age group who are likely to hold full-time official posts have suffered. Given that they have looked at the evidential basis for the measures which they propose, they should be able to satisfy the requirement that it should 'reasonably' appear to compensate for the disadvantages in question.

Positive action and objective justification

As has been seen in Chapter 4, it is possible for the employer to provide objective justification for acts which appear to be discriminatory, with the result that they are not unlawful. In view of this possibility, why would an employer need to make use of the provisions relating to positive action?

The answer is that it is easier to satisfy the positive action conditions contained in reg 29 than it is to show that the action is objectively justified. There are two main reasons for this:

(a)   reg 29 sets out a legitimate aim: preventing or compensating for disadvantages linked to age;

(b)   there is no need to satisfy the objective demands of 'proportionality'. It is sufficient if it 'reasonably appears' to the person putting the positive action into practice that it fulfils the legitimate aim.

The more relaxed test is in itself justifiable because of the strong social reasons for redressing the balance where the effects of age discrimination in the past have had impact upon the present situation. As Age Concern put it in its response to *Equality and Diversity: Coming of Age* (p 26):

'... there are good reasons for enabling organisations to target under-represented groups without having to pass a high threshold, based upon proportionality and their own business needs.'

6 Recruitment and Selection

It is likely that the new law on age discrimination will have a particular impact upon the way in which employers conduct the process of advertising, selecting, interviewing and recruiting new employees. It is within this sphere that much of the litigation surrounding the Regulations is likely to be generated. This chapter covers:

- An outline of the statutory provisions dealing with the recruitment and selection process.

- The danger points where direct or indirect discrimination are likely to appear.

- The possible ways in which an apparently discriminatory recruitment or selection process might be defended as lawful.

- Ways to avoid discrimination in recruitment.

Statutory framework

Regulation 7 sets out the ambit of the prohibition against age discrimination, and the crucial parts of that regulation for the recruitment process are contained in reg 7(1), (3), (4) and (5).

Regulation 7(1) states that:

'It is unlawful for an employer, in relation to employment by him at an establishment in Great Britain, to discriminate against a person:

(a) in the arrangements he makes for the purpose of determining to whom he should offer employment;

(b) in the terms on which he offers that person employment; or

(c) by refusing to offer, or deliberately not offering him employment.'

'Discrimination' is defined by regs 3, 4 and 5 (see Chapter 2 for details), so that it includes:

- direct discrimination;

- indirect discrimination;

- victimisation.

It follows that all these forms of discrimination are outlawed from the selection process. The prohibition on harassment is dealt with in reg 7(3), and it includes not only those whom the employer employs but also anyone who 'has applied to him for employment'. Hence:

- harassment

can be added to the above list.

For the sake of completeness, it should be stressed that employers are liable for any acts of discrimination or harassment committed by their employees in the course of the employment process, and principals are liable for the acts of their agents (see Chapter 2).

There is a specific exemption in relation to recruitment for employment, which is contained in reg 7(4) and (5):

'(4) Subject to paragraph (5), paragraph (1)(a) and (c) does not apply in relation to a person:

(a) whose age is greater than the employer's normal retirement age or, if the employer does not have a normal retirement age, the age of 65; or

(b) who would, within a period of six months from the date of his application to the employer, reach the employer's normal retirement age or, if the employer does not have a normal retirement age, the age of 65.

(5) Paragraph (4) only applies to a person to whom, if he was recruited by the employer, regulation (exception for retirement) could apply …

(8) In paragraph (4) "normal retirement age" is an age of 65 or more which meets the requirements of section 98ZH of the 1996 [Employment Rights] Act.'

This exemption will be dealt with later in this chapter, in the section on Exemptions and justification. For the moment, it should be explained that reg 7(5), by limiting reg 7(4) to those to whom reg 30 applies, in effect restricts it to those who fit the definition of 'employee' within the meaning of s 230 of the Employment Rights Act 1996. It is therefore limited to those with contracts of service, together with Crown employees and Parliamentary staff.

Discrimination in recruitment: the danger points

What forms of discrimination are likely to occur in the recruitment and selection process? What are the danger points which employers and employees ought to watch out for?

Age limits

The obvious form of direct age discrimination is the express age limit, laid down in the advertisement or person description, or set out as an overt condition for those charged with making the selection. For example:

> Personal assistant aged 25 to 35 required for Managing Director.

> Applications for the post of matron in residential home sought. Only those over the age of 40 need apply, in view of the preference of the residents and the need for maturity and experience.

These advertisements can be identified as directly discriminatory without difficulty, but it must be remembered that they may be subject to some exemption, or be objectively justifiable. These possibilities are dealt with later in this chapter.

Qualifications

Less blatantly, the selection process may discriminate indirectly by demanding qualifications which are more likely to be held by people of a particular age group. For example:

> A television company advertises for a research assistant, stating that a degree in media studies is highly desirable. Older applicants are less likely to have such a degree, and may be regarded as subject to indirect discrimination.
>
> (Adapted from *Equality and Diversity: Coming of Age*, the DTI consultation paper on the draft Regulations, paras 4.3.6 to 7.)

> A shipping company seeks applicants for a job as a clerk, stating 'O' levels in English and Mathematics essential (presumably the person placing the advertisement is unaware of the demise of 'O' levels and the birth of the GCSE). Only those over a certain age are likely to have the qualifications in question.

Again, it is possible that one or more of these apparently indirectly discriminatory advertisements could be justified – that possibility is explored later in this chapter.

It should also be emphasised that the recruitment process may be discriminatory if the employer seeks to exclude those who have *too many* qualifications. 'Over-qualified' can be a euphemism for 'too old'.

Experience

Just as a requirement for qualifications may be discriminatory, so may a criterion for appointment which emphasises experience. If a certain number of years' experience is set down as necessary or even desirable to be able to do the job, then it will be indirectly discriminatory on the face of it (subject to justification, etc). A similar problem arises in relation to a specifically negative view being expressed in relation to experience – it may discriminate indirectly against those who are older, because they are disproportionately likely to have experience. In the Irish case of *Tom O'Connor v LIDL Ireland Gmbh (DEC –E-2005/12)* the supermarket sought managers, saying that the ideal candidate would be a graduate with not more than two to three years' experience in a commercial environment. The claimant did not make the shortlist. He complained that he had been indirectly discriminated against as an older person (he was aged 51). The advertisement was held to be indirectly discriminatory on grounds of age.

To provide some further (hypothetical) examples of the way in which experience as a criterion can raise the prospect of discrimination:

> An employer seeks despatch drivers, and requires at least three years' driving experience. Those under the age of 20 will be unable to comply with the requirement for legal reasons and will be directly discriminated against; the numbers of those in their twenties who can apply will be disproportionately smaller than those in older age groups, and they will potentially have claims for indirect discrimination against the employer.

> A firm of solicitors seeks a 'qualified solicitor with between two and four years' post-qualification experience'. They have managed to discriminate indirectly against both the young and the old!

Again, the actions of the employers might be subject to justification (see later).

Maturity

A requirement that applicants 'should be mature' puts the employer in a vulnerable position in much the same way as an indication that experience is a prerequisite. The danger is that this will be perceived by potential applicants (and by a tribunal) as a statement that older people are preferred. If this is joined to a situation where the successful candidate is older than the disappointed applicant, then there may be less favourable treatment coupled with an inference that it was on grounds of age. It may be thought that the employer would readily be able to justify a requirement for maturity (see the section on 'Justification' below). Why is 'maturity' desirable for the job in question? Could a level-headed young person be able to deal with the demands of a challenging job better than an older person (more 'mature' in the ordinary sense of the word) who is in the throes of a marriage breakdown and a personal debt crisis? The employer would be on the back foot, attempting to explain just exactly what he meant by 'maturity' and why it was needed in this particular post.

Requiring dates

It has been common to ask candidates to answer a question on their application form as to their date of birth. Even more universally, candidates are expected to fill in details of dates when jobs were held and qualifications were obtained, from which the deduction as to their age is usually a simple logical step. To ask these questions is not, it is submitted, discriminatory in itself. However, an employer could make use of the information provided to make decisions which are discriminatory on grounds of age. In a case where an allegation of age discrimination is made, it is possible that an inference might be drawn from the inclusion of such information on the application forms, unless a convincing explanation was given as to the reason for its conclusion. In order to avoid such an inference, the cautious employer might move questions from the application form itself to a separate diversity monitoring form. Arrangements would then need to be made to ensure that those who make the recruitment decisions would not see the ethnic monitoring forms. The matter is considered further in the section below which deals with 'Applications'.

Exemptions and justifications

If something done in the course of recruitment or selection is apparently discriminatory, then it is not necessarily unlawful. There are exemptions and defences which an employer can put forward which will exclude any liability. In summary, they are:

(a) the exemption in relation to applicants for employment over 65 or normal retirement age (including those who will reach the requisite age in six months' time);

(b) genuine occupational requirements;

(c)   statutory authority;

(d)   positive action; and

(e)   justification (legitimate aim met by proportionate means).

These exemptions and defences are dealt with in turn in the sections which follow.

Exemption for excluding applicants over 65

The impact of reg 7(4), (5) and (8) (set out above) is that it is not unlawful for an employer to discriminate in the selection process against a person who:

(a)   is over the employer's normal retirement age if that is over 65;

(b)   is over the age of 65 if the employer has no normal retirement age;

(c)   within six months of the date of his application reaches the employer's normal retirement age if that is over 65;

(d)   within six months of the date of his application reaches the age of 65 if the employer has no normal retirement age.

The exemption is confined, by its reference to reg 30, to those who are 'employees' in the narrower sense set out in s 230(1) of the Employment Rights Act 1996, that is to those under a contract of service, together with civil servants and the staff of Parliament. It does not extend to those who are 'under a contract personally to do any work' nor to office-holders, even though the regulations generally apply to these latter categories of workers. For example:

> A church carries out a selection process for a minister, and states that it is excluding all applicants over the age of 65 because it wants to achieve a more balanced age profile among its ministers. The post in question would seem to be an office within the meaning of reg 12 (see Chapter 3), and in any event is unlikely to qualify as employment in the narrow sense described above. Those responsible could not rely on reg 7(4), since it does not apply. It might, however, argue for one of the other defences or justifications which are discussed later in this section.

As far as 'normal retirement age' is concerned, the definition is given in the new s 98ZH of the Employment Rights Act 1996, which is inserted by Schedule 8 of the Regulations:

' "normal retirement age", in relation to an employee, means the age at which employees in the employer's undertaking who hold, or have held, the same kind of position as the employee are normally required to retire.'

Regulation 7(8) makes it clear that, in the context of the exemption, the normal retiring age must be over 65. In other words, if the employer has a normal retiring age under 65, the exemption will only apply in relation to the age of 65.

The scope of the exemption is also limited to discrimination in relation to selection – the arrangements and the decision as to who should be offered the post. It does not cover the terms on which a job is offered to the successful applicant. For example:

> Company A holds interviews and selects B, who is aged 66, as a counter assistant. They decide to offer him a lower wage than they give to C, aged 58, whom they appoint at the same time, because B can make ends meet with his state pension. The company cannot rely on the exemption in reg 7(4), which applies to selection and not to the terms offered for those appointed.

The exemption in respect of job applicants over 65 has been the subject of strong criticism. As part of the consultation process on the draft Regulations, Age Concern produced a response which maintained (p 27) that the exemption was:

> 'an extremely discriminatory policy that cannot be objectively justified. It is a separate issue from Mandatory Retirement ... None of the arguments that have been used to justify Mandatory Retirement Ages apply to a blanket exemption on recruiting people over 65.'

Age Concern went on the examine each of the arguments used to justify mandatory retirement at 65 (see Chapter 8). They maintained that these arguments did not apply to the blanket exemption for recruitment for that age group. In particular, they stated:

(a)   competence and performance did not figure in the equation, because employers were able to recruit and select on merit;

(b)   health and safety concerns could be rigorously assessed during the recruitment process, given that employers tend to carry out more extensive health and safety checks upon new workers than existing employees;

(c)   none of the arguments relating to employment planning apply to the recruitment of older workers;

(d)   employers could ensure that any appointees would be employed for a reasonable period before retirement. In any event, in most jobs, the payback time on recruitment costs was short, and staff turnover was often high, especially among workers in their twenties.

It seems likely that the exemption for applicants over 65 (and those approaching that age) will be subject to challenge on the basis that it does not meet the requirements of the Directive. This possibility is dealt with in Chapter 11.

Genuine Occupational Requirement

Where the employment is subject to a genuine occupational requirement (GOR), reg 7(1)(a) and (c) do not apply to it. As a result, arrangements made by an employer to recruit, and the selection decision itself, will not be unlawful even if they involve less favourable treatment on grounds of age. GORs are dealt with in Chapter 5. In brief, the exemption will only apply if possession of 'a characteristic related to age is a genuine and determining occupational requirement' of the employment in question. In addition, it must be proportionate to apply the GOR in the particular case, and either:

(a)   the applicant to whom the GOR is applied does not meet it; or

(b)   the employer is not satisfied, upon reasonable grounds, that the applicant meets it.

The GOR exemption is available with regard to applications for employment which fulfils the broad definition contained in reg 2: 'employment under a contract of service or of apprenticeship or a contract personally to do any work'. It does not, however, cover the terms upon which an offer of such employment is made.

An example of a GOR:

A theatre company is producing 'Peter Pan' and advertises that a lead actor is required. 'Applicants must be 14 years of age or under'. (The acting example is used by the consultation document *Equality and Diversity: Coming of Age*). A maximum age limit would probably be held to be a GOR, on the grounds that it is difficult to 'age down' (easier for make-up artists to 'age up'). However, it might prove difficult for the company to establish that it is proportionate to apply the requirement to all those over the age of 16. What about an application from a youthful-looking 15-year-old? It might be safer to say: 'The actor must look about 12'.

It should be emphasised that the wise employer will wish to spell out the GOR in the advertisement. It is fair upon potential applicants to make it clear that the employer regards a GOR as applying. In addition, the fact that the employer has been transparent about the view which it takes may be important in any subsequent proceedings. A tribunal would be more likely to find that there was a GOR which the employer regarded as not satisfied if the employer had made it clear from the outset that it considered that a GOR applied. It will still leave the employer to show that 'it was reasonable for him not to be satisfied' (reg 8(2)(c)(ii)) but at least he is halfway there.

Statutory authority

Regulation 27 provides that the regulations do not render unlawful any act done in order to comply with the requirement of any other statutory provision. The ambit of this exception is examined in Chapter 5. In brief, it provides a defence to an employer obliged to discriminate against an individual in order to comply with age limits required by statute or statutory instrument.

Positive action

Regulation 29 permits positive action (not positive discrimination) in certain circumstances, which are dealt with in Chapter 5. It must be aimed at preventing or compensating for disadvantages linked to age among the relevant section of people at whom the positive action is aimed. If the employer is able to establish such a basis for taking positive action, then it can lawfully discriminate against applicants on the ground of their age. For example:

An employer reasonably believes that older people have less opportunity to work in the information technology field due to their age. It embarks upon an advertising campaign which is focussed upon magazines more likely to be read by older people. In its advertisement, it specifically offers facilities for IT training for those who are over 55 and states: 'The company particularly welcomes applications for employment from those who are aged 55 and over'. The arrangements for training, and for job selection, appear to be directly discriminatory, in that they treat less favourably those under 55. However, the company seems to be acting within the terms of reg 29(1), and has a defence against claims that it has discriminated unlawfully.

Justification

In the event that none of the exemptions outlined above applies, the employer can argue that actions in the recruitment process which are apparently discriminatory can be objectively justified (see Chapter 4). This argument can be advanced whether the discrimination in question is direct (e.g. specifying an age group) or indirect (e.g. specifying length of experience). The test is set out in reg 3(1). In sum, the employer must show that the treatment or PCP is:

(a)   to achieve a legitimate aim; and

(b)   is a proportionate means of doing so.

Some examples:

An NHS Trust has a retirement age of 65 for its doctors. The training to become a doctor lasts for seven years. The Trust fixes a maximum age of 51 for recruitment of trainee doctors, so that the doctors will have at least as many years working after qualification as they will have spent training for the qualification. The Trust argues that the bar on those aged 52 and over is justifiable. The retirement age is one laid down by the Regulations as lawful. The Directive (Article 6.1(c)) specifically mentions:

'… the fixing of a maximum age for recruitment which is based on the training requirements of the post in question or the need for a reasonable period of employment before retirement.'

The bar is therefore likely to constitute a legitimate aim. It is arguable that it has been implemented by means which are proportionate, given the expense of training doctors and the balanced way in which the maximum age for recruitment has been calculated. It may well be held to be justifiable, depending on the evidence in support.

A police authority determines that it will retire officers at the age of 55, believing that it is objectively justifiable to do so. Two years' training is required before a police officer becomes fully qualified. The authority sets a maximum age for recruits of 48, claiming that it is justified in so doing, in order to ensure a reasonable period of employment after qualification and before retirement. The authority will first have to justify its retirement age. Any maximum age for recruitment based upon a discriminatory retirement age would itself be discriminatory. Then the authority would need to show that it has a legitimate aim in setting the maximum age for recruitment. They are likely to establish this, using reasoning based on the Directive as in the preceding example. The authority would then need to show that it has sought to achieve the aim by means which are proportionate. The maximum recruitment age does seem to be set with a large margin before retirement (even assuming that compulsory retirement at 55 is lawful). The training period is not as long as that for doctors. Further, evidence would be needed as to the costs of training, and the extent to which a police officer in training could perform at least some of the duties of a trained officer satisfactorily. Given the stated facts, the authority may not be able to satisfy the test of objective justification.

The recruitment process: step by step

What follows is a consideration of the different stages of the recruitment process, and the impact of discriminatory practices at each stage, dealing with legal issues which may arise. A checklist of 'Do's and Don't's' is then set out to assist employers to carry out an age-neutral recruitment policy which will stand up to scrutiny (and enable job applicants to check whether the process of selection was possibly discriminatory).

Advertising

An advertisement can clearly signal the likelihood that the recruitment process taken as a whole is discriminatory. For example:

In 2001, Ryanair advertised for 'a young and dynamic professional', and were fined £8000 in the first case brought under the Irish Employment Equality Act 1998. Their efforts directed at proving that the advertisement was to attract those who were dynamic, rather than those who were young, proved futile.

As the Regulations in this country stand, however, it is doubtful whether an advertisement can in itself constitute an act of discrimination. Our legislation on sex and race discrimination reserves the right to challenge an advertisement directly to the Equal Opportunities Commission and the Commission for Racial Equality respectively, unless an applicant can show that the advertisement constituted part of 'the arrangements made' for determining who should be offered employment. There is no equivalent body to the CRE and the EOC in respect of age discrimination at present, with the result that a challenge to a discriminatory advertisement would have to be made by an applicant. Would he be able to show that it was part of 'the arrangements [the employer] makes for the purpose of determining to whom he should offer employment' (reg 7(1)(a))?

In *Cardiff Women's Aid v Hartup* [1994] IRLR 390, EAT, the applicant complained about an advertisement which specified that the successful candidate would be a black or Asian woman. The EAT held that the employer had not committed any actionable act of discrimination in placing the advertisement. It was unlawful under the Race Relations Act 1976 to cause an advertisement to be published which indicated 'an intention' to commit an act of discrimination, but only the CRE could take action under this provision. The EAT held that it had not been shown that the advertisement was part of the 'arrangements' made to determine who should be offered the job. A crucial point, however, was that the applicant was not interested in the job. It is submitted that, in a general way, an advertisement may constitute part of the arrangements for determining who should be offered a job. If a restriction is laid down as to who will be considered for the post, that will deter applicants who cannot comply with it. The potential applicant who is interested, but is deterred from applying, has been subjected to less favourable treatment, and ought to be able to bring a claim for direct discrimination. The advertisement may amount to a filter system so as to constitute part of the arrangements for selection.

In due course, the Commission for Equality and Human Rights will provide the machinery to prohibit directly advertising that is discriminatory upon grounds of age. In any event, an advertisement in discriminatory terms is likely to provide powerful ammunition for an unsuccessful applicant who brings a claim in tribunal. It will serve to show that the recruitment process was tainted by age discrimination.

Graduate recruitment

If an employer wishes to recruit graduates, is there any element of age discrimination involved? Clearly graduates can be of any age, and a restriction to those who have a degree does not appear likely to constitute age discrimination. Once the desired applicant is said to be a 'recent graduate', however, the picture changes somewhat. Whilst there are a growing number of mature students (and graduates), the age range of the 'recent graduate' will be skewed towards the younger groups. It will be difficult to justify restricting recruitment to 'recent graduates'. In any event, it is worth bearing in mind the ACAS Guidance (see Appendix 3) which states:

'If you ask for graduates, remember that the term can be interpreted as code for someone in their early twenties. Graduates can be almost any age. Make it clear that you are interested in the qualification, and not the age of the applicant.'

Further, recruitment drives specifically directed at the universities ('the milk round') could be seen as indirectly discriminatory. In the consultation document *Equality and Diversity: Coming of Age*, the DTI suggests that they can be justified. If the employer can show that a business need is achieved by using the 'milk round', that would be a legitimate aim. The means employed to achieve the aim could be held to be proportionate provided employers do not exclude applications from other sources. As it was put by the Employers Forum on Age:

'... if employers choose to continue operating a graduate recruitment programme ... there [should be] visible alternative entry methods for "atypical" graduates and others. Employers should also consider the appropriateness and justifications for other programmes such as fast track, leadership and management development programmes.'

Selection criteria

Just as is needed to avoid other forms of discrimination, an employer should be careful to ensure that there are clear selection criteria, and that they do not contravene the age discrimination provisions. In order to ensure that the process of selection will be fair, and that it will withstand subsequent scrutiny, the criteria should be recorded and communicated to all those who will be involved in screening applicants, shortlisting, interviewing, and making the final decisions. The best way of determining criteria is to base them upon a carefully drawn up person specification, linked to the job description. If any criterion appears to be directly or indirectly discriminatory, it should be carefully examined to see whether it is covered by an exemption, or can be objectively justified (see the examples in Chapters 3 and 4).

Application forms

Historically, the typical application form has asked for the applicant's age and/or date of birth. It is not, of course, discriminatory in itself to do so. Further, it can be argued that such information is actually useful in monitoring selection procedures, and hence avoiding discriminatory practices. It helps to provide answers to such questions as: Are we obtaining a range of age groups among our applicants? Is the success rate among applicants skewed towards the young, or the old? Are there good reasons for this?

The problem is that such forms provide information upon which discriminatory decisions can be based. The fact that the decision makers have information relating to age in front of them at the time when they consider e.g. whether to shortlist candidates, may influence them consciously or unconsciously towards age or youth. Even if that is not the case, the fact that they were privy to such information may lead to suspicion on the part of a tribunal if the matter is later litigated. The requirement to provide a date of birth may not be discriminatory in itself, but its absence might help to dispel any inference that there has been age discrimination on the part of those who sift the applications, for example.

Less direct means of acquiring information as to age include a requirement to set out the dates of qualifications, and the dates on which other posts were started and finished. There is also the thought that a request to send a photograph with the application may mean that those who perform the sift will be aware of how old the candidate looks. In the case of this information, there are perhaps stronger reasons to justify the request. The pattern of employment and how recently qualifications were acquired may provide information which is of value. Possession of photographs will sometimes enable those involved in the interview process to jog their memories as to which candidate was which, so as to flesh out the notes made during the course of the interview. However, these practices are capable of being viewed as discriminatory, and if an employer feels strongly that he needs them, he should be prepared to justify their use.

An age-neutral application form can be obtained from the Employers Forum on Age: www.efa.org.uk.

It is based entirely on 'competency', and aims to remove the potential for discrimination. The information on age/date of birth could be removed to appear on the diversity monitoring form. This would provide information for monitoring the selection process, and would not be seen by the decision makers at the time they were shortlisting or interviewing.

Shortlisting

Where a shortlist is prepared, it ought to be done on the basis of the criteria for selection, and is usually carried out on sight of the applications, so the points made in the preceding two sub-sections are relevant to the shortlisting process. Those involved should ensure that, if a minimum or maximum age is set, it is covered by an exemption or is objectively justifiable. Those who are involved should ensure that they do not make decisions based upon unfounded assumptions and stereotypes about age or youth. The ACAS leaflet, *Tackling discrimination and promoting equality – good practice guide for employers*, gives a clear set of recommendations for the sift process, which are incorporated in the 'Checklist' at the end of this chapter.

It is clear that the process of sifting or shortlisting prior to interview is part of the 'arrangements made for the purpose of determining to whom [the employer] should offer the post'. In *Nagarajan v London Regional Transport* [1999] IRLR 572, the House of Lords held that interviewing and assessing candidates for a post could amount to making 'arrangements' within s 4(1)(a) of the Race Relations Act 1976. Those who set up the arrangements may be different from those who carry them out, e.g. by doing the interviews. In *Brennan v J H Dewhurst Ltd* [1983] IRLR 357 (a sex discrimination case), the EAT put it this way:

'[I]f the first filter creamed out all the women, that would be part of the arrangements made and would prevent the woman coming through for consideration.'

Interviews

Whatever the position with regard to advertisements, it seems that an interview should come within the 'arrangements ... for the purpose of determining to whom [the employer] should offer' a job. If that is right, then the decision whether to interview (covered under 'Shortlisting' above) and age discriminatory procedures adopted at the interview would constitute a 'filter' in the term used in the *Brennan* case, so as to bring them within the ambit of reg 7. The case of *Cardiff Women's Aid v Hartup* [1994] IRLR 390 (see above) which dealt with advertisements can be distinguished. The decision whether to apply after seeing an advertisement which shows a bias in terms of age is with the reader (or, at any rate, so it can be argued). However, the decision whether to interview someone or not is clearly in the hands of the employer.

Further, questions which indicated a preoccupation with the age of a particular candidate, and comments which tended to show that this was likely to influence the decision as to whom to appoint, might provide evidence that the decision was taken 'on grounds of [the applicant's] age'. A ready comparison is available from sex discrimination cases, where a focus on the applicant's present and future family plans would be likely to result in an inference that these matters were of importance to the employer and could result in a finding of discrimination.

For example:

An applicant (aged 40) for a position as a pupil in a set of barrister's chambers is asked: 'How would you feel about having someone younger than you as a pupil-master? What would your reaction be to them if you were asked to do the photocopying and make some coffee?' The questions themselves do not necessarily fit the definition of 'less favourable treatment' in reg 3. However, they would provide material from which a tribunal might, in appropriate circumstances, conclude that any less favourable treatment (e.g. a failure to appoint) was 'on grounds of the complainant's age' so as to constitute direct discrimination.

An applicant (aged 50) for a position as a member of cabin crew with an airline is asked at interview: 'How will you take to being given instructions by younger people? How would you feel about starting at the bottom of the ladder? Why didn't you apply for a more senior role?' (adapted from the Irish case of *Hughes v Aer Lingus*). The comments on the previous example are equally relevant here.

Checklist

What follows is a summary of points which should be borne in mind in determining procedures for selection and recruitment. A number of them are taken from the ACAS advice document *Tackling discrimination and promoting equality – good practice guide for employers*. Not all of the points made in that document are relevant for our purposes here, however. In addition, some points have been added. The list that follows contains a number of points which are of relevance to the avoidance of other forms of discrimination (sex, race, etc). What should be remembered overall is that, if the process is transparent and procedurally fair, it will be more effective in selecting the best candidate, as well as better enabling the employer to defend himself in any subsequent proceedings.

Advertising

- Advertise in a cross-section of media to ensure that you are in touch with all age groups.

- Base the advertisement upon the job description and person specification to ensure that you are precise about requirements.

- Think carefully about the language that you use. Avoid phrases such as 'young graduates' or 'mature people'.

- Avoid specifying a minimum/maximum length of experience.

- Clearly state any 'genuine occupational requirement' (GOR) as to age which applies to the job, after carefully checking that it does fulfil the strict criteria for a GOR.

Selection criteria

- Selection criteria should be drafted carefully.

- Criteria should be based upon the job description and person specification.

- Subjective or irrelevant criteria should be avoided.

- Those involved in shortlisting, interviewing, and deciding who should be offered the job should all be aware that they must base their actions on the selection criteria.

- The selection criteria should not be changed during the process in order to assist a candidate who is favoured, for example, at interview.

Application forms

- Avoid asking for age/date of birth (or information which clearly reveals these details) on the application form itself.

- Put information as to age on a separate monitoring form (together with gender, race, etc) which is not seen by those shortlisting, interviewing or deciding on whom to appoint.

- Ensure that the questions on the form give you the information relating to the job and your requirements, i.e. is relevant to the selection criteria.

Shortlisting

- If possible, have more than one person to carry out the 'sift' in order to reduce the risk of bias.

- Adopt a simple marking system based upon the criteria, to show how each candidate has presented evidence to meet your requirements.

- Take each application in turn, and work through the requirements, awarding a mark for each.

- Review the process at the end to ensure that marks are awarded on the basis of evidence on the application form, and record it.

- Invite the candidates with the best scores to interview.

Interviews

- If possible, interviews should be carried out by more than one person.

- Ideally, use an interview panel which mixes ages (sometimes a tall order, particularly if one also wants a mix of genders and races!)

- Interviewers should be aware of the need to focus upon the selection criteria.

- The job description, person specification and the interviewee's application form should provide a useful framework for the interview.

- It will be reasonable to concentrate upon particular points with different candidates, and ask questions in different ways in the light of the information contained on the application forms.

- But interviewers should cover the same topics and issues in depth with each of the candidates.

- Experience outside the workplace (e.g. voluntary activities) is likely to be of relevance, but questions about the candidate's personal circumstances could lead to a perception of bias.

- For that reason, it may avoid misunderstanding to keep away from questions such as 'How old are your children?'

Decision

- The decision should be based on the selection criteria.

- The assessment of each candidate should be recorded.

- The records should be retained for a reasonable period, e.g. a year.

- If references are taken up, it should be done consistently.

- A reference will be more helpful if it is based upon the job description or person specification.

- If you need to be assured of health or fitness of the successful candidate, a medical practitioner or occupational health physician should be consulted.

- Any requirement as to a medical examination should be consistently applied, and no assumption made as to age.

- After the process is over, the results should be monitored by someone independent of the selection process, making use of the separately kept information on the monitoring form as to age, etc.

7 Terms and Conditions

The Regulations provide general protection against discrimination in relation to the terms and conditions under which a worker is employed, subject to certain exemptions. The general prohibition is contained in reg 7(2), which reads:

'It is unlawful for an employer, in relation to a person whom he employs at an establishment in Great Britain, to discriminate against that person:

(a)   in the terms of employment which he affords him;

(b)   in the opportunities which he affords him for promotion, a transfer, training or receiving any other benefit;

(c)   by refusing to afford him, or deliberately not affording him, any such opportunity ...'

The concept of discrimination, which runs throughout the Regulations, is defined in reg 3 and is dealt with in detail in Chapter 2. A difference in terms and conditions, or opportunities, would clearly be capable, in appropriate circumstances, of constituting less favourable treatment such as to amount to direct discrimination.

Equally, such a difference might be found to be a 'particular disadvantage' so as to constitute indirect discrimination. 'Benefits' covers a wide variety of employment-related benefits – not just pay, but other benefits, such as annual leave, sick leave, private health insurance, company cars and staff discount cards. Although pensions are clearly benefits, the treatment of occupational pension schemes is different from that relating to other benefits, and is described in Chapter 9. In any event, reg 32(7) excludes from the operation of this regulation any benefits awarded to a worker when he ceases employment. As a result, it would not cover pensions, or enhanced redundancy payments, which are dealt with in reg 33.

Some examples of the discriminatory provision of benefits:

An employer provides free private health insurance to his employees provided they are aged under 60. Private health insurance is a benefit, and it is being denied to some employees on grounds of their age. The actions of the employer would constitute direct discrimination, unless they could be justified by showing a legitimate aim and a proportionate means of achieving it (see Chapter 4).

The same employer, on receiving advice that his proposal is discriminatory, decides to offer free private health insurance to those with a minimum of ten years in the industry. This puts younger employees at a particular disadvantage, and would seem to be indirectly discriminatory (again subject to a defence of justification). The defence under reg 32 (see the section on 'Benefits and seniority' below) would not be available, as the stated criterion is service in the industry generally, rather than with the particular employer in question.

Chapter 6 dealt with the exemption which entitles employers to exclude those over 65 (or within six months of that age) from the recruitment process. Further, Chapter 8 deals with the default retirement age of 65, which enables an employer to set a compulsory retirement age of 65 or over without having to justify it. In relation to terms and conditions of employment, however, these exemptions do not apply. Once someone is employed, they are entitled to protection from age discrimination, unless the situation falls within the ambit of one of the following provisions:

(a)   benefits also provided to the public or a section of it (reg 7(6));

(b)   the national minimum wage exception (reg 31);

(c)   the exception relating to benefits for seniority (reg 32);

(d)   enhanced redundancy payments (reg 33);

(e)   life assurance after early retirement (reg 34).

Each of these exceptions is dealt with in turn in the sections which follow.

Benefits provided to the public

Excluded from the definition of 'benefits' are certain benefits which the employer provides to the public. They are described in reg 7(6):

'Paragraph (2) [the prohibition against discrimination] does not apply to benefits of any description if the employer is concerned with the provision (for payment or not) of benefits of that description to the public, or to a section of the public which includes the employee in question, unless:

(a)   that provision differs in a material respect from the provision of the benefits by the employer to his employees; or

(b)   the provision of the benefits to the employee in question is regulated by his contract of employment; or

(c)   the benefits relate to training.

The rationale for this exclusion is the fact that the Regulations deal with discrimination in the fields of employment and education, and have not been extended to the supply of goods and services to the public. To take an example of the way in which the exclusion operates:

B is employed by a building society. He applies for a mortgage, and is refused on the grounds that he is too young. On the face of it, this is direct discrimination (less favourable treatment on grounds of age). However, the building society can rely on the exclusion set out in reg 7(6), as they are in the business of supplying mortgages to the public, or a section of it. If the employees of the building society were entitled to specially reduced interest rates, however, then reg 7(6)(a) would apply. The provision of mortgages to the public would 'differ in a material respect from the provision of the benefits by the employer to his employees'. As a result, the discriminatory policy would be unlawful (subject to any possible defence of justification) and B would be able to claim against his employer.

National minimum wage

The National Minimum Wage Regulations 1999 ('the 1999 Regulations') lay down minimum wage bands which differentiate according to the age of the worker concerned. These bands are as follows (the figures in brackets are those in effect from 1 October 2006 – the amounts are usually increased annually):

● Those aged 22 and over: £5.05 (£5.35).

● Those aged 18 to 21: £4.25 (£4.45).

● Those aged 16 and 17: £3 (£3.30).

The rate for those aged 22 and over is designated as the 'single hourly rate'.

Clearly, then, an employer who had workers of these different age groups to whom he paid the minimum wage would be discriminating between them on grounds of age. Such an employer would be able to rely on the defence contained within reg 27 (the exception for statutory authority). However, the Age Regulations go further than this, and reg 31 allows employers to pay:

- Employees aged 22 and over more than those under 22 even where they are doing the same job, provided that those under 22 are paid less than the adult rate.

- Employees aged between 18 and 21 more than those under 18 even where they are doing the same job, provided that those under 18 are paid less than the adult rate.

The reason put forward by the government for this exemption is that it is important to encourage employers to take on young workers and pay them the minimum wage, whilst paying adult workers more, without the fear that this could be unlawful. They cite the report of the Low Pay Commission in 2005, which predicted that 'the application of the adult rate to younger people would have adverse employment consequences, given the distinctive features of the labour market for young people'.

The government claims that the exemption is countenanced by Article 6.1(a) of the Directive which provides that:

'Member States may provide that differences of treatment on grounds of age shall not constitute discrimination if ... they are objectively and reasonably justified by a legitimate aim ... and the means of achieving the aim are appropriate and necessary. Such differences of treatment may include ... (a) the setting of special conditions on access to employment ... including dismissal and remuneration conditions, for young people ... in order to promote their vocational integration.'

Employers are unable to rely on this exemption, however, if they do not base their pay structure upon the national minimum wage bands, because of the way in which reg 31(1) is worded. It states that it is not unlawful for A to be remunerated at a rate lower than B where:

'(a) the hourly rate of the national minimum wage for a person of A's age is lower than that for a person of B's age; and

(b) the rate at which A is remunerated is below the single hourly rate for the national minimum wage . . '

To take a couple of examples:

> The employer pays A, who is 19, less than B, who is 20 and is doing the same job. The difference is based upon the ages of the workers concerned. This situation does not satisfy condition (a) in reg 31(1), as the hourly rate for both A and B is the same, since they are in the same wage band as far as the 1999 Regulations are concerned. It follows that the employer would not be able to rely on the exemption in reg 31(1) and his actions would be unlawful, subject to any defence of justification.

Another employer pays D (aged 17) £8 per hour, E and F (aged 19) £9 per hour, and G (aged 23) £10 per hour. All of them are doing the same job and again the different rates are based upon age. D, E and F would have claims for direct discrimination, subject to any defence of justification. As they are not 'remunerated below the adult rate', the condition in (b) is not satisfied, and the employer cannot rely on the exemption in reg 31(1). This is a strange result. D, E and F have acquired a potentially sound basis for a claim because their employer has paid them more generously than the minimum wage legislation requires. An employer put in this position will be tempted to lower the wages for the workers concerned, in order to avoid the prospect of an age discrimination claim. The net effect is likely to be to depress the wages of younger workers – hardly the outcome which one would expect from a combination of minimum wage and age discrimination legislation.

Regulation 31 also deals with the position of apprentices. Some apprentices are not entitled to the national minimum wage – those under 19, and those in the first year of apprenticeship. Other apprentices can claim the benefit of the minimum wage legislation. Regulation 31(2) enables an employer to pay an apprentice in the first category less than one in the second category. Clearly there is a discriminatory aspect to this treatment – direct discrimination against those under 19, and indirect discrimination (because they are likely to be younger) against those in the first year of apprenticeship. The government claims that this is justified. It states (Explanatory Notes, para 109) that the treatment of apprentices in the 1999 Regulations is designed to encourage employers to offer apprenticeships to young workers in particular. It suggests that this design might be defeated if employers feared legal challenge on grounds of age discrimination.

Benefits and seniority

The major exception to the general rule that there should be no age discrimination with regard to terms and conditions of employment is contained in reg 32. This reads in part:

'(1) Subject to paragraph (2), nothing in Part 2 or 3 shall render it unlawful for a person ('A'), in relation to the award of any benefit by him, to put a worker ('B') at a disadvantage when compared with another worker ('C'), if and to the extent that the disadvantage suffered by B is because B's length of service is less than that of C.'

In other words, it is lawful, subject to what follows, for an employer to give one employee more favourable terms than another on grounds of length of service (seniority). Of course, if there were no such exception, the terms in question would be likely to constitute indirect age discrimination, since the more senior employees in terms of service would also be likely to be older. As a result, younger employees would be subject to a 'particular disadvantage' resulting from a 'provision, criterion or practice' imposed by the employer in awarding the more favourable terms.

The operation of the exemption is limited to an extent by reg 32(2) which states:

> '(2) Where B's length of service exceeds 5 years, it must reasonably appear to A that the way in which he uses the criterion of length of service, in relation to the award in respect of which B is put at a disadvantage, fulfils a business need of his undertaking (for example, by encouraging the loyalty or motivation, or rewarding the experience, of some or all of his workers).'

The first point to note is that reg 32(2) does *not* apply where the service of the person put at a disadvantage (the potential claimant) is less than five years.

If the potential claimant's service is more than five years, then the employer should consider whether the criterion of length of service fulfils 'a business need of his undertaking'. If it reasonably appears to him that it does, then the exemption applies, and it is lawful for him to put the potential claimant (B) at a disadvantage, e.g. by withholding a benefit. This will be an easier test to satisfy than the usual one of 'justification' since all that is required is that it *reasonably appears* to the employer to satisfy a business need. He does not need to establish a legitimate aim (although many business needs will amount to one). More importantly, he does not need to show that the means of achieving the aim is 'proportionate', as reg 3 requires (see Chapter 4 for discussion of 'Justification').

Business needs

This poses the question: what constitutes a business need? Some examples are given in reg 32(2):

(a) encouraging loyalty;

(b) encouraging motivation;

(c) rewarding experience.

These are the obvious reasons why seniority is taken as a benchmark for enhanced benefits. Although the formula is not as demanding as that for justification, an employer should be able to show some basis for concluding that benefits linked to seniority fulfil a business need. By definition, they reward experience. But in what way does experience fulfil a need for that particular business? Is it especially desirable to encourage loyalty? For example, what is the cost of recruiting new staff to the position in question? By answering those questions satisfactorily, an employer is likely to be able to show that he has considered and come to a reasonable conclusion that the benefits accorded to seniority make sound sense. An employer with one eye to the possibility of future claims based upon seniority differentials would no doubt wish to record the perceived benefits of such differentials in the form of a policy statement or the minutes of a meeting at which they were discussed.

Who is affected by the seniority exemption?

As far as the scope of reg 32 is concerned (i.e. to whom does it apply?) that is set out in reg 2, which deals with interpretation. The term 'worker' in reg 32 applies to:

(a)   employees (widely defined so as to include those under contracts of service, contracts personally to do any work, and apprentices);

(b)   office-holders;

(c)   police officers;

(d)   partners, including members of limited liability partnerships;

(e)   those in Crown employment; and

(f)   members of the staff of both Houses of Parliament.

Regulation 32 and the Directive

The exemption contained within reg 32 is a wide-ranging one, and is likely to have far-reaching consequences. Essentially, it is based on a view that, if employers have to justify benefits based on seniority individually, they might take the easy way out, and withdraw the benefits in a process of levelling down. The further assumption is that such benefits are, in general, desirable.

The rationale is set out in more detail in the government's Explanatory Notes, paras 111–119. The Directive provides (Article 6.1(b)) that member states can determine that differences of treatment shall not constitute discrimination if they satisfy the test for objective justification (a legitimate aim achieved by appropriate and necessary means), and goes on to state that:

'Such differences of treatment may include … (b) the fixing of minimum conditions of seniority in service for access … to certain advantages linked to employment.'

It should be noted that the Directive sees any such differences as needing objective justification, whereas reg 32 appears to be posed as an alternative to the normal process of justification.

The Explanatory Notes (para 113) go on to reason that:

'the legitimate aim justifying the retention of service-related benefits is employment planning, in the sense of being able to attract, retain and reward experienced staff. They help maintain workforce stability by rewarding loyalty as distinct from performance and by responding to employees' reasonable expectation that their salary should not remain static. The exact formulation of the exempting provisions ensures that the actual award remains proportionate.'

The Notes suggest that this approach is backed by the European Court of Justice in the case of *Danfoss* [1989] ECR 3199. That was a case in which indirect sex discrimination was alleged, in that the employer awarded pay based partly on length of service. The ECJ concluded that:

'since length of service goes hand in hand with experience and since experience generally enables the employee to perform his duties better, the employer is free to reward him without having to establish the importance it has in the performance of specific tasks entrusted to the employee … [T]he Equal Pay Directive must [therefore] be interpreted as meaning that where it appears that the application of criteria … for the award of pay systematically works to the disadvantage of female employees … the employer does not have to provide special justification for recourse to the criterion of length of service.'

The Notes concede that the principle in *Danfoss* has been eroded by a series of cases in the ECJ. In particular, in *Nimz* [1991] ECR I-297, the ECJ held that, where the effect of using seniority as a criterion is to discriminate indirectly against women, the criterion must be objectively justified by reference to the experience gained in the job in question. However, the Employment Appeal Tribunal in *Health and Safety Executive v Cadman* (Appeal No EAT/0947/02) held that the employer did not have to objectively justify the use of length of service as a criterion in a pay structure, where a disproportionate impact upon women was alleged. The EAT based its decision on *Danfoss* and distinguished *Nimz* on the ground that the crucial feature of the latter case was that the women concerned were part-time workers who took longer to progress up the pay scales because length of service was calculated according to the hours worked by employees. *Cadman* has been referred by the Court of Appeal to the ECJ: [2004] EWCA (Civ) 1317.

At the time of writing, the ECJ had not reached a decision in the *Cadman* case. However, on 18 May 2006, the Opinion of the Advocate General on the case was published. That Opinion (which will form an important part of the material upon which the Court will make its final decision) made it clear that *Danfoss* could not be relied on to support the proposition that seniority could be relied on as a criterion without any specific justification. It stated (para 34):

> 'It is the employer who must ... provide objective justification for that criterion and who must demonstrate that the criterion is both an appropriate means of achieving a legitimate aim and is necessary in order to do so.'

The Opinion went on to indicate (para 63) the standard of proof which the employer must discharge to show that a length-of-service criterion does not lead to indirect discrimination (remembering that the case is essentially one where the claimant alleges less favourable treatment than her male comparators):

> 'In view of the foregoing considerations, the standard of proof which the employer must discharge in order to show that recourse to a length-of-service criterion does not lead to indirect discrimination can be summarised as follows. First, a degree of transparency as to how the length-of-service criterion is applied in the pay system is necessary, so that judicial scrutiny can take place. In particular, it should be clear how much weight is placed, in the determination of pay, on length of service – conceived either as a way of measuring experience or as a means of rewarding loyalty – as compared with other criteria such as merit and qualifications. In addition, the employer should explain why experience will be valuable for a specific job, and why it is rewarded proportionally. In this respect, while an analysis will have to be carried out by the national court, there can be no doubt, for example, that experience will be more valuable – and therefore legitimately rewarded – in the case of posts involving responsibility and management tasks than in the case of repetitive tasks, in respect of which the length-of-service criterion can account for only a small proportion of pay. This criterion may be of particular relevance in the training phase but become less relevant once the employee has acquired sufficient command of his or her job. Finally, the way length of service is accounted for must also minimise the negative impact of the criterion on women. It seems to me, for example, that a system which excludes periods of maternity or paternity leave, although it is prima facie neutral, would result in indirect discrimination against women.'

Clearly the eventual outcome of the case will be important in determining whether reg 32 can be regarded as implementing the Directive. However, it does seem that the clear wording of the Directive is that seniority in service has to be objectively justified. Further, the case of *Nimz* appears to back the need for the employer to complete the justification exercise successfully in order to rely upon seniority in the context of indirect sex discrimination. It is submitted that the European foundations of reg 32 are shaky, and that it may be held not to constitute implementation of the Directive. (As to the implications when the Regulations fail to carry out the terms of the Directive, see Chapter 11 on Enforcement).

There is a further issue with the exemption contained in reg 32, which relates to the five-year watermark. If the potential claimant has less than five years' service, then the reg 32 exemption can be relied on without any requirement for a business need. If he has more than five years' service, then the requirement of seniority must reasonably appear to the employer to fulfil a business need. There is no express rationale for the difference after five years. If it is meant to provide the employer with a sufficient period to satisfy himself that a new employee appears to be capable and intends to be permanent, a much shorter period would seem to be appropriate – for example, the standard probationary period, or the qualifying period for the right not to be unfairly dismissed. On that basis, six months or a year would seem to be the period of service which would require the test set out in reg 32(2). In any event, that test is so undemanding that it would not appear to impose much of a burden to require the employer to consider whether any business need will be fulfilled by tailoring benefits to seniority.

Calculating length of service

Regulation 32(3) explains how an employer should calculate length of service in order to qualify for the exemption. There are two alternatives. He can calculate either:

(a)   the length of time workers have been working for him doing work *at or above a particular level*; or

(b)   the time they have been working for him *in total*.

Where he chooses to calculate the length of time 'at or above a particular level', that level should be assessed in terms of the demands made on the worker, e.g. in terms of effort, skills and decision making. Whenever he chooses to use length of service as a criterion, it is up to him which of these alternatives – (a) or (b) – he adopts.

Regulation 32(4) and (5) clarify the calculation process further, laying down that the employer must calculate the length of time in terms of the number of weeks during which the employee worked for him (reg 32(4)(a)). This ensures that length of service is not calculated according to the number of hours worked by each employee – a system which would disadvantage part-time workers, and fall foul of the decision of the ECJ in *Nimz* [1991] ECR I-297 (see the discussion above in 'Regulation 32 and the Directive'). The employer is allowed to discount any period during which the employee was absent from work, unless it would be unreasonable to do so. In deciding what is reasonable, the way in which the absences of other workers occurring in similar circumstances are treated by the employer should be considered (reg 32(4)(b)). Further, the employer can choose to discount periods when the employee was actually at work, provided that those periods preceded a period of absence and, in all the circumstances, it would be reasonable to discount them (reg 32(4)(c)). Factors which are singled out as reasonable for the employer to take into account in making this choice are the length of the absence in question, the effect it had on the worker's ability to carry out his duties, and the way in which other workers are treated by the employer in similar circumstances.

In calculating length of service, a worker is to be treated as working for his employer if he worked for an associated employer, if there was a transfer of an undertaking, or in various analogous situations (reg 32(5) and (6)).

There are several areas of discretion for the employer in making the calculation of length of service. Although it is not expressly stated in the Regulations, it is submitted that the same method of calculation must be used is respect of B (the potential claimant) and C (his potential comparator) in so far as their circumstances are similar. To do otherwise would make the whole exercise meaningless. Further, whilst a method of calculation by the employer may not be unlawful under the Employment Equality (Age) Regulations 2006, that will not guarantee that it does not fall foul of the Disability Discrimination Act 1995 or other anti-discrimination legislation. One would need to consider, for example, whether a person who is disabled is being treated less favourably on grounds related to his disability when his absence from work is taken into account, or his presence at work after an absence is discounted.

Examples of benefits and seniority

The examples which follow are adapted from the Department of Trade and Industry's consultation paper, *Equality and Diversity: Coming of Age*. The reasoning and some of the results have been altered, however, because the draft regulation upon which the consultation took place was significantly different from the regulation in its final form.

> An employer has a pay scale which gives employees an increase in pay at the end of each year, up to the completion of four years of service. Beyond the fourth year, further pay rises are awarded on the

basis of the performance appraisal of the employee. As far as the rises for the first four years are concerned, they fall within the exemption set out in reg 32(1) and (2). Assume that employee B has been employed for one year, and C for four years. C will have the benefit of an additional three increments based on service. The employer will not need to show that it reasonably appears to him that his use of length of service as a criterion 'fulfils a business need of his undertaking'.

In the situation described in the previous example, assume that C is awarded further increments for the fifth, sixth and seventh years of her service, while B is not awarded any. These increments are awarded in accordance with the performance appraisals of the workers concerned. The use of this criterion is outside the scope of the Regulations – it is not related to age, directly or indirectly. There is no need for the employer to rely on the terms of reg 32, as the difference in treatment is not unlawful.

A law firm uses a three-year pay scale for trainees, a four-year pay scale for junior associates and a five-year pay scale for senior associates. The natural progression for lawyers at this firm is to rise automatically through each of these scales in turn. A trainee who wishes to allege that she has been discriminated against by comparison with, say, a junior associate, would be met by the defence under reg 32(1) – the disadvantage which she suffers is because her length of service is less than that of the junior associate, so it is not unlawful. Further, her case does not fall within reg 32(2), because her length of service is less than five years. As a result, the employer does not need to show that the use of the criterion reasonably appeared to fulfil a business need.

In the same law firm, assume that a junior associate, who has been with the firm for six years (three years as a trainee), wishes to lodge a claim for age discrimination on the basis that she is less favourably treated than a senior associate who has been with the firm for nine years. Neither of the associates has any relevant absences. The employer is entitled, according to reg 32(3), to choose whether to calculate the length of service on the basis of total time with the firm, or on the basis of 'the length of time the worker has been ... doing work ... at or above a particular level'. If the employer can show that he has reasonably assessed the work of a senior associate at or above a particular level, by reference to the demands of the job in relation to effort, skill and decision making, then he can base his case on the claimant's length of service being limited to her three years as a junior associate. If so, he does not have to bother with the need to show a business need (reg 32(2)) and can rely on the exemption in reg 32(1). It would follow that his use of length of service as a criterion for salary increments would not be unlawful, and the claim for age discrimination would fail.

A department store owned by company A has a qualifying period of ten years' employment before members of staff receive an increase in their annual leave entitlement from 25 days to 30 days. B, who has been working for the store for four years, claims that he is discriminated against by comparison with C, who has been working there for eleven years. Prior to commencing work for the store, B worked for company D, which was under the control of company A, for three years. The level of annual leave is a benefit, and B has been less favourably treated than C. Company A can seek to utilise the provisions in reg 32(1) so as to argue that the reliance on length of service is not unlawful. However, B's service with company D must be treated as a period of employment with company A (reg 32(5)). As a result, he has seven years' service in aggregate. Company A will therefore have to satisfy the test in reg 32(2). It must reasonably appear to them that the provision relating to annual leave fulfils a business need of their undertaking, e.g. by encouraging loyalty or motivation, or rewarding experience.

Enhanced redundancy payments

Employers are obliged by statute to make payments to those employees whom they make redundant (Part 11 of the Employment Rights Act 1996). The amount of the payment is determined by the employee's age, length of service and weekly pay. The first two of these criteria are age related, and arguably discriminatory (see Chapter 10). An employer making payments under the statutory scheme, however, can rely upon the defence of statutory authority (reg 27: see Chapter 5).

The exemption related to enhanced redundancy pay has a different focus. Its main aim is to assist employers who base their own redundancy scheme upon the statutory scheme, but are more generous in the terms which they offer. As the government's Explanatory Notes (para 129) point out:

'It would be ironic if employers who did the minimum necessary did not run the risk of a successful challenge under these Regulations, yet a more generous employer – because he was doing more than he was required to do – could be challenged. If this were the position, there is a real risk that more generous employers would simply 'level down'. This would benefit no-one'.

An employer can therefore make an 'enhanced redundancy payment' to any 'qualifying employee'. A qualifying employee is one who:

(a)   is entitled to a redundancy payment in accordance with the statutory scheme; or

(b)   would be entitled to such a payment if he had two years' continuous employment; or

(c)   was not dismissed (whether after two years' continuous employment or not), but agreed to the termination of his employment in circumstances where, had he been dismissed, the dismissal would have been by reason of redundancy.

An enhanced redundancy payment must first be calculated in accordance with the statutory formula contained in s 162 of the Employment Rights Act 1996. Once that calculation has been performed, an employer may:

(a)   pay the amount in question to any qualifying employee; or

(b)   enhance the resultant amount by multiplying it by a figure in excess of one (e.g. applying a multiplier of 1.5, or 2, or 3, etc); or

(c)   raise or remove the maximum amount for a week's pay set out in s 227 of the Employment Rights Act 1996 (currently £290 per week – updated annually); or

(d)   a combination of these processes.

If the employer is able to comply with the conditions set out in reg 33, any less favourable treatment which is meted out as a result of the enhanced redundancy payments will not need to be objectively justified, and will not be unlawful. On the other hand, if an employer uses a formula which is based on length of service, but which does not meet these conditions, it will have to be objectively justified (see Chapter 4). The employer will not be able to utilise the exemption for benefits related to seniority (reg 32) since that does not apply to 'any benefit awarded to a worker by virtue of his ceasing to work for' the employer.

Life assurance cover for retired workers

Regulation 34 provides an exception for employers who provide life assurance cover for workers who have retired early on grounds of ill-health. If the employer arranges for the cover to cease upon the age at which they would normally have retired (or the age of 65 if there was no normal retirement age) then such an arrangement will not be unlawful. The reason for this exception is that life assurance cover becomes more expensive to provide as the probability of death increases. If employers had to provide justification for a cut-off point for the provision of cover for those who retired early, there would be a risk that they would withdraw the cover entirely. The exemption is aimed at avoiding that happening (Explanatory Notes, para 137).

8 Retirement and Dismissal

Retirement can of course be a matter on which employer and employee are agreed, or it can take place as a result of the employee giving notice that he will leave work. In these cases, the Regulations do not come into play. However, where the employee does not want to retire, retirement constitutes a dismissal, and it is this situation which the Regulations deal with. Where the retirement is compulsory, two issues arise:

(a)　Does it constitute age discrimination?

(b)　Is the dismissal unfair?

Is the retirement discriminatory?

On the face of it, any compulsory retirement will constitute age discrimination. The notion of retirement is bound up with the achievement of a particular age, which obviously will vary from one occupation to another and from one employer to another. But the person who has been compulsorily retired has been subjected to less favourable treatment by reason of his age – he can be compared with the younger person who has not reached retirement age, and remains in employment. So, reg 7(2)(d) comes into play:

> 'It is unlawful for an employer, in relation to a person whom he employs at an establishment in Great Britain, to discriminate against that person … (d) by dismissing him, or subjecting him to any other detriment.'

Default retirement age

In view of the fact that all retirement dismissals would be prima facie discriminatory, each one would have to be justified in accordance with reg 3 (see Chapter 4 for details on justification). In other words, the employer would have to show that the retirement age in question was adopted to further a legitimate aim, and that it constituted a proportionate means of furthering that aim.

However, reg 30(2) excludes a large swathe of compulsory retirements from this process. It reads:

'Nothing in Part 2 or 3 shall render unlawful the dismissal of a person to whom this regulation applies at or over the age of 65 where the reason for dismissal is retirement.'

As a result, where the employee is compulsorily retired at the age of 65 or above, the employer does not have to provide justification for that action – it is removed from the scope of the prohibition against age discrimination.

Before examining the rationale for this exception, it should be emphasised that it only applies to 'employees' who are subject to a contract of employment, people who are in Crown employment, and members of Parliamentary staff (reg 30(1)). Those who are under a contract personally to do any work, apprentices, office-holders (including the police), barristers, advocates and partners are not covered by it. It follows that these latter groups of people have protection from dismissal or termination even when they are over 65, unless the dismissal or termination can be objectively justified, or is covered by a statutory exemption.

In addition, it should be emphasised that the effect of reg 30 is to remove compulsory retirements from the ambit of the prohibition on discrimination. The dismissal of someone over the age of 65 for a reason other than retirement may still be unfair (whether it is stated by the employer to be on grounds of retirement or not). That aspect of such dismissals is addressed in the section on 'Unfair dismissal' later in this chapter.

The rationale for the default retirement age

In its Explanatory Notes, the government claims that the default retirement age is within the scope of Article 6.1 of the Directive, i.e. that it is objectively justified, for the following reasons:

(a)   it meets the concerns of employers in relation to workforce planning;

(b)   it avoids adverse impact on the provision of occupational pensions and other work-related benefits;

(c)   it is a target age against which employers can plan their work and employees can plan their careers and their retirement;

(d)   it avoids the blocking of jobs from younger workers; and

(e)   it encourages employees to save now and make provision for their retirement.

This provision has proved particularly controversial. The organisation Age Concern, which aims to represent the interests of older members of the population, has claimed:

'We believe that the government will be unable to complete this process [of objective justification] to the satisfaction of the European

Court of Justice, and the exemption will be found to be incompatible with the Directive under Article 6. This view is enhanced by the government's own Regulatory Impact Assessment which shows that scrapping retirement ages would bring net benefits to the economy.'

(See Age Concern's response to the draft Regulations, published in October 2005, p 32.)

Age Concern goes on to argue that a mandatory retirement age is not necessary for workforce planning, nor relied on heavily, 'because the vast majority of employees retire voluntarily – most well before their employer's mandatory retirement age'. It goes on to suggest that the setting of a default retirement age is incompatible with Article 8.2 of the Directive, which reads:

'The implementation of this Directive shall under no circumstances constitute grounds for a reduction in the level of protection against discrimination already afforded by Member States in the fields covered by this Directive.'

Their argument is that there has never before been a compulsory retirement age in the United Kingdom, with the result that its introduction constitutes a 'reduction in the level of protection'.

As to the merits of the arguments, it does seem that the Article 8.2 point is relatively weak. It is those over 65 who are affected by the default retirement age. As far as protection from age discrimination is concerned, they had none prior to the introduction of the Regulations, so there has been no reduction there. It is inaccurate to characterise this particular provision as 'a compulsory retirement age' in the sense that the government is making it compulsory. It is rather an exemption to allow employers to have a compulsory retirement age. That is something which they have always been entitled to do, subject to the laws relating to unfair dismissal. As far as unfair dismissal is concerned, as will be seen later in this chapter, the position prior to the commencement of the Regulations was that those over the age of 65 could not bring a claim for unfair dismissal. That provision is repealed by the Regulations, so again there has been no reduction in protection.

The more general argument is more difficult for the government to meet. Clearly it is possible to justify objectively the adoption by an individual employer of a compulsory retirement age of 65. The arguments which would be deployed would probably be similar to those which are outlined as (a) to (e) in the list above. But it is much more difficult to rely upon those arguments in relation to employers across all sectors of the economy, all occupations, and all regions of the country, without exception. In effect, that is what reg 30 attempts to do. In addition, it seems to be on shaky ground when it relies upon workforce planning, given the undeniable fact that most people retire before the mandatory retirement age laid down by their employer.

There is a further practical effect of the default retirement age which needs to be fed into the argument. There will be little incentive for an employer to allow employees to work on after the age of 65, particularly where they already have in place a normal retirement age of 65. From the point of view of the cautious employer, it will be far easier to retire an employee at 65 than to allow them to carry on to, say, 68, with the danger that this will result in an argument about whether the later dismissal really is retirement or some other reason. Where an employer has in the past exercised some sort of discretion as to employees continuing to work past a normal retiring age of 65, there is a risk that an abundance of caution may, in effect, lead to a levelling down of the actual age at which retirement takes effect. If this is shown to be the case, it is a powerful argument that the default retirement age is likely to defeat the purpose of the Directive. In paragraph (9) of the Recital to the Directive, for example, reference is made to 'the need to pay particular attention to supporting older workers, in order to increase their participation in the labour force'. Against this must be set the terms of paragraph (14) of the Recital, which states:

'This Directive shall be without prejudice to national provisions laying down retirement ages.'

However, that statement surely cannot give complete freedom to member states to lay down any *compulsory* retirement age (in the sense that the employer makes it compulsory), since such freedom would entirely negate the purpose of the Directive. It may well reflect rather the age which entitles the person retiring to qualify for a state pension and associated benefits. (For the position where the Regulations fail to implement the Directive, see Chapter 11.)

The government has stated that it will review the default retirement age in 2011 (after the Regulations have been in force for five years). It will then (see *Equality and Diversity: Coming of Age* – the consultation paper on the draft Regulations, p 71):

'decide whether it is still necessary. If it is not, we will abolish it. Until then, we will collect relevant information from a number of sources to ensure that our decision is based on evidence …

In 2011, our decision on whether to keep or abolish the default retirement age will focus mainly on two factors:

- whether, in the light of the evidence, the default retirement age remains appropriate and necessary to facilitate workforce planning and to avoid adverse effects on pensions and other employment benefits; and

- the influence of any other social policy objectives.'

As to the information which it will collect, the government stated in *Equality and Diversity: Coming of Age* that it would look at evidence on longevity and the employment patterns of older workers in particular. It will also take into account information relevant to workforce planning, pensions and other employment benefits. In the light of the fact that these are matters which the government is to take into account in determining whether the default retirement age should continue, it is logical to assume that they played a part in the decision to incorporate it within the Regulations in the first place. As far as pensions are concerned, it can safely be assumed that the debate around the report of the Turner Commission will have an important impact upon the eventual fate of the national default retirement age. The central recommendation of the Turner Commission was a deferral of the state pension age (with a substantial lead-in period).

Compulsory retirement under the age of 65

It is of course possible for an employer to have a retirement age which is under the age of 65. That will not be covered by reg 30, with the result that it will be, on the face of it, directly discriminatory. Like any other act of less favourable treatment on grounds of age, it will be open to the employer to put forward objective justification for the policy of retiring its employees (or this particular one) at the age in question. It would seem that the task of establishing justification in these circumstances will be an arduous one, given that the government has set the general benchmark for compulsory retirement at the age of 65. The employer would need to show circumstances particular, for example, to the business or occupation in question which constitute a legitimate aim. In addition, it would need to show that this directly discriminatory means of achieving the legitimate aim was proportionate. For example, is there no less discriminatory way of achieving the aim in question? If the concern relates to health and safety, why not carry out specific tests in order to establish whether the employees at the designated age are for some reason less able to maintain the necessary standards? Although it would be discriminatory to single out employees of a particular age for such tests, such a procedure would not constitute unfavourable treatment to the same extent as retiring them compulsorily, and would be more likely to be viewed as proportionate.

Again, it should be emphasised that compulsory retirement at an age below 65 may well constitute unfair dismissal, and this area is further discussed in the section on 'Unfair dismissal' later in this chapter.

The 'duty to consider' procedure

In setting a default retirement age, with the intention of reviewing it in 2011, the government has also stated that it aims to bring about a 'culture change', so as to move employers away from the notion that they should retire employees even if they can still make a valuable contribution to the enterprise. The major way in which the Regulations attempt to bring about that 'culture change' is by the imposition of a new duty upon the employer – to consider a request by an employee to continue working after the expected retirement date. This duty, together with the procedure which accompanies it, is set out in Sch 6 to the Regulations. In addition, there are certain transitional provisions, contained in Sch 7.

Who is covered by the procedure?

The procedure applies to 'employees' within the meaning of reg 30 (see Sch 6, para 1). As a result it is confined to those who come within the terms of s 230(1) of the Employment Rights Act 1996, to Crown employees and members of Parliamentary staff. Section 230(1) of the Employment Rights Act 1996 states:

> 'In this Act "employee" means an individual who has entered into or works under (or, where the employment has ceased, worked under) a contract of employment.'

It follows that the 'duty to consider' procedure is confined to those who are 'employees' in the narrow sense, i.e. subject to a contract of service. They do not, however, have to have clocked up any qualifying period of employment although, in a general way, they will need a year's qualifying period in order to bring a claim for unfair dismissal.

The duty to notify

The employer must notify the employee of the date upon which he intends the employee to retire, and of the employee's right to request not to be retired on that date (para 2: references in this section are all to Sch 6). The notification must be in writing, and it must be given not more than a year and not less than six months before the intended date of retirement. The duty applies regardless of any term in the employee's contract indicating when retirement is to take place, and irrespective of any other notification about his date of retirement or right to make a request, given at any time. As a result, it is not possible for the employer to avoid compliance with the duty within the six-month – twelve-month window by giving notice within the contract or at any other time.

What about a letter which gives an employee six months' contractual notice (or more)? Can it also serve to fulfil the duty to notify him of the intended date of retirement? There would seem to be no reason why it should not, provided that:

(a)   it is sent no more than 12 months before the retirement date; and

(b)   it informs him of his right to request to continue to work after the stated retirement date.

Paragraph 4 deals with the position where the employer has failed to serve notice within the period of six to twelve months. In such a case, he has a 'continuing duty' to notify the employee in writing of the matters in question until the fourteenth day before the 'operative date of termination'. The 'operative date of termination' is defined (para 1) as the date upon which notice given by the employer expires or, if no notice is given, the date upon which termination of the contract of employment takes effect.

When paras 2 and 4 are read together, their effect is:

(a)   the employer should comply with the duty to notify between six and twelve months before the intended date of retirement;

(b)   if the employer fails to do so, he should nevertheless notify no later than the fourteenth day before dismissal.

As will be seen later (Remedies, Chapter 12), the consequence of failing to comply with (a) is an award to the employee of up to eight weeks' pay (para 11). The consequence of failing to comply with (b) may be much more serious for the employer – the dismissal will be automatically unfair.

The main deadlines contained in the 'duty to consider' procedure are set out in the chart at the end of this chapter.

The right to request

The employee is given a statutory right to request not to retire by para 5, which corresponds to the employer's duty to notify in paras 2 and 4. Just as the notification is about the date of intended retirement, so the right is to request not to retire on the intended date of retirement. The request 'must be in writing and state that it is made under this paragraph'. It is submitted that, whilst the request must be written, a failure to quote the paragraph and schedule number under which it is made is unlikely to be fatal. What is important is that it should be clear that the request is made in accordance with the statutory procedure and in response to the written notification by the employer. In order to avoid any doubt, however, an employee would be well advised to use some formulation such as:

'This request is made in accordance with paragraph 5 to Schedule 6 of the Employment Equality (Age) Regulations 2006 and is in response to the notice of intended retirement received on [insert date].'

The request must propose that the employee should continue in employment:

(a)   indefinitely;

(b)   for a stated period; or

(c)   until a stated date.

It can be made even if the employer has failed to notify. If so, it must identify the date upon which the employee believes that the employer intends to retire him.

If the employer has, in fact, notified in accordance with para 2 (i.e. within the six- to twelve-month window), then the employee is bound by time limits: his request must be made at least three months but not more than six months before the intended date of retirement. If, on the other hand, the employer has failed to notify in accordance with para 2, the employee's request can be made at any time within the six-month period before the intended date of retirement (see the 'duty to consider' procedure: deadlines' chart at the end of this chapter).

The employee is entitled to make only one statutory request in accordance with para 5 in relation to any one intended date of retirement.

Considering the request

Once the employer has received a request under para 5, he is under a duty to consider it in accordance with paras 7 to 9.

Paragraph 7 sets out the procedure for considering the request. The employer must hold a meeting to discuss it with the employee within a reasonable period after receiving it. There is an exception where they reach an agreement that the employee's employment will continue – either indefinitely or to an agreed date. If no such agreement is reached, employer and employee must take all reasonable steps to attend a meeting. In the event that it is impracticable to hold a meeting within a reasonable period, the employer must consider any representations made by the employee.

After the meeting has been held (or the request considered in the event that a meeting is impracticable), the employer must notify the employee of his decision. He does not have to give reasons. All he has to do is:

(a)   where the decision is that the employment will continue indefinitely, state that fact;

(b)   where the decision is that the employment will continue for a further period, state the length of that period or the date on which it will end; or

(c)   where the decision is to refuse the request, confirm that he wishes to retire the employee, and the date on which dismissal is to take effect.

In addition, where he has refused the request, or granted an extension for a period shorter than the employee requested, he must inform the employee of his right to appeal. All notices under para 7 (e.g. accepting or refusing the request to continue in employment, notifying the right to appeal, etc) must be in writing and dated. Useful specimen letters are provided in Annexes 7 to 9 of the ACAS Guidance which is printed as Appendix 3 of this book.

If the employer has:

(a)   received a valid request from the employee not to retire;

(b)   not yet given notice of his decision about that request; and

(c)   dismisses him,

then Sch 6, para 10 applies. This provides that, where the employer dismisses the employee in these circumstances:

'the contract of employment shall continue in force for all purposes, including the purpose of determining for any purpose the period for which the employee has been continuously employed.'

In other words, the dismissal is ineffective. The employee will continue in employment (with the right to be paid, etc) until the day following the day on which notice of the decision is given (para 10(2)).

The employee has a right to appeal from the employer's decision, where it is to refuse his request or to allow a shorter period of continued employment than was requested (para 8). A similar procedure is laid down for the appeal procedure as pertains to the original meeting to consider the request. The employee is supposed to 'set out grounds of appeal'. This is something of a tall order, given that there is no requirement on the employer to set out reasons for the decision which is being appealed against. Again, all notices under para 8 must be written and dated. This includes the notice of appeal, and any acceptance or rejection of the appeal. A specimen letter notifying the result of an appeal is set out as Annex 10 in the ACAS Guidance which is reproduced in Appendix 3 of this book.

Right to be accompanied

The employee has a right to be accompanied to a meeting to consider his request to continue after the intended retirement date, or a meeting to appeal against a refusal to comply with his request (para 9). The right is triggered off where the employee 'reasonably requests to be accompanied at the meeting' by a companion who is 'a worker employed by the same employer as the employee'. A couple of points should be noted:

(a)   The companion must be a 'worker' employed by the same employer (para 9(2)(b)). This would seem to include those within the broad definition in reg 2, namely those under a contract of service or apprenticeship or a contract personally to do any work.

(b)   Trade union officials are not included within the definition of the 'companion', by contrast with the position under the Employment Relations Act 1999, s 10(3), which governs rights at a disciplinary or grievance hearing. Frequently, a trade union official will work for the same employer, and would then fall within the definition. In any event, there is nothing to prevent an employee requesting that he be accompanied by a trade union official who is not a work colleague, or to prevent his employer agreeing to such a request.

(c)   The companion must be permitted to address the meeting, but not to answer questions on behalf of the employee. The companion must also be permitted to confer with the employee during the meeting.

(d)   If the employee's chosen companion is not available at the time proposed by the employer for the meeting, and a convenient alternative time falling within the following seven days is proposed by the employee, the employer must postpone the meeting to that proposed time.

Where the employer fails, or threatens to fail, to comply with a request to be accompanied, the employee may make a claim to an Employment Tribunal. In the event that the claim succeeds, the tribunal can award an amount of up to two weeks' pay (see Remedies, Chapter 12).

Protection for those who exercise their right to be accompanied is provided by para 13. An employee is entitled not to be subjected to a detriment for doing so, and the companion whom he chooses is similarly protected. Further, an employee is entitled to be regarded as unfairly dismissed if the reason (or principal reason) for his dismissal is that he used (or tried to use) the right to be accompanied in para 9. Again, the companion is provided with similar protection, although it is worth pointing out that the right not to be unfairly dismissed is confined to employees (within the meaning of s 230(1) of the Employment Rights Act 1996), whereas any worker (see above) can be a companion.

Duty to consider – the transitional provisions

Once the Regulations are fully in place, the duty to notify of the intended date of retirement will have to be complied with between six and twelve months before that date. This creates an obvious problem in relation to dismissals which are to occur shortly after the date of commencement of the Regulations (1 October 2006). This issue is dealt with in Sch 7, which modifies Sch 6 in respect of dismissals which are to occur after 1 October 2006, but before 1 April 2007. It sets out (in paras 2 to 4 of Sch 7) the circumstances in which an employer is to be treated as having complied with para 2 (six to twelve months' notification) or para 4 (notification up to the fourteenth day prior to dismissal) of Sch 6.

Paragraph 6 of Sch 7 then sets out the consequences, as far as the right to request not to be retired on the intended date of retirement is concerned, for dismissals where notice is given on or after 1 October 2006, with notice expiring before 1 April 2007. The employer is under a duty to consider requests which are made in accordance with para 6 of Sch 7.

In summary, the position is as follows in respect of notice given before 1 October 2006. If the employer gives the employee notice that they are to be retired in the period between 1 October 2006 and 31 March 2007:

(a)   notice must be either that required by the contract, or, where the period required by the contract exceeds four weeks, at least four weeks;

(b)   the employer must write to the employee on 1 October or as soon as possible afterwards, telling him of his right to request to work longer;

(c)   the employee's request can be made before, or up to four weeks after, their contract has terminated;

(d)   a meeting to discuss the request and an appeal should then be held in the same way as has been described above under the 'duty to consider' procedure set out in Sch 6.

As far as notice given after 1 October 2006 and before 1 April 2007 is concerned, the position can be summarised as follows:

(a)   the employee must be notified of the intended retirement date, giving him the notice to which he is entitled by statute or by contract, whichever is the longer;

(b)   the employee must be told in writing of his right to request working longer;

(c)   an employee who wishes to exercise this right should make a written request to do so either:

    (i)   where possible, four weeks before the intended retirement date, or

    (ii)   as soon as reasonably practicable after being notified of his 'right to request';

(d)   any request can be made before, or up to four weeks after, the employee's contract has been terminated;

(e)   a meeting to discuss the request and an appeal should then be held in the same way as has been described above under the 'duty to consider' procedure set out in Sch 6.

The question whether there is a remedy of up to eight weeks' pay for failure to notify under the transitional provisions in Sch 7 (in the same way as there is under Sch 6) is considered in Chapter 12 in the section entitled 'Failure to notify'.

Unfair dismissal

The law relating to unfair dismissal is altered radically by the Regulations. The combined effect of the major changes contained in Schs 6 and 8, is:

(a)   the upper age limit upon claims for unfair dismissal is repealed;

(b)   'retirement of the employee' becomes a fair reason for dismissal;

(c)   various presumptions are laid down as to whether retirement has been established as the reason for dismissal;

(d)   there is a special test for fairness in respect of retirement dismissals and the 'duty to consider' procedure replaces the statutory Dismissal and Disciplinary Procedure (DDP) in respect of retirement dismissals.

The subsequent sections deal with each of these topics in turn. The flowchart at the end of this chapter entitled 'Retirement and Unfair Dismissal' shows how the concepts are inter-related. A more detailed representation of the process is contained in the flowchart in Annex 5 of the ACAS Guidance (see Appendix 3 of this book) provides a useful diagrammatic summary of the retirement process in the context of unfair dismissal law.

Removal of age limit for unfair dismissal

Schedule 8, para 25 of the Regulations repeals s 109 of the Employment Rights Act 1996. The repealed section excluded the right to bring a claim for unfair dismissal where the employee had attained:

(a)   the normal retiring age for an employee holding the position held by him; and

(b)   in any other case, the age of 65.

As a result, an employee who has attained the normal retiring age and/or the age of 65 will now be able to claim unfair dismissal. As outlined in the section above on the default retirement age, a dismissal of an employee over the age of 65 on the ground of retirement will not, in terms of the Regulations, amount to unlawful age discrimination (reg 30). However, it may constitute some other form of unfair dismissal, and if the dismissal takes place after the commencement of the Regulations, the employee will be entitled (subject to the usual qualifying period) to bring a claim.

Retirement becomes a fair reason

The fairness of a dismissal is primarily governed by s 98 of the Employment Rights Act 1996. Until now, there have in effect been five potentially fair reasons for dismissal:

1   a reason relating to capability or qualifications;

2   a reason relating to the conduct of the employee;

3   redundancy;

4   continuation in post would contravene a statutory duty or restriction; or

5   some other substantial reason.

The Regulations (Sch 8, para 22) insert a sixth reason: 'retirement of the employee'.

It follows that, if the employer establishes that the reason (or the principal reason) for the dismissal was retirement, the dismissal will potentially be a fair one. The question must then be resolved as to whether the dismissal itself (as well as the reason) was in fact fair.

Presumptions as to when retirement is the reason for dismissal

Given the formulaic determination of fairness in retirement dismissals (see the section on 'Test of fairness for retirement' below), the way in which the tribunal determines whether the reason for a dismissal is retirement assumes great importance. That importance is underlined when one considers that the employer is obliged to operate different procedures depending on whether:

(a)   the reason for dismissal is retirement (in which case the duty to consider procedure must be followed); or

(b)   there is some other reason for dismissal (in which case the statutory dismissal and disciplinary procedure (DDP) laid down in the Employment Act 2002 must be followed).

Following the wrong procedure will place the employer in jeopardy of an automatic finding of unfair dismissal.

The Regulations have introduced into the Employment Rights Act 1996 a set of presumptions which determine in a number of instances whether a dismissal is by reason of retirement. These presumptions are to be found in ss 98ZA to 98ZF, which are inserted in the Employment Rights Act 1996 by Sch 8, para 23.

The presumptions make a number of references to the 'normal retirement age' (NRA). This is defined in s 98ZH as 'the age at which employees in the employer's undertaking who hold, or have held, the same kind of position as the employee are normally required to retire'. This would appear to differ from the way in which the phrase 'normal retiring age' as it appeared in the (now repealed) s 109(1) of the Employment Rights Act 1996 has been interpreted. In *Waite v Government Communications Headquarters* [1983] IRLR 341, HL, it was stated that the test for ascertaining normal retiring age is what would be the reasonable expectation of employees holding the relevant position at the relevant time. This was held to differ from the contractual retiring age. However, the statutory definition in s 98ZH, which now applies to retirement dismissals, appears to place the emphasis upon the contractual position, by the use of the phrase 'required to retire'.

As far as the presumptions are concerned, retirement is deemed to be the *only* reason for dismissal where:

(a)   the employee has no normal retirement age (NRA), the employer gives the required notice (i.e. six to twelve months in accordance with para 2 of Sch 6) and the dismissal takes effect on or after the employee's 65th birthday and on the intended date of retirement (s 98ZB(2));

(b)   the employee has an NRA which is over 65, the employer gives the required notice under para 2 of Sch 6 and the dismissal takes effect on or after the employee has reached the NRA and on the intended date of retirement (s 98ZD(2));

(c)   the employee has an NRA which is below 65 but which does not amount to unlawful age discrimination, the employer has given the required notice under para 2 of Sch 6 and the dismissal takes effect on or after the employee has reached the NRA and on the intended date of retirement (s 98ZE(4)).

There are various sets of circumstances where retirement is deemed *not* to be the reason for dismissal:

(a)   where the employee has no normal retirement age, but the dismissal takes effect before the employee reaches the age of 65 (s 98ZA(2));

(b)   where the employee has no normal retirement age, the employer gives notice in accordance with para 2 of Sch 6, but the dismissal takes effect before the intended date of retirement notified to the employee (s 98ZB(3));

(c) where the employee has a normal retirement age (whether above or below 65), but the dismissal takes effect before the employee reaches that age (s 98ZC(2));

(d) where the employee has a normal retirement age of 65 or over, the employer gives notice in accordance with para 2 of Sch 6, but the dismissal takes effect before the intended date of retirement date so notified (s 98ZD(3));

(e) where the employer does not notify the employee in accordance with para 2 of Sch 6, but he does notify the employee of an intended date of retirement, but the dismissal takes effect before that intended date of retirement (s 98ZD(4));

(f) where the employer has a normal retirement age which is below the age of 65, the dismissal takes effect after the NRA, but it is unlawful age discrimination for the employee to have that retirement age (i.e. the retirement age is not objectively justified) (s 98ZE(2));

(g) where the employer has a normal retirement age which is below the age of 65, that retirement age is objectively justified, the employer has notified the employee in accordance with para 2 of Sch 6, but the dismissal takes effect before the intended retirement date (s 98ZE(5)).

There are a few cases which are not governed by the presumptions, so that it is left to the tribunal to decide whether retirement is the reason for dismissal:

(a) where the employer has not notified the employee in accordance with para 2 of Sch 6 – perhaps he notified late or not at all (whether or not the employee has a normal retirement age) (s 98ZB(5), 98ZD(5), 98ZE(7)); or

(b) where the employer notified the employee in accordance with para 2 of Sch 6, but the dismissal takes effect after the intended date of retirement.

Where (a) above applies, the tribunal *must* take the matters listed in s 98ZF of the Employment Rights Act 1996 into account. Where (b) applies, it may take them into account. The matters in question are:

(a) whether or not the employer has notified the employee in accordance with para 4 of Sch 6 to the 2006 Regulations (which lays down that notice must be given by the fourteenth day before termination);

(b) if notice was given in accordance with that paragraph, how long before the intended retirement date it was given; and

(c) whether or not the employer followed, or sought to follow, the procedures in para 7 of Sch 6 (meeting to consider the request not to retire).

Test of fairness for retirement

The usual test as to whether a dismissal is unfair is contained within s 98(4) of the Employment Rights Act 1996. Once the employer has established a potentially fair reason for dismissal (e.g. misconduct):

'the determination of the question whether the dismissal is fair or unfair (having regard to the reason shown by the employer):

(a) depends on whether in the circumstances (including the size and administrative resources of the employer's undertaking) the employer acted reasonably or unreasonably in treating it as a sufficient reason for dismissing the employee, and

(b) shall be determined in accordance with equity and the substantial merits of the case.'

The test is, therefore, one where the tribunal has to make a judgment, taking all the circumstances into account, as to whether the employer acted reasonably or unreasonably in deciding to dismiss. Typically, this will involve an examination of the fairness of the procedure, and the appropriateness of the decision to dismiss (rather than, say, to issue a warning in a case of misconduct, or to redeploy in a case of redundancy). In coming to its conclusion, the tribunal must avoid substituting its own judgment for that of the employer, and must rather decide whether the actions of the employer fell within the 'band of reasonableness'. Nevertheless there are judgments to be made about what is reasonable, and a number of different factors have to be weighed in the balance. The test of fairness contained in s 98(4) of the Employment Rights Act 1996 continues to govern all dismissals other than those which are by reason of retirement.

As far as retirement dismissals are concerned, a new s 98ZG of the Employment Rights Act 1996 (inserted by para 23 of Sch 8 to the Regulations) determines whether the dismissal is fair or not. Of course, it applies only where the employer has established (with or without the help of the presumptions set out in the previous section) that the dismissal was by reason of retirement. Section 98ZG reads:

'1 This section applies if the reason (or principal reason) for a dismissal is the retirement of the employee.

2 The employee shall be regarded as unfairly dismissed if, and only if, there has been a failure on the part of the employer to

comply with an obligation imposed on him by any of the following provisions of Schedule 6 to the 2006 Regulations:

(a)   paragraph 4 (notification of retirement, if not already given under paragraph 2),

(b)   paragraphs 6 and 7 (duty to consider employee's request not to be retired),

(c)   paragraph 8 (duty to consider appeal against decision to refuse a request not to be retired).'

The test for retirement dismissals, then, is one of procedural fairness. The issue for the tribunal to determine is whether the employer complied with the core obligations contained within the 'duty to consider' procedure in Sch 6. Those core obligations are:

- to serve notice of the date of intended retirement and of the right to make a request, at least by the fourteenth day before the date in question;

- consideration of any request to continue in employment after the intended date of retirement (usually by holding a meeting, but considering the request in any event where a meeting is not practicable);

- considering any appeal against a decision to refuse a request.

The requirements are purely formal. Concepts such as 'reasonableness', 'equity' and 'merits' do not enter into the equation. If the core obligations are complied with, the retirement dismissal is deemed to be fair. If they are not, it is automatically unfair.

The operation of s 98ZG is similar in conception to that of s 98A(1) of the Employment Rights Act 1996. Section 98A(1), which applies to dismissals other than retirement dismissals, lays down that a dismissal is automatically unfair if the employer fails to complete the requirements of the statutory DDP, where one applies in relation to the dismissal. However, there is one crucial difference. If a non-retirement dismissal is conducted in accordance with the statutory DDP, whilst it will not be automatically unfair, it is still subject to the test in s 98(4) (set out above) – in other words, it may be unfair, even though not automatically unfair.

As a result, the failure of the employer to date a notice of his decision in relation to a request to continue working after the intended date of retirement (para 7(8) of Sch 6) might conceivably result in a finding of automatically unfair dismissal. On the other hand, a decision by the employer to uphold a retirement date, notwithstanding powerful reasons adduced by the employee, will be deemed to be fair, provided that the reason for dismissal is genuinely retirement and the 'duty to consider' procedure is followed.

Retirement dismissals and the Polkey reduction

In the case of *Polkey v A E Dayton Service Ltd* [1987] AC 344, the House of Lords decided that, in a case where an employee had been dismissed by a procedure involving proven irregularity, the question whether carrying out a proper procedure would have made no difference was irrelevant to the fairness or otherwise of the dismissal. In other words, an unfair dismissal would not become fair merely because the employee could have been dismissed fairly. At the same time, the House of Lords held that it would in some circumstances be just and equitable to reduce the compensatory award of an employee who would have been dismissed in any event, if a fair procedure had been adopted. This is commonly referred to as a *Polkey* reduction, i.e. a reduction in the compensatory award to reflect the chance that the employee would have been dismissed in any event, if a fair procedure had been adopted.

Section 98A(1) of the Employment Rights Act 1996 deals with this situation in respect of dismissals generally, and partially reverses the *Polkey* principle. Section 98A(1) lays down that a dismissal to which the statutory DDP applies will be automatically unfair if procedure is not completed due to the failure of the employer. Section 98A(2) lays down that in respect of all other dismissals:

> 'failure by an employer to follow a procedure in relation to the dismissal of an employee shall not be regarded for the purposes of section 98(4)(a) as by itself making the employer's action unreasonable if he shows that he would have decided to dismiss the employee if he had followed the procedure.'

None of s 98A applies to retirement dismissals. As indicated in the section above on 'Retirement dismissals and the test of fairness', the statutory DDPs do not apply where the dismissal is by reason of retirement – instead the 'duty to consider' procedure applies. As far as s 98A(2) is concerned, that is specifically stated to be relevant to the operation of s 98(4)(a), which again does not operate in respect of retirement dismissals, the fairness of which is determined by the new s 98ZG.

A *Polkey* reduction will still be of relevance in some cases of retirement dismissals. For example:

The employer, A, notifies his employee, B, on 10 November that he intends him to retire on 31 March the following year and informs him of his right to request to continue working after that date. On receipt of the notice, B requests to continue working for a further year. A meets him and decides to refuse his request. A sends B a notice setting out his decision. However, A fails to inform B of his right to appeal, contrary to para 7(8) of Sch 6. There is a formal defect in A's compliance with the core obligations in the 'duty to consider' procedure which leads to a finding of unfair dismissal, in accordance with s 98ZG of the Employment Rights Act 1996. However, the tribunal finds that the defect makes no difference to the outcome, and that, if A had complied with the requirement to inform B of his right to appeal, B would still have been retired on 31 March. The tribunal decides that B should receive no compensatory award. However, reduction in accordance with the *Polkey* principle affects the compensatory award only. B is still entitled to the basic award (see 'Remedies', Chapter 12).

Compliance with the retirement procedures

The interlocking sets of rules set out above mean that employers and employees (and those who advise them) need to consider with care how to adapt their practices to ensure compliance with the Regulations.

The employer's duties

It would be as well for employers to:

- Ensure that there is no ambiguity about the normal retirement age in respect of any particular employee.

- Consider whether any retirement age below 65 is objectively justifiable (does it achieve a legitimate aim by means which are proportionate?).

- Keep records of the age of each employee, so as to fix the point at which they would normally retire.

- Set up a diary system to ensure that there is a clear reminder of the point at which a notice of intended date of retirement should be sent, e.g. one year in advance of the date on which the employee is due to reach retirement age.

- Be clear about the reason why a particular employee is to be dismissed. Remember that there are different procedures to follow where the employee is to be retired from those for other dismissals.

- Where the intended dismissal is for some potentially fair reason other than retirement (e.g. redundancy, conduct, capability), then ensure that the statutory DDP is followed, and that the procedure is fair in other respects.

- Where the intended dismissal is genuinely a retirement, follow the 'duty to consider' procedure diligently.

- Make sure that all deadlines are entered into the diary, and that they are met.

- Ensure that all notices are written and dated.

- Where an employee wishes to be accompanied, comply with that request. In any event, as a matter of good practice, inform the employee prior to the appropriate meetings that he may be accompanied.

- Make use of the specimen letters in Annexes 7 to 11 of the ACAS Guidance (see Appendix 3 of this book).

The 'duty to consider' procedure does not require that any reasons should be given for a refusal of a request to continue working after the intended date of retirement. However, the employer will often wish to give reasons, and it may be regarded as a matter of good practice. It will avoid a position where the employee is aggrieved because he is not aware of perfectly sound logical business reasons why it is not possible for him to continue working beyond normal retirement age. As a result, it may avoid fruitless litigation, particularly where there is some doubt in the mind of the employee that what is involved is a genuine retirement. In appropriate cases, it may assist in establishing that the dismissal was a retirement. In the event of any formal defect in the 'duty to consider' procedure, it may show that the employee would have been dismissed in any event, with the result that a *Polkey* reduction applies.

Requests by the employee

The concerns of the employee are likely to be more narrowly focused upon the intended date of retirement as set out in the notice from the employer. Many employees will be content to retire on that date, but if not, the following points should be borne in mind:

- Ensure that the request is made within the deadline (less than six months before the intended date of retirement and, if the employer has given proper notice, more than three months before that date).

- Make the request that employment continue in writing, and date it.

- State that the request is made under para 5 of Sch 6 to the Employment Equality (Age) Regulations 2006.

- Propose that employment should continue indefinitely, for a stated period, or until a stated date.

- Give reasons for the proposal, setting out the advantages both to the employee and to the employer.

- Ensure that all reasonable steps are taken to attend the meeting called by the employer to consider the request.

- Request a companion (a work colleague) if that is felt to be of assistance (it often will be).

- If the request is refused, look at any reasons given in the notice from the employer (there may not be any) and decide whether to appeal.

- If deciding to appeal, give notice as soon as possible, setting out the grounds of appeal, i.e. the reasons why the request should have been agreed.

- Make any application to the tribunal within the appropriate deadline (see the chart at the end of this chapter entitled 'The 'duty to consider' procedure: deadlines').

The 'duty to consider' procedure: deadlines

DATE (and authority)	EVENT
12 months before intended date of retirement (sch 6, para 2)	Earliest date for employer to issue notice of intended retirement
Six months before intended date of retirement (sch 6, para 2)	Latest date for employer to issue notice of intended retirement without incurring penalty of up to eight weeks' wages* AND Earliest date for employee to make request to continue working
Three months before intended date of retirement (sch 6, para 5(5))	Latest date for employee to make request to continue working if employer gave notice between six and twelve months before intended date of retirement
14 days before date of dismissal (sch 6, para 4 and s 98ZG of ERA 1996)	If employer has not issued date of intended retirement, any dismissal for retirement will be automatically unfair
Intended date of retirement/dismissal	Employee will be dismissed OR Date of retirement altered
Three months after * above or the date on which the employee knew (or should have known) that date (sch 6, para 11)	Deadline for claim in respect of failure to issue notice under sch 6, para 2 (subject to any extension because it was 'not reasonably practicable' to present claim, etc)

The table above summarises the provisions in Sch 6 of the Regulations. See the transitional provisions in Sch 7 where the conditions specified in that Schedule are met, and notice expires on or before 31 March 2007.

Retirement and Unfair Dismissal

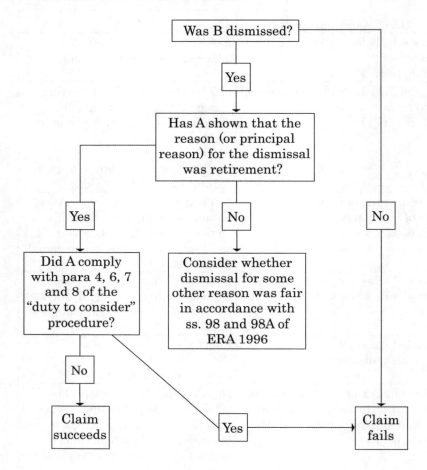

A = employer
B = employee
The chart assures that B has the right to claim unfair dismissal
e.g. in terms of length of service, meeting time limits etc.

9 Pension Schemes

The Directive covers pay and terms and conditions of employment, with the result that pensions fall within its ambit. It does not, however, apply to state pensions (Article 3(3)). All aspects of occupational pensions schemes are covered by Sch 2 to the Regulations, but there are wide-ranging exemptions (references to paragraph numbers in this chapter refer to Sch 2). Where an age-related provision in a pension scheme is covered by an exemption, this means that the Regulations do not require it to be justified objectively by the trustees or the employer. The wide-ranging scope of these exemptions reflects a belief that many age-related rules and practices are necessary for pension schemes to operate effectively.

As far as personal pension schemes are concerned, the only aspect which the Regulations deal with is employer contributions. Other aspects of personal pensions are not covered, because a personal pension is essentially an arrangement between the worker and the personal pension provider, and does not form part of the worker's pay and conditions.

Where a pension scheme contains an age-related provision which is not exempted, it may amount to direct or indirect discrimination. For example:

> The rules of a company's pension scheme only allow workers to join if their pensionable pay is in excess of £300 per week. Within the company there are proportionately far fewer workers under the age of 40 with pensionable pay over £300 than there are workers over the age of 40 whose pay is above the threshold. On the face of it, the rule is indirectly discriminatory, as workers under 40 are treated worse than those over 40, and it will have to be objectively justified.

Further examples of such discrimination are provided in the DTI's *Guidance: the Impact of Age Regulations on Pension Schemes*. This document is available on their website www.dti.gov.uk, and a number of the illustrations in this chapter are taken from it.

Coverage of the Regulations

The definition of 'worker' relevant to Sch 2 is contained in reg 2, and includes:

(a)   employees (in the wide sense, so as to include those under a contract of service, Crown employees, members of Parliamentary staff, apprentices, and those with a contract personally to do any work);

(b)   office-holders to whom reg 12 applies;

(c)   police officers; and

(d)   partners, including members of limited liability partnerships.

Partners

The way in which the Regulations will apply to partners will depend on the pension arrangement in place for them. For example:

(a)   If partners make their own voluntary contributions to a personal pension, that will not be subject to the Regulations.

(b)   If a partnership allows partners to join an occupational pension scheme set up for its employees, that arrangement will be covered by the Regulations. Any exemptions available in respect of employees can also be used in relation to partners (see the section on 'Exemptions' below).

(c)   If partners are required to pay a portion of their profits into a pension arrangement, that will come within the Regulations, with the result that any age-related provisions will have to be objectively justified unless subject to an exemption.

(d)   If a partnership makes payments to retired partners, for example by way of a partnership annuity, any age-based practices will have to be objectively justified. The specific pension exemptions under the Regulations will not be available.

The non-discrimination rule

The Regulations deem all occupational pension schemes to contain a 'non-discrimination rule', which overrides any discriminatory provisions in the scheme rules. In addition, trustees are given the power to amend the rules of their scheme to ensure that they comply with the Regulations. However, where amendments would require the employer's consent if made under the rules, the trustees should obtain such consent (Sch 2, para 2).

If the trustees believe a rule is discriminatory, and is not covered by any of the specific exemptions (see 'Exemptions' below), they can choose whether to:

(a)   objectively justify the rule (see Chapter 4);

(b)   amend the rule; or

(c)   remove the rule.

Where a worker or a pensioner member of a scheme presents a complaint to an Employment Tribunal, it should be against the trustees of the scheme if it relates to powers exercised by the trustees under the scheme rules. The employer will then be treated as a party to the complaint. On the other hand, claims relating to conduct by the employer (e.g. employer contributions or minimum periods of waiting imposed on workers before an employer allows them to join the scheme) must be brought against the employer (para 5).

For details about tribunal claims, see Chapter 11, and for an account of the remedies available, see Chapter 12.

Exemptions

A wide range of exemptions is provided in respect of occupational pensions (paras 7 to 30 of Sch 2). In addition, there are some exemptions in relation to contributions to personal pension schemes. Employers (but not trustees) may also be able to make use of the exemption for benefits based on length of service in reg 32 and this is dealt with in the section below entitled 'Benefits based on length of service'.

Where no exemption covers a particular provision in a scheme which treats members of different ages less favourably, then it must be objectively justified. Where there is an exemption, then the government has presumably come to a decision that the proper implementation of the Directive has not been prejudiced by that exemption. In the description of the exemptions contained in Sch 2, which is set out below, the examples given draw upon the Guidance from the DTI cited above. The final part of this chapter makes some comments on the extent to which the exemptions appear to be permitted by the Directive.

Admissions

Paragraph 7(a) of Sch 2 allows a scheme to set a minimum or maximum age for admission, including setting different ages for different groups of worker. For example:

A scheme allows employees to join if they are between the ages of 25 and 60. Under the Regulations, this practice can continue.

109

Paragraph 7(b) allows a scheme to set a minimum level of pensionable pay for admission, provided that this minimum is not above the lower earnings limit (£4368 per annum in 2006–7). For example:

> A scheme prevents employees who earn less than £4,000 per annum from joining. The Regulations permit this.

Age criteria using actuarial calculations

Paragraph 8(a) allows any age-related benefit to be reduced because it starts before any early retirement pivot age, or enhanced because it starts after any late retirement pivot age. An early retirement pivot age is defined in para 1(5) as the earliest age at which a worker can draw a pension (other than in cases of ill-health) without it being reduced for early payment. A late retirement pivot age is defined in para 1(5) as the age above which a member can take a pension which is actuarially enhanced for late payment. For example:

> A scheme allows members to take retirement at 60 on full pension. Members are also allowed to take early retirement before this age, subject to an actuarial reduction, which is based on the number of years the member is under 60. This practice can continue under the Regulations.

Paragraph 8(b) allows member or employer contributions to be calculated on the basis of an actuarial reduction. For example:

> In a money purchase scheme, employer contributions differ according to the age of the member. This is determined by an actuary in order to produce equal pensions for workers with the same salary and length of service. The Regulations allow this.

Paragraph 8(c) allows the use of age criteria in the actuarial calculation of any age-related benefit commuted in exchange for the payment of any age-related lump sum. For example:

> Lower conversion rates are used for older members when calculating by how much a pension should be reduced when a lump sum benefit is taken. The Regulations permit this.

Contributions

Paragraph 9 exempts differences in contributions payable where this is attributable to differences in the pensionable pay of members. The exemption applies to contributions whether by the employer or the member.

Paragraph 10 deals with contributions in money purchase schemes (those where benefits are determined by the investment returns on contributions). It allows for different rates of member or employer contributions depending on the age of the members, provided that the aim is to make more equal the amount of benefit that members of different ages in comparable situations are entitled to. It also allows equal rates of contribution, irrespective of the age of the member.

Paragraph 11 deals with defined benefits arrangements, such as final salary schemes. It allows different rates of member or employer contributions according to the age of the members, provided that:

(a)   each year of pensionable service entitles members in a comparable situation to accrue a right to defined benefits based on the same fraction of pensionable pay; and

(b)   the aim of the different rates is to reflect the increasing cost of providing defined benefits in respect of members as they get older.

Benefits

Paragraph 12 allows a scheme to set a minimum age for members to become entitled to age-related benefits. However, where an age-related benefit is paid under a defined benefits scheme before the early retirement pivot age:

(a)   the benefit must be actuarially reduced for early payment; and

(b)   the member must not be credited with extra years of pensionable service.

(The early retirement pivot age is defined above in the section on 'Age criteria using actuarial calculations).

For example:

An occupational pension scheme provides that benefits can be taken on early retirement provided that the worker is aged at least 50. This is exempted, provided there is an actuarial reduction, and no credit of 'additional years' of service.

There is a transitional exemption in para 13 which allows the setting of a minimum age for early retirees, above which a benefit can be paid without an actuarial reduction and/or with credit for additional years of service. It applies only to existing and prospective members on 1 October 2006, and not to new joiners. (A 'prospective member' is an individual who can join the scheme either immediately or if he continues in employment for a sufficient period of time: para 1(5).)

Paragraph 14 allows a scheme to have an early retirement pivot age, or a late retirement pivot age. It can also set different ages for different groups or categories of members (the terms are defined above in the section on 'Age criteria using actuarial calculations'). For example:

> A scheme lays down that senior executives can be paid full scheme retirement benefits without actuarial reduction at the age of 55. The rest of the workforce is also entitled to this benefit, but only at the age of 60. The usual age for retirement within the company is 65. The provisions in question are permitted by the Regulations.

Paragraph 15 allows the enhancement of an age-related benefit where a member retires before any early retirement pivot age on ill-health grounds. The enhancement must be calculated according to the years of pensionable service the member would have completed if he had continued to work until the age which the scheme rules specify. For example:

> A and B both take ill-health retirement. A is aged 52, B is 42. Both have worked for the company for the same length of time, and are on the same salary. Each is awarded the pension that he would have received if he had worked to age 60. A might complain that he has suffered discrimination because he has not been given the same amount of enhancement as B. However, the exemption prevents him from bringing a claim.

Paragraph 16 allows a scheme to provide a male member with a bridging pension, e.g. a pension paid to retired men aged 60–64 to compensate for the fact that they do not yet receive the basic state pension. Men over 65 cannot complain under the Regulations that they do not receive such a bridging pension.

Paragraph 17 allows the reduction of a pension paid to a dependant where the dependant is more than a specified number of years younger than the member. For example:

> A scheme states that, where a dependant spouse is more than ten years younger than the member, the spouse's pension is reduced. The Regulations permit this.

Paragraph 18 permits the discontinuance of life assurance cover for members retiring on ill-health grounds before early retirement pivot age (defined above in the section on 'Age criteria using actuarial calculations') once they reach 65, or the normal retirement age applicable to that member.

Paragraph 19 permits rules which provide that entitlement to benefits under a defined benefits arrangement may be calculated on the basis of the number of years' pensionable service which the member has completed. For example:

> A final salary scheme provides pensions on the basis of 1/60th of final salary for each year of pensionable service. A (with 20 years' service) gets double the pension which B gets (he has 10 years' service). The Regulations allow this.

Paragraph 20 permits differences in benefit related to differences over time of pensionable pay. For example:

> A and B both retire after 10 years' service. The scheme allows for a pension of 1/60th of final pensionable salary per year's service. A's final salary is £40,000; B's final salary is £20,000. As a result, A's pension will be double that of B. This is permitted by the Regulations.

Paragraph 21 allows the imposition of a maximum number of years of service when calculating benefits, e.g. so as to limit benefits to a maximum of 40 years' service.

Paragraph 22 allows a scheme to restrict benefits to members who have completed a minimum period of two years' qualifying service.

Paragraph 23 allows a scheme to impose a minimum level of pay used to calculate benefits, provided that level is not above the lower earnings limit (£4368 for 2006–07). Paragraph 24 allows a scheme to restrict benefits payable to its members by reference to a maximum level of pensionable pay specified in the scheme rules. For example:

> A scheme has rules which state that it will only provide benefits for members if their pensionable pay exceeds £3,000. Further, it decides that only £50,000 of pensionable pay will be used to calculate benefits. Both of these limitations are permitted by the Regulations.

Other rules and practices exempted

Paragraph 25 enables a scheme to close, from a particular date, to workers who have not already joined it.

Paragraph 26 allows increases to pensions (e.g. rises in accordance with the retail price index) made to workers over 55 but not below that age.

Paragraph 27 permits a different rate of increase of pensions which are being paid to members of different ages, where the purpose is to maintain the relative value of members' pensions. For example:

> A scheme pays a higher increase to pensioners once they reach the age of 75, because they have been worse affected than younger pensioners by increases in the cost of living since their retirement.

Paragraph 28 allows a scheme to set a different rate of increase of pensions in payment for those who have been receiving pensions for different lengths of time, where the purpose is to maintain the relative value of members' pensions.

Paragraph 29 enables a scheme to set an age limit for the transfer of a member's accrued rights into or out of the scheme (provided that any limit is not more than one year before normal pension age). For example:

> A scheme has a normal pension age of 65. It can specify in its rules that it will not allow transfers to be paid out of the scheme, or accepted by the scheme, after age 64.

Registered pension schemes

Pension schemes may be registered by HM Revenue and Customs, or acquire registered status automatically by being 'approved' pension schemes on 5 April 2006.The Finance Act 2004 confers favourable tax status upon such schemes. A registered scheme is allowed by the Regulations to do anything in order to secure tax relief or prevent any charge to tax (para 30). This exemption does not cover the setting of a minimum age for receiving benefits, which is dealt with in paras 12 and 13 – see the section on 'Benefits' above. For example:

> A scheme provides that a pension payable to any dependant children on death-in-service ceases at age 23. Older members may be less likely to have children under 23. However, they cannot complain that

114

they are disadvantaged by the rule, because it is in place in order to prevent a charge to tax.

Personal pension schemes

Personal pension schemes are generally outside the ambit of the Regulations, as they are a matter between the member and the provider. Contributions by employers to personal pension schemes, however, are benefits related to employment. Exemptions apply in two cases.

First, by para 31, employers can make contributions at different rates according to the age of the worker, where the aim is to make more equal the amount of benefit to which members of different ages in comparable situations are entitled to. This mirrors a similar provision for occupational pensions – see the section on 'Contributions' in relation to para 10, above.

Second, employers can make contributions at different rates for different workers, where this is due to any difference in pensionable pay. For example:

A company pays a contribution of 6% of pay to workers earning £30,000 or more, and 5% of pay to those earning less than £30,000. The difference in the employer contribution rate is exempted.

Benefits based on length of service

In Chapter 7, the effects of reg 32 are set out. In brief, it enables an employer to award benefits to an employee on the basis of length of service, even if this amounts to more favourable treatment on grounds of age (and therefore constitutes less favourable treatment for an employee who does not receive the benefit in question).

Regulation 32(1) permits an employer to award benefits based on a length of service requirement of up to five years. This exemption is not available to trustees, however. It would cover, for instance, the imposition of a period of waiting before allowing an employee to join the scheme, or a more favourable rate of contribution. For example:

A company restricts membership of its occupational pension scheme to those with four years' service. This is permitted under reg 32. However, the trustees cannot rely on this exemption, and will need to

> justify objectively any scheme rules which discriminate indirectly against younger members in this way.

Regulation 32(2) states that, where a benefit is awarded on a length of service requirement which exceeds five years, the requirement must reasonably appear to fulfil a business need of the undertaking. For example:

> Once an employee has been with the company for ten years, the employer contributions to his pension are increased. The employer would need to show that this difference in treatment, which disadvantages those who have been with the company for less than ten years, reasonably appears to fulfil a business need of the company, e.g. by encouraging loyalty or motivation, or by rewarding experience. Again, this partial exemption is not available to trustees of the scheme.

The Directive in relation to pensions

The Directive permits direct or indirect discrimination on grounds of age, provided that it is objectively justified or, as the Regulations put it, the person discriminating can show it to be 'a proportionate means of achieving a legitimate aim'. In the document *Guidance: the Impact of Age Regulations on Pension Schemes* issued by the DTI, it is suggested that this test is met if there is a legitimate aim, and there is no way of achieving the aim with a lesser degree of discrimination (see the flowchart on p 5 of that document). This is a misleading oversimplification, and reference should be made to the commentary in Chapter 4 of this book for an analysis of what is involved in showing that the means of achieving the legitimate aim are 'appropriate and necessary' as the Directive puts it (Article 6(1)).

Article 6(2) has specific relevance to pensions, and states:

> 'Notwithstanding Article 2(2), Member States may provide that the fixing for occupational social security schemes of ages for admission or entitlement to retirement or invalidity benefits, including the fixing under those schemes of different ages for employees or groups or categories of employees, and the use, in the context of such schemes, of age criteria in actuarial calculations, does not constitute discrimination on the grounds of age, provided that this does not result in discrimination on the grounds of sex.'

In sum, this enables a Member State to legislate to allow occupational pension schemes to treat some members less favourably than others on the following grounds:

(a) by fixing different ages for admission;

(b) by fixing different ages for entitlement to retirement or invalidity benefits;

(c) by using age criteria in actuarial calculations.

Exemptions which fall within these categories do not require objective justification by the Member State when it legislates. Other exemptions require the Member State to justify them if its legislation is to be seen to implement the Directive.

Some of the exemptions set out in Sch 2 appear to fall within the specific exemptions permitted by the Directive. For example:

• para 7 allowing the setting of different ages for admission;

• para 8 permitting the use of age criteria in actuarial calculations;

• para 12 enabling a scheme to set a minimum age for payment of age-related benefits; and

• para 14 permitting the setting of early and late retirement pivot ages.

Other exemptions within Sch 2, however, are more difficult to bring within the scope of Article 6(2) of the Directive. For example:

• paras 9, 10 and 11 in relation to contributions; and

• para 29, which permits a scheme to lay down a maximum age limit for transferring a member's accrued rights into or out of the scheme.

Some of the practices allowed by the Regulations may well constitute direct or indirect discrimination. Of course, it is possible that they may be objectively justified, but the Regulations purport to exempt employers and trustees from the necessity to justify, by providing an unconditional exemption. For further discussion of the position where the Regulations fail to implement the Directive, see Chapter 11 on Enforcement.

10 Changes to other Legislation

Some legislation which is already on the statute books discriminates on the basis of age. Article 16 of the Directive obliges member states to repeal or amend such legislation, so that the statute book no longer offends against the principle of equal treatment. Further, implementing the Regulations will in itself require additional statutory machinery, which entails amendment to existing legislation.

The government has attempted to achieve these objectives in Schedules 8 and 9. In so far as an entire provision (e.g. a section or sub-section of an Act) can be identified, it is included in the tables in Sch 9. This is divided into Part 1, which deals with the repeal of statutes, and Part 2, which deals with the revocation of statutory instruments. Schedule 8 deals with amendments to existing legislation, including the omission of particular words from within a provision. In addition, where words within a provision are to be omitted, they are dealt with in Sch 8, alongside amendments. Further, where a piece of legislation requires both sorts of amendment, all the changes appear sequentially in Sch 8 (e.g. the Employment Rights Act 1996).

Some of the changes to other legislation are analysed elsewhere in this book. In particular, the major changes to unfair dismissal legislation are dealt with in Chapter 8. Changes to enforcement machinery are looked at in Chapter 11. A number of amendments have been made to the remedies available in respect of unfair dismissal and allied claims, and they are dealt with in Chapter 12. The current chapter looks at the other pieces of legislation which are affected. The section which follows this introduction is devoted to the changes which have taken place in relation to statutory redundancy payments, the section after that to various pieces of legislation in the field of social security, and the final section deals with miscellaneous pieces of legislation which have undergone relatively minor changes.

Redundancy payments

The statutory redundancy scheme which has been in force for a number of years has contained a number of age-related features. Some of these have seemed on the face of it to be directly discriminatory, and others indirectly discriminatory, on grounds of age. The basic framework of the scheme is to oblige the employer to make a payment to a redundant employee who qualifies by having two years or more continuous employment with that employer. For a qualifying employee, the amount of the payment is determined by the number of years' continuous employment with that employer. The particular features which were identified as being age related in the DTI's consultation paper in 2005 around the draft Regulations *Equality and Diversity: Coming of Age* were:

(a)   The lower age limit of 18 for computing the period of continuous employment. This feature, which was contained in s 211(2) of the ERA 1996, has been repealed by the Regulations. As a result, all continuous service with the employer will count in the calculation (Sch 8, para 35).

(b)   The upper age limit on entitlement – s 156 of the ERA 1996 set this at the normal retirement age of the business in question, or at the age of 65 if the business does not have a retirement age. This is repealed by the Regulations (Sch 8, para 30). As a result, employees over the age of 65 are able to claim a redundancy payment after the commencement of the Regulations.

(c)   Section 162(4) and (5) of the ERA 1996 provide that the statutory redundancy payment should gradually taper down to zero for employees aged between 64 and 65. This tapering down rule is removed by Sch 8, para 32 of the Regulations.

(d)   The requirement for two years of continuous service before entitlement starts is likely to affect certain age groups more than others. As a result, it might constitute indirect age discrimination. This qualifying period has not been revoked by the legislation, and remains in place. The failure to abolish it is commented on below.

(e)   The calculation of the redundancy payment uses a multiplier with age bands. The payment is determined by marking each year of service with half a week's pay (for years when the worker was under 22), one and a half weeks' pay (where the worker was over 41) and one week's pay (in respect of other years – broadly speaking those between the ages of 22 and 41). This scheme is retained, and the failure to abolish it is commented on below.

Redundancy: do the Regulations comply with the Directive?

In *Equality and Diversity: Coming of Age*, the government indicated that 'the Age Regulations will remove the multiplier based on wide age brackets'. They stated that they had not yet determined the common multiplier which was to replace the three multipliers in force, and it was assumed that it would come down to a choice between a common multiplier of one week's pay per week of service, or one and a half week's pay. During the consultation period, those representing the interests of employees, such as the TUC, pushed for a common multiplier of one and a half, while employers' organisations pressed for a unified one week per year of service entitlement.

At the end of the consultation process, Mr Gerry Sutcliffe (Parliamentary Under-Secretary of State for Trade and Industry) announced on behalf of the government that the existing three age bands would be retained (House of Commons, 2 March 2006). He stated by way of explanation:

> 'Evidence the government have gathered demonstrates that younger, prime age and older workers fall into three distinct economic categories, with older workers facing a particularly difficult position in the employment market. Young workers tend not to be out of work for long, and see only a small fall in pay when switching jobs. Older workers are much more likely to become long-term unemployed, and to experience a substantial fall in pay when finding a new job. Prime age workers fall into the middle. We therefore believe that it is sensible for the level of support provided through the scheme to reflect these three categories. A system using a single multiplier would leave a significant group of older workers substantially worse off than at present, and we believe this would be unacceptable. Even if a substantial amount of money were injected into the scheme so as to leave older workers no worse off, the enhanced benefits to younger workers are not justified by their position in the employment market.'

He went on to state the government's position that this age-related distinction was objectively and reasonably justified by a legitimate aim, citing 'employment policy' as the aim in question. He suggested that the retention of the age bands was therefore permitted by the Directive. Whether that is the case is clearly controversial. Even if the retention of the age bands does fulfil a legitimate aim, as the government suggests, there remains the question whether the means adopted to achieve that aim is proportionate. In addition, no reference was made to the detail of the evidence upon which the government based its apparent conclusion that its employment policy required that younger workers, up to early middle age, should be directly discriminated against in terms of the redundancy payments which they were offered. To make the obvious point, it would be an amazing coincidence if that evidence suggested that the age at which long-term unemployment became a greater risk was 41 – precisely the age at which the long-standing statutory scheme had always increased the entitlement per year of employment.

There are other features of the statutory redundancy scheme which are age related, and which have been retained, such as the requirement for two years' qualifying service, and the relationship between the amount of the payment and the number of years' continuous employment. These features are likely to be indirectly discriminatory, but have not proved as controversial as the age bands. In relation to all these features, and the age bands in particular, it is likely that the failure to repeal will be the subject of future challenge, and the implications of that prospect are looked at in Chapter 11. It should be pointed out at this stage, however, that employers act within the Regulations if they pay the statutory amounts, because of the protection of reg 27 (exception for statutory authority). Indeed, an enhanced redundancy payment which is based upon the age bands contained in the statutory scheme is also protected by reg 33 (exception for provision of enhanced redundancy payments to employees). Both of these exceptions are dealt with in more detail in Chapter 5.

Social security legislation

The Social Security Contributions and Benefits Act 1992 (SSCBA 1992) is amended in order to remove age limits relating to entitlement to sick, maternity, paternity and adoption pay. With respect to statutory maternity pay, the crucial date for determining the employer's liability is whether a woman was employed by him in the fifteenth week before her expected week of confinement. As a result, the amended provisions apply to women whose expected week of confinement begins on or after 14 January 2007 (15 weeks after 1 October 2006). Equivalent provisions for commencement are set out with respect to statutory paternity pay and statutory adoption pay (Sch 8, paras 8 to 12).

The upper age limit of 65 for entitlement to statutory sick pay (SSP) is removed. This is done by Sch 8, para 13, repealing that portion of the SSCBA 1992 which prevents a period of incapacity for work arising where a person is over the age of 65. Employees over 65 who have a period of incapacity beginning after the Regulations take effect on 1 October 2006 may therefore be entitled to SSP.

In addition, there are changes to the Statutory Sick Pay (General) Regulations 1982 to enable those under 16 to be treated in the same way as those aged 16 and over. The Statutory Maternity Pay (General) Regulations 1986 are amended with similar effect (applying to women whose expected week of confinement begins on or after 14 January 2007). Equivalent changes are made to the Statutory Paternity Pay and Statutory Adoption Pay (General) Regulations 2002, in each case removing discrimination against those under 16.

Miscellaneous legislation

Certain statutes are amended to abolish the age limits which they impose, including:

Changes to other Legislation

(a) The Mines and Quarries Act 1954 and the Pilotage Act 1987 (removing lower age limits for certain posts, but retaining the stipulation that the operators in question should be competent).

(b) The Parliamentary Commissioner Act 1967 and the Health Service Commissioners Act 1993 (changing these from appointments with a retirement age of 65 to non-renewable fixed-term appointments of no more than seven years).

11 Enforcement

This chapter deals with the way in which the Regulations are enforced. It begins by looking at the jurisdiction of the employment tribunals and the courts. It then goes on to deal with particular procedural matters – the burden of proof, the role of questionnaires, applicable time limits and the particular procedural issues in connection with pensions. The validity of various terms in contracts, agreements and rules is then dealt with. Finally, there is discussion of the implications where any aspect of the Regulations fails to implement the Directive – the role of judicial review and of the European Court of Justice.

Employment tribunals

Regulation 36 confers general jurisdiction to hear complaints under the Regulations upon employment tribunals. There are two exceptions:

(a) complaints that an act of discrimination or harassment is unlawful by virtue of reg 23 (institutions of further and higher education) should be brought in the sheriff or county court (reg 39); and

(b) complaints against qualifications bodies covered by reg 19 cannot be brought in the employment tribunals if there is a statutory appeal already available against the decision of the body in question.

With regard to point (a), it should be noted that claims relating to vocational training provided by employers for employees will be dealt with by the employment tribunals, since that will fall within the scope of reg 7. Complaints against institutions of further and higher education will be dealt with in the county or sheriff courts.

The usual tribunal rules of procedure apply to claims brought under the Regulations. ACAS is given power to conciliate in the same way as in other cases, as a result of an amendment to the Employment Tribunals Act 1996 (Sch 8, para 19 of the Regulations). The Employment Appeals Tribunal has jurisdiction to hear appeals arising from claims under the Regulations (Sch 8, para 20).

It is worth noting that the statutory grievance procedure applies to claims under the Regulations brought by employees (other than for dismissal). A claimant will therefore have to bring a grievance and wait 28 days before presenting a discrimination claim to the tribunal (Employment Act 2002, s 32 and Sch 4 as amended by Sch 8, para 36(4) of the Regulations).

Certain claims in respect of other strands of discrimination are sometimes brought by the Commission of Racial Equality, the Equal Opportunities Commission or the Disability Rights Commission. There is no equivalent official body in respect of age discrimination at present. However, the Commission for Equality and Human Rights is expected to be operative in October 2007, and will perform these functions.

County and sheriff courts

Regulation 39 provides that complaints under reg 23 against institutions of further and higher education should be brought in the county court in England and Wales, or in a sheriff court in Scotland. The usual court rules of procedure apply, as they would to any other claim in tort (England and Wales) or reparation (Scotland) for breach of statutory duty.

Burden of proof

Regulation 37 makes provision concerning the burden of proof for claims brought in the employment tribunals, arising out of Part 2 of the Regulations. Similar provision is made by reg 39 in respect of claims brought in the county or sheriff courts. The provisions in question relate to claims of discrimination and harassment, including victimisation and instructions to discriminate. They do not apply to claims of unfair dismissal and other claims which arise out of the 'duty to consider' procedure.

In brief, reg 37 states that, once the person making the complaint has made out a prima facie case (where the tribunal or court could consider that discrimination or harassment has taken place) it is for the respondent (e.g. the employer) to prove that he did not commit the act of discrimination or harassment. Regulation 39 is to similar effect in relation to the courts.

This provision is now common to the various strands of discrimination, based upon the Burden of Proof Directive (Council Directive 97/80/EC). Important guidance as to its application in cases of sex discrimination was provided by the Court of Appeal in *Igen Ltd v Wong* [2005] IRLR 258. Although the references in the extract which follows are to sex discrimination, the provisions in the Employment Equality (Age) Regulations 2006 are identical in all material respects to those in the Sex Discrimination Act 1975, and the guidance is equally applicable:

'(1)   Pursuant to s 63A of the SDA [Sex Discrimination Act 1975], it is for the claimant who complains of discrimination to prove on the balance of probabilities facts from which the tribunal could conclude, in the absence of an adequate explanation, that the respondent has committed an act of discrimination against the claimant which is unlawful by virtue of s 41 or 42 of Part II or which by virtue of s 41 or 42 of the SDA to be treated as having been committed against the claimant. These are referred to below as "such facts".

(2)   If the claimant does not prove such facts he or she will fail.

(3)   It is important to bear in mind in deciding whether the claimant has proved such facts that it is unusual to find direct evidence of sex discrimination. Few employers would be prepared to admit such discrimination, even to themselves. In some cases the discrimination will not be an intention but merely based on the assumption that "he or she would not have fitted in".

(4)   In deciding whether the claimant has proved such facts, it is important to remember that the outcome at this stage of the analysis by the tribunal will therefore usually depend on what inferences it is proper to draw from the primary facts found by the tribunal.

(5)   It is important to note the word "could" in [the burden of proof provision]. At this stage the tribunal does not have to reach a definitive determination that such facts would lead it to the conclusion that there was an act of unlawful discrimination. At this stage a tribunal is looking at the primary facts before it to sees what inferences of secondary fact could be drawn from them.

(6)   In considering what inferences or conclusions can be drawn from the primary facts, the tribunal must assume that there is no adequate explanation for those facts.

(7)   These inferences can include, in appropriate cases, any inferences that it is just and equitable to draw in accordance with section 74(2)(b) of the SDA [see reg 41(2)(b) of the Employment Equality (Age) Regulations 2006] from an evasive or equivocal reply to a questionnaire or any other questions that fall within section 74(2) of the SDA [reg 41(2) of the Regulations].

(8)   Likewise, the tribunal must decide whether any provision of any relevant code of practice is relevant and if so, take it into account in determining, such facts pursuant to section 56A(10) of the SDA [there is no equivalent in the Regulations]. This means that inferences may also be drawn from any failure to comply with any relevant code of practice.

(9)   Where the claimant has proved facts from which conclusions

could be drawn that the respondent has treated the claimant less favourably on the ground of sex, then the burden of proof moves to the respondent.

(10) It is then for the respondent to prove that he did not commit, or as the case may be, is not to be treated as having committed, that act.

(11) To discharge that burden it is necessary for the respondent to prove, on the balance of probabilities, that the treatment was in no sense whatsoever on the grounds of sex, since "no discrimination whatsoever" is compatible with the Burden of Proof Directive.

(12) That requires a tribunal to assess not merely whether the respondent has proved an explanation for the facts from which such inferences can be drawn, but further that it is adequate to discharge the burden of proof on the balance of probabilities that sex was not a ground for the treatment in question.

(13) Since the facts necessary to prove an explanation would normally be in the possession of the respondent, a tribunal would normally expect cogent evidence to discharge that burden of proof. In particular, the tribunal will need to examine carefully explanations for failure to deal with the questionnaire procedure and/or code of practice.'

How does this apply in the field of age discrimination? Take an example where age discrimination is alleged in the appointment of a manager. The claimant puts forward the successful candidate as her comparator. Inevitably, they are of different ages. That fact alone will not prove sufficient to satisfy the first step in the reasoning process. It is not sufficient material by itself 'from which the tribunal could conclude, in the absence of an adequate explanation, that the respondent has committed an act of [unlawful] discrimination'. However, if it is also established, for example, that the claimant had better qualifications than the successful candidate, that would form the basis upon which the tribunal *could* infer that age was the reason for the difference in treatment. In accordance with point (9) above, the burden of proof would then shift to the respondent.

Questionnaires

Regulation 41 allows a complainant to serve a questionnaire upon the respondent, e.g. their employer. The purpose is to obtain information which will help in pursuing any claim (or prospective claim). Standard forms for the questionnaire and the reply are set out in Schs 3 and 4 to the Regulations. It is possible for the questions and any reply by the respondent to be admitted as evidence in subsequent proceedings before a tribunal or court. Further, where the respondent deliberately and without unreasonable excuse fails to reply within eight weeks of service of the questions, or if his reply is evasive or equivocal, the court or tribunal may draw adverse inferences from that fact. The evidence will only be admissible if the questionnaire is served within the time limits laid down in reg 41(3) and (4). In an employment tribunal, it is only admissible:

(a)   where served before the claim has been presented to the tribunal, if it is served within three months beginning when the act complained of was done;

(b)   where served after a claim has been presented to the tribunal, if it is served within 21 days of presentation or later with the leave of the tribunal.

In the case of proceedings in court, the period in (a) is six months, and the leave of the court is always required for service of the questionnaire after proceedings are commenced.

As is clear from the case of *Igen* (above), the responses (or lack of them) to a questionnaire can play a critical part in establishing a case.

Time limits

The time limit for proceedings under the Regulations is set out in reg 42. A complaint to a tribunal must be presented within three months of the alleged act, and a complaint to the county or sheriff court within six months. Regulation 42(3) defines the 'act' from which time begins to run, in the same way as has become familiar in other strands of discrimination law. In particular, 'any act extending over a period shall be treated as done at the end of that period'. In other words, where there has been a continuing act of age discrimination, the act extends over a period of time, and the three-month limit will only begin to run at the end of that period.

Even if the claim is out of time (i.e. presented to the tribunal more than three months after the act complained of), the tribunal may still accept the claim and adjudicate on it if it concludes that it is just and equitable to do so. The court is given a similar discretion in relation to claims presented after six months.

Regulation 42 and the points made above apply to claims which are based on an act which is allegedly unlawful in terms of the Regulations. It covers, in other words, claims of discrimination, harassment, victimisation and instructions to discriminate, including those where an employer or principal is asserted to be liable for the act of their employee or agent. Claims for unfair dismissal attract a different set of provisions relating to time limits, which are set out in s 111 of the Employment Rights Act 1996. In brief, the limit is three months from the effective date of termination, and the tribunal has a more limited discretion to allow late claims. It can only do so where it was not reasonably practicable for the claimant to present the claim before the end of three months, and the claim was then presented within such further period as was reasonable. Claims for failure to comply with the duty to notify or failure to allow accompaniment under the 'duty to consider' procedure have time limits which are similar to those for unfair dismissal (paras 11 and 12 of Sch 6).

Validity of contracts, rules and agreements

Part 1 of Sch 5 to the Regulations contains provisions relating to terms in contracts. It lays down that certain terms in a contract are void or unenforceable. Among unenforceable terms are those which try to exclude or limit the operation of the Regulations (Sch 5, para 1(3)) – such a term is unenforceable by the person in whose favour it purports to operate. There is an exception, however, contained in the provisions relating to compromise agreements. Where these meet the safeguards set out in Sch 5, para 2, they are valid. The safeguards are similar to those contained in other employment law statutes, and enable claims to be settled provided that it is done so within the statutory framework.

Part 2 of Sch 5 deals with the terms of collective agreements and rules made by employers, trade organisations (including trade unions) and qualifications bodies. An individual is entitled to bring a complaint about a term which is alleged to be unlawful by virtue of the Regulations, if he believes that it may affect him in the future (paras 4 to 7). A tribunal may declare a discriminatory term or rule to be void, but it may also preserve the rights of certain persons under the agreement or rule (paras 8 and 9).

Pensions

There are some distinct features about claims relating to occupational pensions. First, a claim will be against the trustees if it relates to powers exercised by the trustees under the scheme rules. The employer will be treated as a party to any complaint brought against the trustees (Sch 2, para 5). However, claims relating to conduct by the employer, e.g. relating to employer contributions or waiting periods imposed by an employer before workers are allowed to join an occupational scheme, must be brought against the employer.

Second, individuals are entitled to pursue an alternative route in making their complaint. They can lodge a complaint against either the trustees or the employer with the Pensions Ombudsman. This should only be done after any internal dispute resolution procedure has been exhausted. A complaint to the Pensions Ombudsman must normally be brought within three years of the act complained of. The Pensions Ombudsman will not consider a complaint if a claim has been made to the employment tribunal (unless the claim is discontinued). Prior to referring the matter to the Pensions Ombudsman, individuals should seek advice from the Pensions Advisory Service. Usually the Pensions Ombudsman will not investigate a complaint until the Pensions Advisory Service has been consulted.

The Regulations and the Directive

During the preceding chapters of this book, various points have been identified where it can be argued that the Regulations fail to implement the Directive. Among these are:

(a) The default retirement age of 65 (Chapter 8).

(b) The exemption for discriminatory benefits based upon length of service (Chapter 7).

(c) The exemption for recruitment of job applicants approaching the age of 65 (Chapter 6).

(d) Some of the provisions relating to occupational pensions (Chapter 9).

(e) The retention of an age multiplier in relation to the statutory redundancy scheme (Chapter 10).

(f) The absence of a clear remedy in Sch 7 in respect of the duty to notify during the transitional period (Chapter 12).

There are two ways in which these matters may be litigated so as to ensure that the United Kingdom's obligation to implement the Directive has been put into effect. First, the Regulations themselves can be challenged by way of judicial review. Second, the courts and tribunals can interpret the Regulations in such a way as to give effect to the Directive.

Judicial review

The Regulations make it clear that they do not purport to exclude an application for judicial review in the High Court (reg 35). This was the means chosen by various trade unions to challenge the implementation of the Directive in respect of the Employment Equality (Sexual Orientation) Regulations 2003 in *R (on the application of Amicus – MSF section) v Secretary of State for Trade and Industry* [2004] IRLR 430. In that case, the challenge was defeated, and Richards J held that the Sexual Orientation Regulations were compatible with the Directive. The judgment is based upon the fundamental point, however, that the domestic courts would, in applying the Sexual Orientation Regulations, be bound to construe them purposively so as to conform as far as possible with the Directive. The same principle will apply in relation to the Employment Equality (Age) Regulations 2006, and that is the subject of the next section.

Interpretation

As a general principle, the effect of European Community law is to overrule inconsistencies or ambiguities found in domestic statutes, rather than provide free-standing rights: *Barber v Staffordshire County Council* [1996] IRLR 209. This means that, where regulations have been made in order to give effect to a Community obligation, the courts and tribunals have a duty to give effect to the legislative intention, and implement the Community obligation: *Pickstone v Freemans plc* [1988] IRLR 357, HL. The legislature is presumed to have had, as its purpose, the implementation of the Directive in question. That purpose must be put into effect by adopting a *purposive* interpretation of the legislation. *Pickstone* was applied in *Litster v Forth Dry Docks Co Ltd* [1989] IRLR 161, HL in relation to regulations made for the express purpose of implementing a Directive, just as the Employment Equality (Age) Regulations 2006 are. In *Litster* (at p 165), Lord Oliver put it this way:

> 'If the legislation can reasonably be construed so as to conform with those obligations – obligations which are to be ascertained not only from the wording of the relevant Directive but from the interpretation placed upon it by the European Court of Justice in Luxembourg – such a purposive construction will be applied even though, perhaps, it may involve some departure from the strict and literal application of the words which the legislature has elected to use.'

When did age discrimination become unlawful?

The question posed in the heading is bound up with the relationship between domestic law and the law of the European Community. The obvious answer (from the perspective of domestic law) is that it becomes unlawful on the commencement of the Regulations, that is on 1 October 2006. However, the German case of *Mangold v Helm* [2006] IRLR 143 suggests that the answer may not be so simple. In that case, Mr Mangold at the age of 56 entered into a fixed-term contract with his employer. The German law implementing the Fixed Term Work Directive (99/70/EC) provides that a fixed-term contract must be justifiable on objective grounds. However, this condition does not apply where the worker is aged 52 or over at the time when the employment commences. (The age in question was lowered from 58 to 52 on 1 January 2003.) Mr Mangold asserted in the German Labour Court that his contract was incompatible with the Equal Treatment Framework Directive (2000/78/EC), and the case was referred to the European Court of Justice (ECJ).

The background is that the Equal Treatment Framework Directive gave Member States until 2 December 2003 to implement the majority of its provisions. As far as the provisions on age discrimination were concerned, however, an additional period of grace of three years (until 2 December 2006) was permitted. Like the United Kingdom, Germany took advantage of this additional period.

The ECJ was asked whether the removal of the condition requiring objective justification in the case of older workers was incompatible with Community law. The ECJ examined the aim of the German government in removing the condition and decided it was 'to promote the vocational integration of older workers, in so far as they encounter considerable difficulties in finding work'. The ECJ concluded that this was a legitimate aim. They went on to consider whether it was 'an appropriate and necessary' means of achieving that aim. The ECJ took the view that the exclusion of workers over the age of 52 from the protection of legislation on fixed-term work denied a significant number of workers the benefit of stable employment during a substantial part of their working lives. It distinguished between workers solely on the ground of their age, regardless of other relevant factors, e.g. the structure of the labour market, the personal circumstances of the workers in question. As a result, it went beyond what was necessary to attain the objective pursued, could not be justified, and was incompatible with the Directive.

At the time that Mr Mangold concluded his contract, Germany had not yet implemented those parts of the Directive relating to age discrimination. Further, it was not obliged to do so until 2 December 2006. However, the ECJ stated that, during the period prescribed for implementing a Directive, member states were obliged to 'refrain from taking any measures liable seriously to compromise the result prescribed by that Directive'. The domestic legislation which was inconsistent with the Directive therefore had to be set aside.

It would seem, therefore, that a worker could claim the protection of the Directive, even before the commencement of the Regulations, in certain limited circumstances. In essence, such claims would have to be based upon discriminatory domestic legislation introduced after the date of the Directive (2 December 2000).

12 Remedies

The main thrust of the Regulations is to prohibit age discrimination, and the next section of this chapter deals with the remedies available to the victim of age discrimination. The Regulations also have an impact upon the law relating to unfair dismissal. Two sections thereafter deal with unfair dismissal. The first attempts to give an overview of the remedies available for unfair dismissal, since this will be of general relevance to a number of claims under the Regulations. The second deals with the specific changes which the Regulations have made to remedies for unfair dismissal. Short sections then follow on the remedies available for failure to notify under the 'duty to consider' procedure, failure to permit accompaniment under that procedure, and failure to provide a statement of particulars of terms of employment. Finally, certain points relevant to remedies for discrimination in relation to pensions are dealt with.

Discrimination

Article 17 of the Directive is entitled 'Sanctions', and reads (in so far as relevant) as follows:

'Member States shall lay down the rules on sanctions applicable to infringements of the national provisions adopted pursuant to this Directive and shall take all measures necessary to ensure that they are applied. The sanctions, which may comprise the payment of compensation to the victim, must be effective, proportionate and dissuasive.'

The Regulations implement the Directive primarily through reg 38, which sets out the remedies available for a complaint brought in an employment tribunal. The tribunal may make:

(a)   a declaration;

(b)   a recommendation; and/or

(c)   an order that compensation should be paid.

Declarations and recommendations

As far as a declaration is concerned, it is a declaration as to the 'rights of the complainant and the respondent in relation to the act to which the complaint relates'. This would typically consist of that part of the tribunal's judgment on liability which states that the respondent discriminated against the claimant contrary to the Regulations (or did not do so where the claim is dismissed).

With regard to recommendations, the power is set out in reg 38(1)(c), and must be:

> 'that the respondent take within a specified period action appearing to the tribunal to be practicable for the purpose of obviating or reducing the adverse effect on the complainant of any act of discrimination or harassment to which the complaint relates.'

The power is somewhat limited by the phrase 'adverse effect on the complainant'. If the complainant has been dismissed, for example, there are few recommendations which the tribunal can make to assist him. In *Ministry of Defence v Jeremiah* [1978] IRLR 402, EAT, it was held (in respect of the equivalent provision in the Sex Discrimination Act 1975) that the tribunal had no power to order an employer to discontinue a discriminatory practice. Even where its recommendation is confined to matters which would benefit the victim, the powers of the tribunal are circumscribed. In *British Gas plc v Sharma* [1991] IRLR 101 (a case under the Race Relations Act 1976), the EAT held that a tribunal did not have the power to make a recommendation that the employers promote a successful claimant to the next suitable vacancy. That would constitute positive discrimination, contrary to the RRA. Any recommendation in respect of a successful claimant in an age discriminatory case would come up against the same limitation.

If a recommendation is made but not complied with, the tribunal can award compensation, or increase any award already made (reg 38(3)).

Compensation

Compensation is the central core of the remedies which are awarded to the claimant. As is the case with the other strands of discrimination (sex, race, etc) there is no limit on the amount which can be awarded in a claim for age discrimination.

The measure of compensation is that which could be ordered in the ordinary courts. It is compensation for the statutory tort of discrimination, and the principles applicable to the law of tort are applied in determining compensation (like a claim for personal injury). The calculation of compensation may cover the following heads:

- *Financial loss.* The principle is to ask what would have happened if it had not been for the discriminatory act. The claimant should then be put in the same position as they would have been, but for the unlawful act. In a case where women were dismissed on grounds of pregnancy, the Court of Appeal held that the tribunal should calculate the sum they would have earned had they remained in post. Then it had to deduct the amount they earned (or should have earned) elsewhere. Finally, it had to discount the net loss by a percentage to reflect the chance that they might have left the job in any event: *Ministry of Defence v Wheeler* [1998] IRLR 23, CA. A similar process would be employed in the case of a discriminatory dismissal on grounds of age.

The claimant is entitled to be compensated for the loss which arises naturally and directly from the wrong. It is not necessary for him to show that the particular type of loss was reasonably foreseeable (in contrast to a case for the tort of negligence): *Essa v Laing* [2004] IRLR 313, CA.

The employee is obliged to mitigate his loss. The burden of proving failure to mitigate is on the party asserting it.

- *Injury to feelings*. The principles in relation to discrimination cases generally are set out in *Armitage v Johnson* [1997] IRLR 162, EAT and may be summarised as follows:

(a) The award is to be compensatory, not punitive. It should not be inflated by feelings of indignation at the wrongdoer's conduct.

(b) Awards should not be so low as to diminish respect for the anti-discrimination legislation. Nor should they be so excessive as to be seen as a way to untaxed riches.

(c) Awards should bear some broad general similarity to the whole range of awards in personal injury cases (rather than any particular type of such award).

(d) Tribunals should remind themselves of the value in everyday life of the sum which they have in mind, e.g. by reference to purchasing power, or earnings.

The leading case on the levels which should be awarded under this head is *Vento v Chief Constable of West Yorkshire Police (No 2)* [2003] IRLR, CA. This set out three bands for compensation for injury to feelings (as distinct from psychiatric injury), as follows:

(a) The top band between £15,000 and £25,000 to be awarded in the most serious cases, e.g. where there has been a lengthy campaign of harassment. Only in the most exceptional case should an award of compensation for injury to feelings exceed £25,000.

(b) The middle band of £5,000 – £15,000 should be used for serious cases other than those in the top band.

(c) Awards of between £500 and £5,000 are appropriate for less serious cases, such as where the act of discrimination is an isolated or one-off occurrence. Awards lower than this should generally be avoided.

In *Voith Turbo Ltd v Stowe* [2005] IRLR 228, the EAT upheld a tribunal which had assessed compensation for injury to feelings in the middle band where the act of racial discrimination was dismissal. HHJ McMullen stated that dismissal on grounds of race discrimination is a very serious incident, and cannot be described as one-off or isolated. There is nothing to suggest that tribunals will view a dismissal which is discriminatory on grounds of age in a less serious light.

In assessing injury to feelings, the willingness of the employer to admit that it has acted in breach of the law may help to reduce the hurt felt by sparing the claimant from the indignity and further hurt of rehearsing the nature of his treatment: *Orlando v Didcot Power Station Sports and Social Club* [1996] IRLR 262, EAT.

- *Psychiatric injury.* This is a different concept from injury to feelings. The tribunal has power to award both. However, it is not always easy to separate the two, and care must be taken to avoid the risk of double compensation. As already indicated, since the award is based on the statutory tort of discrimination, rather than common law tort of negligence, the injury does not need to have been reasonably foreseeable. What is necessary is causation: *Sheriff v Klyne Tugs (Lowestoft) Ltd* [1999] IRLR 481. The existence and extent of psychiatric injury are matters of fact to be determined by the tribunal, which may (not must) be assisted by psychiatric evidence: *HM Prison Service v Salmon* [2001] IRLR 425, EAT.

- *Aggravated damages.* These are awarded where the respondent behaved in a high-handed, malicious, insulting or oppressive manner in committing the act of discrimination: *Alexander v Home Office* [1988] IRLR 190, CA. It may also cover cases where an employer has failed to investigate a complaint of discrimination, or used his power to inflict further distress, or acted insensitively and treated a serious matter as trivial. Conduct in the course of litigation (including unsatisfactory answers to a statutory questionnaire: see Chapter 11) may be taken into account in deciding whether to make an award of aggravated damages: *City of Bradford Metropolitan Council v Arora* [1989] IRLR 442, EAT.

  Aggravated damages should not be aggregated with, or treated as part of, the damages for injury to feelings: *Scott v Commissioners of Inland Revenue* [2004] IRLR 713, CA. Aggravated damages should be distinguished from exemplary damages which are punitive in nature and cannot be awarded in discrimination cases, as they are limited to those torts for which exemplary damages had been awarded prior to the decision of *Rookes v Barnard* in 1964: *Deane v London Borough of Ealing* [1993] IRLR 209, EAT.

- *Interest.* The rules are different from those for unfair dismissal, breach of contract, etc where interest only begins to accumulate after the judgment is sent to the parties. In discrimination cases, the award itself normally includes an element of interest relating to the period between the unlawful act and the judgment.

Any calculation by the tribunal is governed by the Employment Tribunals (Interest on Awards in Discrimination Cases) Regulations 1996, which is extended to cover cases of age discrimination by Sch 8, para 56. For injury to feelings, interest should be awarded for the period starting with the date of the act of discrimination, and ending on the day on which the amount of interest is calculated. For the other elements of the award, interest is calculated from the date at the midpoint between the act of discrimination and the date of calculation. The rate of interest is the rate for the Special Investment Account (currently 6%).

Unintentional indirect discrimination

As far as indirect discrimination is concerned, there is an additional hurdle for the claimant to clear before he can obtain compensation. The rule (which mirrors that applicable to other strands of discrimination with the exception of sex discrimination in employment) is set out in reg 38(2). In summary, it lays down that if the respondent (usually the employer) can prove that the provision, criterion or practice was not applied with the intention of treating the complainant unfavourably on grounds of age, the tribunal can only award compensation if:

(a)   it has made a declaration or recommendation (or both); and

(b)   it considers it just and equitable to award compensation.

In any case where a recommendation is made and not complied with, the tribunal can award compensation, or increase any award already made (reg 38(3)).

The relevant point at which the intention is to be gauged is when the provision, criterion or practice is applied, rather than the time at which it was introduced. The intention to apply the provision, criterion or practice together with knowledge of its impact upon the claimant as a member of the disadvantaged group, is sufficient to establish intention: *London Underground v Edwards* [1995] IRLR 355, EAT. Intention can be inferred from the knowledge of the consequences: *Walker Ltd v Hussain* [1996] IRLR 1.

Joint and several awards

It is not generally appropriate for a tribunal to make a joint and several award (i.e. 100% against each respondent). It ought not to do so on the basis of the relative financial resources of the respondents. It should apportion liability between the employer and the individual employee who has discriminated. Apportionment should be based upon the responsibility of each of the respondents bearing in mind their relative culpability and the extent to which they caused the damage. If the tribunal does make a joint and several award, it should make clear its reasons for doing so: *Way v Crouch* [2005] IRLR 603.

Remedies for unfair dismissal: an overview

As is described in Chapter 7 on Dismissal and Retirement, the Regulations make major changes to the law on unfair dismissal, and some of these relate to remedies. In addition, if a dismissal is also an act of discrimination prohibited by the Regulations, then the rules on remedies for unfair dismissal may be of relevance in calculating the claimant's entitlement. It should be noted at the outset, however, that where an act is both unfair dismissal and discrimination or harassment under the Regulations, compensation cannot be awarded twice for the same loss (s 126 of the Employment Rights Act 1996, as amended by Sch 8, para 29 of the Regulations).

This section looks at the remedies for unfair dismissal generally, because these general rules will be of relevance where there has been a dismissal which is unfair in terms of the Regulations.

If a tribunal decides that the claimant has been unfairly dismissed, it can order:

(a) *reinstatement* – the claimant returns to his old job, with arrears of pay, etc from a date specified by the tribunal;

(b) *re-engagement* – the claimant must be engaged in employment comparable to that from which he was dismissed, or other suitable employment; or

(c) *financial compensation.*

It must consider the remedies available in the above order. However, before making an order for reinstatement or re-engagement, the tribunal must consider:

(a) the claimant's wishes;

(b) whether the order is practicable; and

(c) whether it would be just if the claimant caused or contributed to the dismissal.

Coupled with any order for reinstatement or re-engagement, there needs to be an order for compensation for the period since the claimant was unfairly dismissed. This is assessed on principles broadly similar to those set out under the heading 'Financial compensation' below. If reinstatement or re-engagement is ordered, and the employer fails to comply, compensation will be increased by an 'additional award' of between 26 and 52 weeks – a special form of punitive damages (s 117(3)(b) of the Employment Rights Act 1996).

Financial compensation

This is the remedy for unfair dismissal in the great majority of cases. It consists of a basic and a compensatory award.

Basic award

This represents a number of weeks gross pay, calculated in accordance with s 119 of the Employment Rights Act 1996 ('ERA 1996'), which lays down that the unfairly dismissed employee should receive:

(a)   one and a half weeks' pay for each year of employment in which the employee was not below the age of 41;

(b)   one week's pay for each year of employment not within (a) above, in which he was not below the age of 22; and

(c)   half a week's pay for each year of employment not within (a) or (b) above.

The formula for calculation (like that for statutory redundancy payments) is itself age related and arguably discriminatory. (See the section entitled 'Redundancy: do the Regulations comply with the Directive?' in Chapter 10.)

There are various points to note about the formula. In particular:

(a)   The weekly pay in question is gross wages, i.e. before deduction of tax, etc and includes allowances and commission if contractual.

(b)   It is subject to a limit which is raised annually (£290 with effect from 1 February 2006).

(c)   Only complete years are counted.

Deductions may be made from the basic award where it would be 'just and equitable to reduce the basic award' (ERA 1996, s 122(3)). But no deduction should be made because of a failure by the employee to mitigate, nor should it be reduced because the employee has suffered no financial loss. The principle is that the employee should receive the basic award, even if he steps straight into another job immediately after being unfairly dismissed, and even if the new job is more highly paid than the one which he has lost. For example:

A dismissal takes place which is automatically unfair because the employer has failed to comply with the 'duty to consider' procedure. The employee is aged 60, had 12 years' continuous employment with the employer, and was paid £350 gross per week at the time of the dismissal. He finds alternative employment, which is better paid, immediately. Leaving to one side any compensatory award, he should receive £290 (the statutory maximum) x 12 x 1.5 by way of basic award – £5220. In fact, where an older employee with substantial service is dismissed, the basic award will usually amount to a substantial sum.

Compensatory award

The basic principle is that this element of the award should compensate the employee for financial loss suffered as a result of the dismissal. A statutory cap is placed on most forms of unfair dismissal by s 124 of the Employment Rights Act 1996. This limits the compensatory award to £58,400 for cases where the effective date of termination (EDT) is on or after 1 February 2006.

The compensatory award includes:

(a) *Immediate loss of wages.* This deals with the period from the EDT to the remedy part of the hearing. The loss is the net amount which the employee would have earned, less the amount earned in fresh employment (if any).

(b) *Future loss of wages.* This covers loss after the remedy hearing. The tribunal will look at whether the employee will suffer continuing loss, after reasonable efforts at mitigation are taken into consideration.

(c) *Loss of statutory protection.* A figure (e.g. £250) to compensate for the loss of the right not to be unfairly dismissed from a future job.

Elements (a) and (b) above will include, where appropriate, loss of fringe benefits and pension rights.

Adjustments to the compensatory award, where applicable, should be made in the following order (*Digital Equipment Ltd v Clements* (*No 2*) [1998] IRLR 134, CA, as modified by s 31(5) of the Employment Act 2002 ('EA 2002'):

1 Deduct any payment already made by the employer as compensation for the dismissal (e.g. as an ex gratia payment), other than an enhanced redundancy payment.

2   Deduct any sums earned by way of mitigation, or to reflect the employee's failure to take reasonable steps in mitigation.

3   Make any percentage reduction under the principle in *Polkey v AE Dayton Services* [1988] AC 344 (see below).

4   Increase or reduce where either employer or employee failed to comply with a relevant grievance procedure (GP) (EA 2002, s 31).

5   Increase for any failure by the employer to provide written particulars (EA 2002, s 38: see the section on Statement of particulars below).

6   Make any percentage reduction for the employee's contributory fault (ERA 1996, s 123(6)).

7   Deduct any enhanced redundancy payment to the extent that it exceeds the basic award.

8   Apply the statutory cap: £58,400 if the EDT is on or after 1 February 2006.

The employee has a duty to mitigate his or her loss (ERA 1996, s 123(4)). In particular, reasonable steps must be taken to get another job. The dismissed employee need not necessarily take the first job which comes along. It may sometimes be reasonable to wait if there is a likelihood that better paid employment will come along. But, after a period of unemployment, it will become increasingly reasonable for an employee to accept a job at a lower rate of pay than before.

In *Polkey v AE Dayton Services* [1988] AC 344, the House of Lords considered the position where the employer's failure to follow a fair procedure did not affect the outcome, i.e. the employee would have been dismissed anyway. Lord Bridge (at 365) stated that, if the tribunal was in doubt about whether the employee would have been dismissed, that doubt 'can be reflected by reducing the normal amount of compensation by a percentage representing the chance that the employee would still have lost his employment'.

If the relevant grievance procedure was not completed before proceedings were commenced, the tribunal is obliged to adjust the level of the compensatory (but not the basic) award (EA 2002, s 31, extended by Sch 8, para 36(2)(a) of the Regulations). If the reason for non-completion was wholly or mainly due to a failure by the employee to comply with requirements or to exercise a right of appeal under the relevant procedure, the award must be reduced. If it was due to a failure by the employer, the award must be increased. The standard level of adjustment is 10%. If 'just and equitable in all the circumstances', that adjustment may be up to 50%. On the other hand, if there are 'exceptional circumstances' why a 10% adjustment would be unjust or inequitable, the tribunal may make a lesser adjustment, or none at all.

Unfair dismissal: the changes

This section deals with the specific changes made by the Regulations to the remedies available for unfair dismissal. They are to be found in Sch 8.

First, where the dismissal is automatically unfair as a result of the employer's failure to comply with the 'duty to consider' procedures in Sch 6 to the Regulations, and the tribunal orders the employee to be reinstated or re-engaged, it should order the payment of a minimum of four weeks' compensation, subject to the interests of justice. This change is effected by Sch 8, para 26, which amends s 112(5) of the Employment Rights Act 1996. It puts failure to comply with the 'duty to consider' procedure on the same footing in this respect as a failure in relation to the statutory dismissal and disciplinary procedure (DDP).

More generally, provision is made for the payment of a minimum of four weeks' compensation where the dismissal is automatically unfair as a result of the employer's failure to comply with the 'duty to consider' procedure (Sch 8, para 28, amending s 120(1A) of the Employments Rights Act 1996). In other words, where the basic award for unfair dismissal would be less than four weeks' pay, the tribunal may increase it to four weeks' pay, subject once again to the interests of justice. This provision applies to all such unfair dismissals, and, unlike the amendment described in the preceding paragraph, is not confined to those where the tribunal orders reinstatement and re-engagement. Again, it reflects an equivalent provision in relation to the statutory DDP.

Section 119(4) and (5) of the Employment Rights Act 1996 are repealed by Sch 8, para 27. These provided for the gradual tapering of the basic award where the employee was dismissed after his 64th birthday.

Failure to notify

As described in Chapter 8, the 'duty to consider' procedure contains a duty to notify an employee of his impending retirement. According to Sch 6, para 2, the employer must notify such an employee in writing of:

(a) the employee's right to make a request to continue working after that date; and

(b) the date upon which he intends the employee to retire.

The notification must take place not more than one year, and not less than six months, before the intended date of retirement. For breach of this duty, the tribunal 'shall order the employer to pay compensation to the employee of such amount, not exceeding eight weeks' pay, as the tribunal considers just and equitable in all the circumstances' (Sch 6, para 11(3)). The maximum amount of a week's pay is limited in accordance with s 227(1) of the Employment Rights Act 1996 (currently £290, updated annually). The tribunal would no doubt, in exercising its judgment as to what is just and equitable, take into account any disadvantage which might have been incurred by the claimant. It seems that the formulation is also broad enough to take into account the degree of culpability on the part of the employer. The tribunal might therefore consider such questions as: Was there some notice given other than in writing? Was notice given at some stage outside the statutory period and, if so, how late was it? Did the actions of the employer amount to a calculated attempt to deprive the employee of his rights?

The duty to notify continues after the expiry of the six-month deadline in para 2, until the fourteenth day before termination of the contract. If the employer fails to meet this second deadline, the dismissal is automatically unfair.

It is uncertain whether there is a remedy for failure to comply with the duty to give notice under para 2 of Sch 6 during the currency of the transitional provisions (which are set out in Sch 7, and discussed in Chapter 8). The remedy of up to eight weeks' pay is set out in para 11(1) of Sch 6, which confines it to the situation where the employer has 'failed to comply with the duty to notify him [the employee] in paragraph 2' of Sch 6. In transitional cases where paras 2 and 3 of Sch 7 apply, 'the duty to notify in accordance with paragraph 2 of Schedule 6 does not apply'. In those cases covered by paras 4 and 5 of Sch 7, 'the employer shall be treated as complying with the duty under paragraph 2 of Schedule 6'. If these deeming provisions are read in isolation, then there is no failure by the employer to comply with the duty to notify under para 2 of Sch 6.

If this is right, it is a surprising result. In order to give effect to Article 17 of the Directive, there should be some effective sanction for an employer's failure to comply with the primary duty to notify, even where the expiry date falls before 1 April 2007. In addition, the duty to notify well in advance is a central plank in the 'duty to consider' procedure, which is in turn the means chosen by the government to bring about the desired culture change of seeking to employ those willing and able to work beyond normal retiring age. Those supporting such a purposive statutory construction can point to the absence of any provision in Sch 7 for the disapplication of para 11 of Sch 6, and argue that this surely means that the award applies to the transitional period. The absence of any such disapplication is particularly notable given that para 10 of Sch 6 is expressly disapplied by para 6 of Sch 7.

Failure to permit accompaniment

The employee is entitled to be accompanied by a work colleague at the meeting to consider his request to continue working after the intended date of retirement. There is a similar right in respect of the meeting to consider any appeal which he might make. If the employer fails to comply with the right to be accompanied, and the employee makes a claim in respect of that failure, the tribunal is required to order the employer to pay compensation of an amount not exceeding two weeks' pay (Sch 6, para 12). The amount of a week's pay is limited to the maximum laid down in s 227(1) of the Employment Rights Act 1996 (currently £290, updated annually). In deciding whether to award the maximum of two weeks or some lesser amount, the tribunal might take into account any mitigation which the employer could put forward, e.g. any genuine and reasonable confusion with regard to whether the employee was making such a request.

Statement of particulars

By s 38 of the Employment Act 2002 ('EA 2002'), where an employer has failed to give a statement of employment particulars to an employee, the tribunal must make an additional award of compensation to the employee (over and above any award for discrimination or unfair dismissal, for example). The provision applies to those claims listed in EA 2002, Sch 5. Age discrimination is added to the list of such claims by Sch 8, para 36(2)(c) of the Regulations. The award must be of a minimum amount of two weeks' pay, and, if it is just and equitable in all the circumstances, it may be the higher amount of four weeks' pay. The amount of a week's pay is limited to the maximum laid down in s 227(1) of the Employment Rights Act 1996 (currently £290, updated annually). What is just and equitable will no doubt depend partly on the circumstances surrounding the failure to issue the particulars in question, and the size and resources of the employer. Any fruitless request by the employee for such a written statement would no doubt weigh in the scales in favour of the higher award.

Pensions

In considering the remedies available for discrimination in relation to occupational pensions, reg 38 (which deals with remedies generally) is augmented by Sch 2, para 6 (which deals with remedies in the field of pensions).

Paragraph 6 provides for the situation where a complainant succeeds in showing that the terms on which a person may become a member of the scheme, or the terms upon which a member is treated, are unlawful in terms of the Regulations. The complainant must be a member or a prospective member of the pension scheme in question.

In this situation, the tribunal may make an order:

(a) giving the complainant a right to be admitted to the scheme, if the complaint related to the terms upon which people can become members; or

(b) giving the complainant the right to be granted membership without discrimination, if the complaint related to the terms on which members of the scheme were treated.

The order may be backdated, but not to a date before the commencement of the Regulations on 1 October 2006.

An order that the complainant be granted membership without discrimination amounts in effect to 'levelling up' his benefits. In due course, the trustees may alter the rules so as to 'level down' the benefit in question. Subject to the other rules in the scheme, they would be entitled to do this, provided that the new rule is not unlawful in itself.

The tribunal may not make an order for compensation in relation to a complaint under para 6, other than compensation for injury to feelings or for failure to comply with a recommendation made under reg 38(3).

APPENDIX 1
Employment Equality (Age) Regulations 2006

No 1031

Part 1
General

1 Citation, commencement and extent

(1) These Regulations may be cited as the Employment Equality (Age) Regulations 2006, and shall come into force on 1st October 2006.

(2) Any amendment, repeal or revocation made by these Regulations has the same extent as the provision to which it relates.

(3) Subject to that, these Regulations do not extend to Northern Ireland.

2 Interpretation

(1) In these Regulations, references to discrimination are to any discrimination falling within regulation 3 (discrimination on grounds of age), regulation 4 (discrimination by way of victimisation) or regulation 5 (instructions to discriminate) and related expressions shall be construed accordingly, and references to harassment shall be construed in accordance with regulation 6 (harassment on grounds of age).

(2) In these Regulations—

'1996 Act' means the Employment Rights Act 1996;

'act' includes a deliberate omission;

'benefit', except in regulation 11 and Schedule 2 (pension schemes), includes facilities and services;

'commencement date' means 1st October 2006;

'Crown employment' means—

    (a) service for purposes of a Minister of the Crown or government department, other than service of a person holding a statutory office; or

    (b) service on behalf of the Crown for purposes of a person holding a statutory office or purposes of a statutory body;

'detriment' does not include harassment within the meaning of regulation 6;

'employment' means employment under a contract of service or of apprenticeship or a contract personally to do any work, and related expressions (such as 'employee' and 'employer') shall be construed accordingly, but this definition does not apply in relation to regulation 30 (exception for retirement) or to Schedules 2, 6, 7 and 8;

'Great Britain' includes such of the territorial waters of the United Kingdom as are adjacent to Great Britain;

'Minister of the Crown' includes the Treasury and the Defence Council;

'proprietor', in relation to a school, has the meaning given by section 579 of the Education Act 1996;

'relevant member of the House of Commons staff' means any person who was appointed by the House of Commons Commission or who is a member of the Speaker's personal staff;

'relevant member of the House of Lords staff' means any person who is employed under a contract of employment with the Corporate Officer of the House of Lords;

'school', in England and Wales, has the meaning given by section 4 of the Education Act 1996, and, in Scotland, has the meaning given by section 135(1) of the Education (Scotland) Act 1980, and references to a school are to an institution in so far as it is engaged in the provision of education under those sections;

'service for purposes of a Minister of the Crown or government department' does not include service in any office mentioned in Schedule 2 (Ministerial offices) to the House of Commons Disqualification Act 1975;

'statutory body' means a body set up by or in pursuance of an enactment, and 'statutory office' means an office so set up; and

'worker' in relation to regulations 32 and 34 and to Schedule 2, means, as the case may be—

    (a)   an employee;

    (b)   a person holding an office or post to which regulation 12 (office-holders etc) applies;

    (c)   a person holding the office of constable;

    (d)   a partner within the meaning of regulation 17 (partnerships);

    (e)   a member of a limited liability partnership within the meaning of that regulation;

    (f)   a person in Crown employment;

    (g)   a relevant member of the House of Commons staff;

    (h)   a relevant member of the House of Lords staff.

(3)   In these Regulations references to 'employer', in their application to a person at any time seeking to employ another, include a person who has no employees at that time.

3 Discrimination on grounds of age

(1) For the purposes of these Regulations, a person ('A') discriminates against another person ('B') if—

(a) on grounds of B's age, A treats B less favourably than he treats or would treat other persons, or

(b) A applies to B a provision, criterion or practice which he applies or would apply equally to persons not of the same age group as B, but—

(i) which puts or would put persons of the same age group as B at a particular disadvantage when compared with other persons, and

(ii) which puts B at that disadvantage,

and A cannot show the treatment or, as the case may be, provision, criterion or practice to be a proportionate means of achieving a legitimate aim.

(2) A comparison of B's case with that of another person under paragraph (1) must be such that the relevant circumstances in the one case are the same, or not materially different, in the other.

(3) In this regulation—

(a) 'age group' means a group of persons defined by reference to age, whether by reference to a particular age or a range of ages; and

(b) the reference in paragraph (1)(a) to B's age includes B's apparent age.

4 Discrimination by way of victimisation

(1) For the purposes of these Regulations, a person ('A') discriminates against another person ('B') if he treats B less favourably than he treats or would treat other persons in the same circumstances, and does so by reason that B has—

(a) brought proceedings against A or any other person under or by virtue of these Regulations;

(b) given evidence or information in connection with proceedings brought by any person against A or any other person under or by virtue of these Regulations;

(c) otherwise done anything under or by reference to these Regulations in relation to A or any other person; or

(d) alleged that A or any other person has committed an act which (whether or not the allegation so states) would amount to a contravention of these Regulations,

or by reason that A knows that B intends to do any of those things, or suspects that B has done or intends to do any of them.

(2) Paragraph (1) does not apply to treatment of B by reason of any allegation made by him, or evidence or information given by him, if the allegation, evidence or information was false and not made (or, as the case may be, given) in good faith.

Appendix 1

5 Instructions to discriminate

For the purposes of these Regulations, a person ('A') discriminates against another person ('B') if he treats B less favourably than he treats or would treat other persons in the same circumstances, and does so by reason that—

    (a)   B has not carried out (in whole or in part) an instruction to do an act which is unlawful by virtue of these Regulations, or

    (b)   B, having been given an instruction to do such an act, complains to A or to any other person about that instruction.

6 Harassment on grounds of age

(1)   For the purposes of these Regulations, a person ('A') subjects another person ('B') to harassment where, on grounds of age, A engages in unwanted conduct which has the purpose or effect of—

    (a)   violating B's dignity; or

    (b)   creating an intimidating, hostile, degrading, humiliating or offensive environment for B.

(2)   Conduct shall be regarded as having the effect specified in paragraph (1)(a) or (b) only if, having regard to all the circumstances, including in particular the perception of B, it should reasonably be considered as having that effect.

Part 2
Discrimination in Employment and Vocational Training

7 Applicants and employees

(1)   It is unlawful for an employer, in relation to employment by him at an establishment in Great Britain, to discriminate against a person—

    (a)   in the arrangements he makes for the purpose of determining to whom he should offer employment;

    (b)   in the terms on which he offers that person employment; or

    (c)   by refusing to offer, or deliberately not offering, him employment.

(2)   It is unlawful for an employer, in relation to a person whom he employs at an establishment in Great Britain, to discriminate against that person—

    (a)   in the terms of employment which he affords him;

    (b)   in the opportunities which he affords him for promotion, a transfer, training, or receiving any other benefit;

    (c)   by refusing to afford him, or deliberately not affording him, any such opportunity; or

    (d)   by dismissing him, or subjecting him to any other detriment.

(3)   It is unlawful for an employer, in relation to employment by him at an establishment in Great Britain, to subject to harassment a person whom he employs or who has applied to him for employment.

(4)   Subject to paragraph (5), paragraph (1)(a) and (c) does not apply in relation to a person—

(a)   whose age is greater than the employer's normal retirement age or, if the employer does not have a normal retirement age, the age of 65; or

(b)   who would, within a period of six months from the date of his application to the employer, reach the employer's normal retirement age or, if the employer does not have a normal retirement age, the age of 65.

(5)   Paragraph (4) only applies to a person to whom, if he was recruited by the employer, regulation 30 (exception for retirement) could apply.

(6)   Paragraph (2) does not apply to benefits of any description if the employer is concerned with the provision (for payment or not) of benefits of that description to the public, or to a section of the public which includes the employee in question, unless—

(a)   that provision differs in a material respect from the provision of the benefits by the employer to his employees; or

(b)   the provision of the benefits to the employee in question is regulated by his contract of employment; or

(c)   the benefits relate to training.

(7)   In paragraph (2)(d) reference to the dismissal of a person from employment includes reference—

(a)   to the termination of that person's employment by the expiration of any period (including a period expiring by reference to an event or circumstance), not being a termination immediately after which the employment is renewed on the same terms; and

(b)   to the termination of that person's employment by any act of his (including the giving of notice) in circumstances such that he is entitled to terminate it without notice by reason of the conduct of the employer.

(8)   In paragraph (4) 'normal retirement age' is an age of 65 or more which meets the requirements of section 98ZH of the 1996 Act.

8   Exception for genuine occupational requirement etc

(1)   In relation to discrimination falling within regulation 3 (discrimination on grounds of age)—

(a)   regulation 7(1)(a) or (c) does not apply to any employment;

(b)   regulation 7(2)(b) or (c) does not apply to promotion or transfer to, or training for, any employment; and

(c)   regulation 7(2)(d) does not apply to dismissal from any employment,

where paragraph (2) applies.

(2)   This paragraph applies where, having regard to the nature of the employment or the context in which it is carried out—

(a) possessing a characteristic related to age is a genuine and determining occupational requirement;

(b) it is proportionate to apply that requirement in the particular case; and

(c) either—

(i) the person to whom that requirement is applied does not meet it, or

(ii) the employer is not satisfied, and in all the circumstances it is reasonable for him not to be satisfied, that that person meets it.

9 Contract workers

(1) It is unlawful for a principal, in relation to contract work at an establishment in Great Britain, to discriminate against a contract worker—

(a) in the terms on which he allows him to do that work;

(b) by not allowing him to do it or continue to do it;

(c) in the way he affords him access to any benefits or by refusing or deliberately not affording him access to them; or

(d) by subjecting him to any other detriment.

(2) It is unlawful for a principal, in relation to contract work at an establishment in Great Britain, to subject a contract worker to harassment.

(3) A principal does not contravene paragraph (1)(b) by doing any act in relation to a contract worker where, if the work were to be done by a person taken into the principal's employment, that act would be lawful by virtue of regulation 8 (exception for genuine occupational requirement etc).

(4) Paragraph (1) does not apply to benefits of any description if the principal is concerned with the provision (for payment or not) of benefits of that description to the public, or to a section of the public to which the contract worker in question belongs, unless that provision differs in a material respect from the provision of the benefits by the principal to his contract workers.

(5) In this regulation—

'principal' means a person ('A') who makes work available for doing by individuals who are employed by another person who supplies them under a contract made with A;

'contract work' means work so made available; and

'contract worker' means any individual who is supplied to the principal under such a contract.

10 Meaning of employment and contract work at establishment in Great Britain

(1) For the purposes of this Part ('the relevant purposes'), employment is to be regarded as being at an establishment in Great Britain if the employee—

(a) does his work wholly or partly in Great Britain; or

(b) does his work wholly outside Great Britain and paragraph (2) applies.

(2)   This paragraph applies if—

(a)   the employer has a place of business at an establishment in Great Britain;

(b)   the work is for the purposes of the business carried on at that establishment; and

(c)   the employee is ordinarily resident in Great Britain—

(i)   at the time when he applies for or is offered the employment, or

(ii) at any time during the course of the employment.

(3)   The reference to 'employment' in paragraph (1) includes—

(a)   employment on board a ship only if the ship is registered at a port of registry in Great Britain, and

(b)   employment on an aircraft or hovercraft only if the aircraft or hovercraft is registered in the United Kingdom and operated by a person who has his principal place of business, or is ordinarily resident, in Great Britain.

(4)   Subject to paragraph (5), for the purposes of determining if employment concerned with the exploration of the sea bed or sub-soil or the exploitation of their natural resources is outside Great Britain, this regulation has effect as if references to Great Britain included—

(a)   any area designated under section 1(7) of the Continental Shelf Act 1964 except an area or part of an area in which the law of Northern Ireland applies; and

(b)   in relation to employment concerned with the exploration or exploitation of the Frigg Gas Field, the part of the Norwegian sector of the Continental Shelf described in Schedule 1.

(5)   Paragraph (4) shall not apply to employment which is concerned with the exploration or exploitation of the Frigg Gas Field unless the employer is—

(a)   a company registered under the Companies Act 1985;

(b)   an oversea company which has established a place of business within Great Britain from which it directs the exploration or exploitation in question; or

(c)   any other person who has a place of business within Great Britain from which he directs the exploration or exploitation in question.

(6)   In this regulation—

'the Frigg Gas Field' means the naturally occurring gas-bearing sand formations of the lower Eocene age located in the vicinity of the intersection of the line of latitude 59 degrees 53 minutes North and of the dividing line between the sectors of the Continental Shelf of the United Kingdom and the Kingdom of Norway and includes all other gas-bearing strata from which gas at the start of production is capable of flowing into the above-mentioned gas-bearing sand formations;

'oversea company' has the same meaning as in section 744 of the Companies Act 1985.

(7) This regulation applies in relation to contract work within the meaning of regulation 9 as it applies in relation to employment; and, in its application to contract work, references to 'employee', 'employer' and 'employment' are references to (respectively) 'contract worker', 'principal' and 'contract work' within the meaning of regulation 9.

11 Pension schemes

(1) It is unlawful, except in relation to rights accrued or benefits payable in respect of periods of service prior to the coming into force of these Regulations, for the trustees or managers of an occupational pension scheme to discriminate against a member or prospective member of the scheme in carrying out any of their functions in relation to it (including in particular their functions relating to the admission of members to the scheme and the treatment of members of it).

(2) It is unlawful for the trustees or managers of an occupational pension scheme, in relation to the scheme, to subject to harassment a member or prospective member of it.

(3) Schedule 2 (pension schemes) shall have effect for the purposes of—

(a) defining terms used in this regulation and in that Schedule;

(b) exempting certain rules and practices in or relating to pension schemes from Parts 2 and 3 of these Regulations;

(c) treating every occupational pension scheme as including a non-discrimination rule;

(d) giving trustees or managers of an occupational pension scheme power to alter the scheme so as to secure conformity with the non-discrimination rule;

(e) making provision in relation to the procedures, and remedies which may be granted, on certain complaints relating to occupational pension schemes presented to an employment tribunal under regulation 36 (jurisdiction of employment tribunals).

12 Office-holders etc

(1) It is unlawful for a relevant person, in relation to an appointment to an office or post to which this regulation applies, to discriminate against a person—

(a) in the arrangements which he makes for the purpose of determining to whom the appointment should be offered;

(b) in the terms on which he offers him the appointment; or

(c) by refusing to offer him the appointment.

(2) It is unlawful, in relation to an appointment to an office or post to which this regulation applies and which is an office or post referred to in paragraph (8)(b), for a relevant person on whose recommendation (or subject to whose approval) appointments to the office or post are made, to discriminate against a person—

(a)   in the arrangements which he makes for the purpose of determining who should be recommended or approved in relation to the appointment; or

(b)   in making or refusing to make a recommendation, or giving or refusing to give an approval, in relation to the appointment.

(3)   It is unlawful for a relevant person, in relation to a person who has been appointed to an office or post to which this regulation applies, to discriminate against him—

(a)   in the terms of the appointment;

(b)   in the opportunities which he affords him for promotion, a transfer, training or receiving any other benefit, or by refusing to afford him any such opportunity;

(c)   by terminating the appointment; or

(d)   by subjecting him to any other detriment in relation to the appointment.

(4)   It is unlawful for a relevant person, in relation to an office or post to which this regulation applies, to subject to harassment a person—

(a)   who has been appointed to the office or post;

(b)   who is seeking or being considered for appointment to the office or post; or

(c)   who is seeking or being considered for a recommendation or approval in relation to an appointment to an office or post referred to in paragraph (8)(b).

(5)   Paragraphs (1) and (3) do not apply to any act in relation to an office or post where, if the office or post constituted employment, that act would be lawful by virtue of regulation 8 (exception for genuine occupational requirement etc); and paragraph (2) does not apply to any act in relation to an office or post where, if the office or post constituted employment, it would be lawful by virtue of regulation 8 to refuse to offer the person such employment.

(6)   Paragraph (3) does not apply to benefits of any description if the relevant person is concerned with the provision (for payment or not) of benefits of that description to the public, or a section of the public to which the person appointed belongs, unless—

(a)   that provision differs in a material respect from the provision of the benefits by the relevant person to persons appointed to offices or posts which are the same as, or not materially different from, that which the person appointed holds; or

(b)   the provision of the benefits to the person appointed is regulated by the terms and conditions of his appointment; or

(c)   the benefits relate to training.

(7)   In paragraph (3)(c) the reference to the termination of the appointment includes a reference—

(a)   to the termination of the appointment by the expiration of any period (including a period expiring by reference to an event or circumstance), not being a termination immediately after which the appointment is renewed on the same terms and conditions; and

    (b)   to the termination of the appointment by any act of the person appointed (including the giving of notice) in circumstances such that he is entitled to terminate the appointment without notice by reason of the conduct of the relevant person.

(8)   This regulation applies to—

    (a)   any office or post to which persons are appointed to discharge functions personally under the direction of another person, and in respect of which they are entitled to remuneration; and

    (b)   any office or post to which appointments are made by (or on the recommendation of or subject to the approval of) a Minister of the Crown, a government department, the National Assembly for Wales or any part of the Scottish Administration,

but not to a political office or a case where regulation 7 (applicants and employees), 9 (contract workers), 15 (barristers), 16 (advocates) or 17 (partnerships) applies, or would apply but for the operation of any other provision of these Regulations.

(9)   For the purposes of paragraph (8) (a) the holder of an office or post—

    (a)   is to be regarded as discharging his functions under the direction of another person if that other person is entitled to direct him as to when and where he discharges those functions;

    (b)   is not to be regarded as entitled to remuneration merely because he is entitled to payments—

        (i)   in respect of expenses incurred by him in carrying out the function of the office or post; or

        (ii)   by way of compensation for the loss of income or benefits he would or might have received from any person had he not been carrying out the functions of the office or post.

(10)   In this regulation—

    (a)   appointment to an office or post does not include election to an office or post;

    (b)   'political office' means—

        (i)   any office of the House of Commons held by a member of it;

        (ii)   a life peerage within the meaning of the Life Peerages Act 1958, or any office of the House of Lords held by a member of it;

        (iii)   any office mentioned in Schedule 2 (Ministerial offices) to the House of Commons Disqualification Act 1975;

        (iv)   the offices of Leader of the Opposition, Chief Opposition Whip or Assistant Opposition Whip within the meaning of the Ministerial and other Salaries Act 1975;

        (v)   any office of the Scottish Parliament held by a member of it;

    (vi)   a member of the Scottish Executive within the meaning of section 44 of the Scotland Act 1998, or a junior Scottish Minister within the meaning of section 49 of that Act;

    (vii)   any office of the National Assembly for Wales held by a member of it;

    (viii)   in England, any office of a county council, a London borough council, a district council, or a parish council held by a member of it;

    (ix)   in Wales, any office of a county council, a county borough council, or a community council held by a member of it;

    (x)   in relation to a council constituted under section 2 of the Local Government etc (Scotland) Act 1994 or a community council established under section 51 of the Local Government (Scotland) Act 1973, any office of such a council held by a member of it;

    (xi)   any office of the Greater London Authority held by a member of it;

    (xii)   any office of the Common Council of the City of London held by a member of it;

    (xiii)   any office of the Council of the Isles of Scilly held by a member of it;

    (xiv)   any office of a political party;

(c)   'relevant person', in relation to an office or post, means—

    (i)   any person with power to make or terminate appointments to the office or post, or to determine the terms of appointment,

    (ii)   any person with power to determine the working conditions of a person appointed to the office or post in relation to opportunities for promotion, a transfer, training or for receiving any other benefit, and

    (iii)   any person or body referred to in paragraph (8)(b) on whose recommendation or subject to whose approval appointments are made to the office or post;

(d)   references to making a recommendation include references to making a negative recommendation; and

(e)   references to refusal include references to deliberate omission.

13 Police

(1)   For the purposes of this Part, the holding of the office of constable shall be treated as employment—

    (a)   by the chief officer of police as respects any act done by him in relation to a constable or that office;

    (b)   by the police authority as respects any act done by it in relation to a constable or that office.

(2)   For the purposes of regulation 25 (liability of employers and principals)—

    (a)   the holding of the office of constable shall be treated as employment by the chief officer of police (and as not being employment by any other person); and

    (b)   anything done by a person holding such an office in the performance, or purported performance, of his functions shall be treated as done in the course of that employment.

(3)   There shall be paid out of the police fund—

    (a)   any compensation, costs or expenses awarded against a chief officer of police in any proceedings brought against him under these Regulations, and any costs or expenses incurred by him in any such proceedings so far as not recovered by him in the proceedings; and

    (b)   any sum required by a chief officer of police for the settlement of any claim made against him under these Regulations if the settlement is approved by the police authority.

(4)   Any proceedings under these Regulations which, by virtue of paragraph (1), would lie against a chief officer of police shall be brought against the chief officer of police for the time being or in the case of a vacancy in that office, against the person for the time being performing the functions of that office; and references in paragraph (3) to the chief officer of police shall be construed accordingly.

(5)   A police authority may, in such cases and to such extent as appear to it to be appropriate, pay out of the police fund—

    (a)   any compensation, costs or expenses awarded in proceedings under these Regulations against a person under the direction and control of the chief officer of police;

    (b)   any costs or expenses incurred and not recovered by such a person in such proceedings; and

    (c)   any sum required in connection with the settlement of a claim that has or might have given rise to such proceedings.

(6)   Paragraphs (1) and (2) apply to a police cadet and appointment as a police cadet as they apply to a constable and the office of constable.

(7)   Subject to paragraph (8), in this regulation—

'chief officer of police'—

    (a)   in relation to a person appointed, or an appointment falling to be made, under a specified Act, has the same meaning as in the Police Act 1996;

    (b)   in relation to a person appointed, or an appointment falling to be made, under the Police (Scotland) Act 1967, means the chief constable of the relevant police force;

    (c)   in relation to any other person or appointment means the officer or other person who has the direction and control of the body of constables or cadets in question;

'police authority'—

(a)   in relation to a person appointed, or an appointment falling to be made, under a specified Act, has the same meaning as in the Police Act 1996;

(b)   in relation to a person appointed, or an appointment falling to be made, under the Police (Scotland) Act 1967, has the meaning given in that Act;

(c)   in relation to any other person or appointment, means the authority by whom the person in question is or on appointment would be paid;

'police cadet' means any person appointed to undergo training with a view to becoming a constable;

'police fund'—

(a)   in relation to a chief officer of police within sub-paragraph (a) of the above definition of that term, has the same meaning as in the Police Act 1996;

(b)   in any other case means money provided by the police authority; and

'specified Act' means the Metropolitan Police Act 1829, the City of London Police Act 1839 or the Police Act 1996.

(8)   In relation to a constable of a force who is not under the direction and control of the chief officer of police for that force, references in this regulation to the chief officer of police are references to the chief officer of the force under whose direction and control he is, and references in this regulation to the police authority are references to the relevant police authority for that force.

(9)   This regulation is subject to regulation 14.

14   Serious Organised Crime Agency

(1)   For the purposes of this Part, any constable or other person who has been seconded to SOCA to serve as a member of its staff shall be treated as employed by SOCA.

(2)   For the purposes of regulation 25 (liability of employers and principals)—

(a)   the secondment of any constable or other person to SOCA to serve as a member of its staff shall be treated as employment by SOCA (and not as employment by any other person); and

(b)   anything done by a person so seconded in the performance, or purported performance, of his functions shall be treated as done in the course of that employment.

(3)   In this regulation 'SOCA' means the Serious Organised Crime Agency established under section 1 of, and Schedule 1 to, the Serious Organised Crime and Police Act 2005.

15   Barristers

(1)   It is unlawful for a barrister or barrister's clerk, in relation to any offer of a pupillage or tenancy, to discriminate against a person—

(a) in the arrangements which are made for the purpose of determining to whom the pupillage or tenancy should be offered;

(b) in respect of any terms on which it is offered; or

(c) by refusing, or deliberately not offering, it to him.

(2) It is unlawful for a barrister or barrister's clerk, in relation to a pupil or tenant in the set of chambers in question, to discriminate against him—

(a) in respect of any terms applicable to him as a pupil or tenant;

(b) in the opportunities for training, or gaining experience, which are afforded or denied to him;

(c) in the benefits which are afforded or denied to him; or

(d) by terminating his pupillage, or by subjecting him to any pressure to leave the chambers or other detriment.

(3) It is unlawful for a barrister or barrister's clerk, in relation to a pupillage or tenancy in the set of chambers in question, to subject to harassment a person who is, or has applied to be, a pupil or tenant.

(4) It is unlawful for any person, in relation to the giving, withholding or acceptance of instructions to a barrister, to discriminate against any person by subjecting him to a detriment, or to subject him to harassment.

(5) In this regulation—

'barrister's clerk' includes any person carrying out any of the functions of a barrister's clerk;

'pupil', 'pupillage' and 'set of chambers' have the meanings commonly associated with their use in the context of barristers practising in independent practice; and

'tenancy' and 'tenant' have the meanings commonly associated with their use in the context of barristers practising in independent practice, but also include reference to any barrister permitted to work in a set of chambers who is not a tenant.

(6) This regulation extends to England and Wales only.

16 Advocates

(1) It is unlawful for an advocate, in relation to taking any person as his pupil, to discriminate against a person—

(a) in the arrangements which he makes for the purpose of determining whom he will take as his pupil;

(b) in respect of any terms on which he offers to take any person as his pupil; or

(c) by refusing to take, or deliberately not taking, a person as his pupil.

(2) It is unlawful for an advocate, in relation to a person who is his pupil, to discriminate against him—

(a) in respect of any terms applicable to him as a pupil;

(b) in the opportunities for training, or gaining experience, which are afforded or denied to him;

(c) in the benefits which are afforded or denied to him; or

(d) by terminating the relationship, or by subjecting him to any pressure to terminate the relationship or other detriment.

(3) It is unlawful for an advocate, in relation to a person who is his pupil or taking any person as his pupil, to subject such a person to harassment.

(4) It is unlawful for any person, in relation to the giving, withholding or acceptance of instructions to an advocate, to discriminate against any person by subjecting him to a detriment, or to subject him to harassment.

(5) In this regulation—

'advocate' means a member of the Faculty of Advocates practising as such; and

'pupil' has the meaning commonly associated with its use in the context of a person training to be an advocate.

(6) This regulation extends to Scotland only.

17 Partnerships

(1) It is unlawful for a firm, in relation to a position as partner in the firm, to discriminate against a person—

(a) in the arrangements they make for the purpose of determining to whom they should offer that position;

(b) in the terms on which they offer him that position;

(c) by refusing to offer, or deliberately not offering, him that position; or

(d) in a case where the person already holds that position—

(i) in the way they afford him access to any benefits or by refusing to afford, or deliberately not affording, him access to them; or

(ii) by expelling him from that position, or subjecting him to any other detriment.

(2) It is unlawful for a firm, in relation to a position as partner in the firm, to subject to harassment a person who holds or has applied for that position.

(3) Paragraphs (1)(a) to (c) and (2) apply in relation to persons proposing to form themselves into a partnership as they apply in relation to a firm.

(4) Paragraph (1) does not apply to any act in relation to a position as partner where, if the position were employment, that act would be lawful by virtue of regulation 8 (exception for genuine occupational requirement etc).

(5) In the case of a limited partnership references in this regulation to a partner shall be construed as references to a general partner as defined in section 3 of the Limited Partnerships Act 1907.

(6) This regulation applies to a limited liability partnership as it applies to a firm; and, in its application to a limited liability partnership, references to a partner in a firm are references to a member of the limited liability partnership.

(7)   In this regulation, 'firm' has the meaning given by section 4 of the Partnership Act 1890.

(8)   In paragraph (1)(d) reference to the expulsion of a person from a position as partner includes reference—

(a)   to the termination of that person's partnership by the expiration of any period (including a period expiring by reference to an event or circumstance), not being a termination immediately after which the partnership is renewed on the same terms; and

(b)   to the termination of that person's partnership by any act of his (including the giving of notice) in circumstances such that he is entitled to terminate it without notice by reason of the conduct of the other partners.

18 Trade organisations

(1)   It is unlawful for a trade organisation to discriminate against a person—

(a)   in the terms on which it is prepared to admit him to membership of the organisation; or

(b)   by refusing to accept, or deliberately not accepting, his application for membership.

(2)   It is unlawful for a trade organisation, in relation to a member of the organisation, to discriminate against him—

(a)   in the way it affords him access to any benefits or by refusing or deliberately omitting to afford him access to them;

(b)   by depriving him of membership, or varying the terms on which he is a member; or

(c)   by subjecting him to any other detriment.

(3)   It is unlawful for a trade organisation, in relation to a person's membership or application for membership of that organisation, to subject that person to harassment.

(4)   In this regulation—

'trade organisation' means an organisation of workers, an organisation of employers, or any other organisation whose members carry on a particular profession or trade for the purposes of which the organisation exists;

'profession' includes any vocation or occupation; and

'trade' includes any business.

19 Qualifications bodies

(1)   It is unlawful for a qualifications body to discriminate against a person—

(a)   in the terms on which it is prepared to confer a professional or trade qualification on him;

(b)   by refusing or deliberately not granting any application by him for such a qualification; or

(c)   by withdrawing such a qualification from him or varying the terms on which he holds it.

(2)   It is unlawful for a qualifications body, in relation to a professional or trade qualification conferred by it, to subject to harassment a person who holds or applies for such a qualification.

(3)   In this regulation—

'qualifications body' means any authority or body which can confer a professional or trade qualification, but it does not include—

(a)   a governing body of an educational establishment to which regulation 23 (institutions of further and higher education) applies, or would apply but for the operation of any other provision of these Regulations, or

(b)   a proprietor of a school;

'confer' includes renew or extend;

'professional or trade qualification' means any authorisation, qualification, recognition, registration, enrolment, approval or certification which is needed for, or facilitates engagement in, a particular profession or trade;

'profession' and 'trade' have the same meaning as in regulation 18.

20   The provision of vocational training

(1)   It is unlawful, in relation to a person seeking or undergoing training, for any training provider to discriminate against him—

(a)   in the arrangements he makes for the purpose of determining to whom he should offer training;

(b)   in the terms on which the training provider affords him access to any training;

(c)   by refusing or deliberately not affording him such access;

(d)   by terminating his training; or

(e)   by subjecting him to any other detriment during his training.

(2)   It is unlawful for a training provider, in relation to a person seeking or undergoing training, to subject him to harassment.

(3)   Paragraph (1) does not apply if the discrimination concerns training that would only fit a person for employment which, by virtue of regulation 8 (exception for genuine occupational requirement etc), the employer could lawfully refuse to offer the person seeking training.

(4)   In this regulation—

'professional or trade qualification' has the same meaning as in regulation 19;

'registered pupil' has the meaning given by section 434 of the Education Act 1996;

'training' means—

 (a) all types and all levels of training which would help fit a person for any employment;

 (b) vocational guidance;

 (c) facilities for training;

 (d) practical work experience provided by an employer to a person whom he does not employ; and

 (e) any assessment related to the award of any professional or trade qualification;

'training provider' means any person who provides, or makes arrangements for the provision of, training, but it does not include—

 (a) an employer in relation to training for persons employed by him;

 (b) a governing body of an educational establishment to which regulation 23 (institutions of further and higher education) applies, or would apply but for the operation of any other provision of these Regulations; or

 (c) a proprietor of a school in relation to any registered pupil.

21 Employment agencies, careers guidance etc

(1) It is unlawful for an employment agency to discriminate against a person—

 (a) in the terms on which the agency offers to provide any of its services;

 (b) by refusing or deliberately not providing any of its services; or

 (c) in the way it provides any of its services.

(2) It is unlawful for an employment agency, in relation to a person to whom it provides its services, or who has requested it to provide its services, to subject that person to harassment.

(3) Paragraph (1) does not apply to discrimination if it only concerns employment which, by virtue of regulation 8 (exception for genuine occupational requirement etc), the employer could lawfully refuse to offer the person in question.

(4) An employment agency shall not be subject to any liability under this regulation if it proves that—

 (a) it acted in reliance on a statement made to it by the employer to the effect that, by reason of the operation of paragraph (3), its action would not be unlawful; and

 (b) it was reasonable for it to rely on the statement.

(5) A person who knowingly or recklessly makes a statement such as is referred to in paragraph (4)(a) which in a material respect is false or misleading commits an offence, and shall be liable on summary conviction to a fine not exceeding level 5 on the standard scale.

(6) For the purposes of this regulation—

(a) 'employment agency' means a person who, for profit or not, provides services for the purpose of finding employment for workers or supplying employers with workers, but it does not include—

  (i) a governing body of an educational establishment to which regulation 23 (institutions of further and higher education) applies, or would apply but for the operation of any other provision of these Regulations; or

  (ii) a proprietor of a school; and

(b) references to the services of an employment agency include guidance on careers and any other services related to employment.

22 Assisting persons to obtain employment etc

(1) It is unlawful for the Secretary of State to discriminate against any person by subjecting him to a detriment, or to subject a person to harassment, in the provision of facilities or services under section 2 of the Employment and Training Act 1973 (arrangements for assisting persons to obtain employment).

(2) It is unlawful for Scottish Enterprise or Highlands and Islands Enterprise to discriminate against any person by subjecting him to a detriment, or to subject a person to harassment, in the provision of facilities or services under such arrangements as are mentioned in section 2(3) of the Enterprise and New Towns (Scotland) Act 1990 (arrangements analogous to arrangements in pursuance of the said Act of 1973).

(3) This regulation does not apply in a case where—

(a) regulation 20 (the provision of vocational training) applies or would apply but for the operation of any other provision of these Regulations, or

(b) the Secretary of State is acting as an employment agency within the meaning of regulation 21 (employment agencies, careers guidance etc).

23 Institutions of further and higher education

(1) It is unlawful, in relation to an educational establishment to which this regulation applies, for the governing body of that establishment to discriminate against a person—

(a) in the terms on which it offers to admit him to the establishment as a student;

(b) by refusing or deliberately not accepting an application for his admission to the establishment as a student; or

(c) where he is a student of the establishment—

  (i) in the way it affords him access to any benefits,

  (ii) by refusing or deliberately not affording him access to them, or

(iii)   by excluding him from the establishment or subjecting him to any other detriment.

(2)   It is unlawful, in relation to an educational establishment to which this regulation applies, for the governing body of that establishment to subject to harassment a person who is a student at the establishment, or who has applied for admission to the establishment as a student.

(3)   Paragraph (1) does not apply if the discrimination concerns training that would only fit a person for employment which, by virtue of regulation 8 (exception for genuine occupational requirement etc), the employer could lawfully refuse to offer the person in question.

(4)   This regulation applies to the following educational establishments in England and Wales, namely—

(a)   an institution within the further education sector (within the meaning of section 91(3) of the Further and Higher Education Act 1992);

(b)   a university;

(c)   an institution, other than a university, within the higher education sector (within the meaning of section 91(5) of the Further and Higher Education Act 1992).

(5)   This regulation applies to the following educational establishments in Scotland, namely—

(a)   a college of further education within the meaning of section 36(1) of the Further and Higher Education (Scotland) Act 1992 under the management of a board of management within the meaning of Part I of that Act;

(b)   a college of further education maintained by an education authority in the exercise of its further education functions in providing courses of further education within the meaning of section 1(5)(b)(ii) of the Education (Scotland) Act 1980;

(c)   any other educational establishment (not being a school) which provides further education within the meaning of section 1 of the Further and Higher Education (Scotland) Act 1992;

(d)   an institution within the higher education sector (within the meaning of Part 2 of the Further and Higher Education (Scotland) Act 1992);

(e)   a central institution (within the meaning of section 135 of the Education (Scotland) Act 1980).

(6)   In this regulation—

'education authority' has the meaning given by section 135(1) of the Education (Scotland) Act 1980;

'governing body' includes—

(a)   the board of management of a college referred to in paragraph (5)(a), and

(b)   the managers of a college or institution referred to in paragraph (5)(b) or (e);

'student' means any person who receives education at an educational establishment to which this regulation applies; and

'university' includes a university college and the college, school or hall of a university.

24 Relationships which have come to an end

(1) In this regulation a 'relevant relationship' is a relationship during the course of which an act of discrimination against, or harassment of, one party to the relationship ('B') by the other party to it ('A') is unlawful by virtue of any preceding provision of this Part.

(2) Where a relevant relationship has come to an end, it is unlawful for A—

(a) to discriminate against B by subjecting him to a detriment; or

(b) to subject B to harassment;

where the discrimination or harassment arises out of and is closely connected to that relationship.

(3) In paragraph (1), reference to an act of discrimination or harassment which is unlawful includes, in the case of a relationship which has come to an end before the coming into force of these Regulations, reference to an act of discrimination or harassment which would, after the coming into force of these Regulations, be unlawful.

Part 3
Other Unlawful Acts

25 Liability of employers and principals

(1) Anything done by a person in the course of his employment shall be treated for the purposes of these Regulations as done by his employer as well as by him, whether or not it was done with the employer's knowledge or approval.

(2) Anything done by a person as agent for another person with the authority (whether express or implied, and whether precedent or subsequent) of that other person shall be treated for the purposes of these Regulations as done by that other person as well as by him.

(3) In proceedings brought under these Regulations against any person in respect of an act alleged to have been done by an employee of his it shall be a defence for that person to prove that he took such steps as were reasonably practicable to prevent the employee from doing that act, or from doing in the course of his employment acts of that description.

26 Aiding unlawful acts

(1) A person who knowingly aids another person to do an act made unlawful by these Regulations shall be treated for the purpose of these Regulations as himself doing an unlawful act of the like description.

(2) For the purposes of paragraph (1) an employee or agent for whose act the employer or principal is liable under regulation 25 (or would be so liable but for regulation 25(3)) shall be deemed to aid the doing of the act by the employer or principal.

(3)   A person does not under this regulation knowingly aid another to do an unlawful act if—

(a)   he acts in reliance on a statement made to him by that other person that, by reason of any provision of these Regulations, the act which he aids would not be unlawful; and

(b)   it is reasonable for him to rely on the statement.

(4)   A person who knowingly or recklessly makes a statement such as is referred to in paragraph (3)(a) which in a material respect is false or misleading commits an offence, and shall be liable on summary conviction to a fine not exceeding level 5 on the standard scale.

Part 4
General Exceptions from Parts 2 and 3

27   Exception for statutory authority

(1)   Nothing in Part 2 or 3 shall render unlawful any act done in order to comply with a requirement of any statutory provision.

(2)   In this regulation 'statutory provision' means any provision (whenever enacted) of—

(a)   an Act or an Act of the Scottish Parliament;

(b)   an instrument made by a Minister of the Crown under an Act;

(c)   an instrument made under an Act or an Act of the Scottish Parliament by the Scottish Ministers or a member of the Scottish Executive.

28   Exception for national security

Nothing in Part 2 or 3 shall render unlawful an act done for the purpose of safeguarding national security, if the doing of the act was justified by that purpose.

29   Exceptions for positive action

(1)   Nothing in Part 2 or 3 shall render unlawful any act done in or in connection with—

(a)   affording persons of a particular age or age group access to facilities for training which would help fit them for particular work; or

(b)   encouraging persons of a particular age or age group to take advantage of opportunities for doing particular work;

where it reasonably appears to the person doing the act that it prevents or compensates for disadvantages linked to age suffered by persons of that age or age group doing that work or likely to take up that work.

(2)   Nothing in Part 2 or 3 shall render unlawful any act done by a trade organisation within the meaning of regulation 18 in or in connection with—

(a)   affording only members of the organisation who are of a particular age or age group access to facilities for training which would help fit them for holding a post of any kind in the organisation; or

(b)   encouraging only members of the organisation who are of a particular age or age group to take advantage of opportunities for holding such posts in the organisation,

where it reasonably appears to the organisation that the act prevents or compensates for disadvantages linked to age suffered by those of that age or age group holding such posts or likely to hold such posts.

(3)   Nothing in Part 2 or 3 shall render unlawful any act done by a trade organisation within the meaning of regulation 18 in or in connection with encouraging only persons of a particular age or age group to become members of the organisation where it reasonably appears to the organisation that the act prevents or compensates for disadvantages linked to age suffered by persons of that age or age group who are, or are eligible to become, members.

30   Exception for retirement

(1)   This regulation applies in relation to an employee within the meaning of section 230(1) of the 1996 Act, a person in Crown employment, a relevant member of the House of Commons staff, and a relevant member of the House of Lords staff.

(2)   Nothing in Part 2 or 3 shall render unlawful the dismissal of a person to whom this regulation applies at or over the age of 65 where the reason for the dismissal is retirement.

(3)   For the purposes of this regulation, whether or not the reason for a dismissal is retirement shall be determined in accordance with sections 98ZA to 98ZF of the 1996 Act.

31   Exception for the national minimum wage

(1)   Nothing in Part 2 or 3 shall render it unlawful for a relevant person ('A') to be remunerated in respect of his work at a rate which is lower than the rate at which another such person ('B') is remunerated for his work where—

(a)   the hourly rate of the national minimum wage for a person of A's age is lower than that for a person of B's age, and

(b)   the rate at which A is remunerated is below the single hourly rate for the national minimum wage prescribed by the Secretary of State under section 1(3) of the National Minimum Wage Act 1998.

(2)   Nothing in Part 2 or 3 shall render it unlawful for an apprentice who is not a relevant person to be remunerated in respect of his work at a rate which is lower than the rate at which an apprentice who is a relevant person is remunerated for his work.

(3)   In this regulation—

'apprentice' means a person who is employed under a contract of apprentice-ship or, in accordance with regulation 12(3) of the National Minimum Wage Regulations 1999, is to be treated as employed under such a contract;

'relevant person' means a person who qualifies for the national minimum wage (whether at the single hourly rate for the national minimum wage prescribed by the Secretary of State under section 1(3) of the National Minimum Wage Act 1998 or at a different rate).

32 Exception for provision of certain benefits based on length of service

(1) Subject to paragraph (2), nothing in Part 2 or 3 shall render it unlawful for a person ('A'), in relation to the award of any benefit by him, to put a worker ('B') at a disadvantage when compared with another worker ('C'), if and to the extent that the disadvantage suffered by B is because B's length of service is less than that of C

(2) Where B's length of service exceeds 5 years, it must reasonably appear to A that the way in which he uses the criterion of length of service, in relation to the award in respect of which B is put at a disadvantage, fulfils a business need of his undertaking (for example, by encouraging the loyalty or motivation, or rewarding the experience, of some or all of his workers).

(3) In calculating a worker's length of service for these purposes, A shall calculate—

(a) the length of time the worker has been working for him doing work which he reasonably considers to be at or above a particular level (assessed by reference to the demands made on the worker, for example, in terms of effort, skills and decision making); or

(b) the length of time the worker has been working for him in total;

and on each occasion on which he decides to use the criterion of length of service in relation to the award of a benefit to workers, it is for him to decide which of these definitions to use to calculate their lengths of service.

(4) For the purposes of paragraph (3), in calculating the length of time a worker has been working for him—

(a) A shall calculate the length of time in terms of the number of weeks during the whole or part of which the worker was working for him;

(b) A may discount any period during which the worker was absent from work (including any period of absence which at the time it occurred was thought by A or the worker to be permanent) unless in all the circumstances (including the way in which other workers' absences occurring in similar circumstances are treated by A in calculating their lengths of service) it would not be reasonable for him to do so;

(c) A may discount any period of time during which the worker was present at work ('the relevant period') where—

(i) the relevant period preceded a period during which the worker was absent from work, and

(ii) in all the circumstances (including the length of the worker's absence, the reason for his absence, the effect his absence has had on his ability to discharge the duties of his work, and the way in which other workers are treated by A in similar circumstances) it is reasonable for A to discount the relevant period.

(5)   For the purposes of paragraph (3)(b), a worker shall be treated as having worked for A during any period during which he worked for another if—

(a)   that period is treated as a period of employment with A for the purposes of the 1996 Act by virtue of the operation of section 218 of that Act; or

(b)   were the worker to be made redundant by A, that period and the period he has worked for A would amount to 'relevant service' within the meaning of section 155 of that Act.

(6)   In paragraph (5)—

(a)   the reference to being made redundant is a reference to being dismissed by reason of redundancy for the purposes of the 1996 Act;

(b)   the reference to section 155 of that Act is a reference to that section as modified by the Redundancy Payments (Continuity of Employment in Local Government, etc) (Modification) Order 1999.

(7)   In this regulation—

'benefit' does not include any benefit awarded to a worker by virtue of his ceasing to work for A; and

'year' means a year of 12 calendar months.

33   Exception for provision of enhanced redundancy payments to employees

(1)   Nothing in Part 2 or 3 shall render it unlawful for an employer—

(a)   to give a qualifying employee an enhanced redundancy payment which is less in amount than the enhanced redundancy payment which he gives to another such employee if both amounts are calculated in the same way;

(b)   to give enhanced redundancy payments only to those who are qualifying employees by virtue of sub-paragraph (a) or (c)(i) of the definition of qualifying employee below.

(2)   In this regulation—

'the appropriate amount', 'a redundancy payment' and 'a week's pay' have the same meaning as they have in section 162 of the 1996 Act;

'enhanced redundancy payment' means a payment of an amount calculated in accordance with paragraph (3) or (4);

'qualifying employee' means—

(a)   an employee who is entitled to a redundancy payment by virtue of section 135 of the 1996 Act;

(b)   an employee who would have been so entitled but for the operation of section 155 of that Act;

(c)   an employee who agrees to the termination of his employment in circumstances where, had he been dismissed—

(i)   he would have been a qualifying employee by virtue of sub-paragraph (a) of this definition; or

169

        (ii)   he would have been a qualifying employee by virtue of sub-paragraph (b).

(3)   For an amount to be calculated in accordance with this paragraph it must be calculated in accordance with section 162(1) to (3) of the 1996 Act.

(4)   For an amount to be calculated in accordance with this paragraph—

    (a)   it must be calculated as in paragraph (3);

    (b)   however, in making that calculation, the employer may do one or both of the following things—

        (i)   he may treat a week's pay as not being subject to a maximum amount or as being subject to a maximum amount above the amount laid down in section 227 of the 1996 Act;

        (ii)   he may multiply the appropriate amount allowed for each year of employment by a figure of more than one;

    (c)   having made the calculation as in paragraph (3) (whether or not in making that calculation he has done anything mentioned in sub-paragraph (b)) the employer may increase the amount thus calculated by multiplying it by a figure of more than one.

(5)   For the purposes of paragraphs (3) and (4), the reference to 'the relevant date' in section 162(1)(a) of the 1996 Act is to be read, in the case of a qualifying employee who agrees to the termination of his employment, as a reference to the date on which that termination takes effect.

34 Exception for provision of life assurance cover to retired workers

(1)   Where a person ('A') arranges for workers to be provided with life assurance cover after their early retirement on grounds of ill health, nothing in Part 2 or 3 shall render it unlawful—

    (a)   where a normal retirement age applied in relation to any such workers at the time they took early retirement, for A to arrange for such cover to cease when such workers reach that age;

    (b)   in relation to any other workers, for A to arrange for such cover to cease when the workers reach the age of 65.

(2)   In this regulation, 'normal retirement age', in relation to a worker who has taken early retirement, means the age at which workers in A's undertaking who held the same kind of position as the worker held at the time of his retirement were normally required to retire.

Part 5
Enforcement

35 Restriction of proceedings for breach of Regulations

(1)   Except as provided by these Regulations no proceedings, whether civil or criminal, shall lie against any person in respect of an act by reason that the act is unlawful by virtue of a provision of these Regulations.

(2) Paragraph (1) does not prevent the making of an application for judicial review or the investigation or determination of any matter in accordance with Part 10 (investigations: the Pensions Ombudsman) of the Pension Schemes Act 1993 by the Pensions Ombudsman.

36 Jurisdiction of employment tribunals

(1) A complaint by any person ('the complainant') that another person ('the respondent')—

    (a) has committed against the complainant an act to which this regulation applies; or

    (b) is by virtue of regulation 25 (liability of employers and principals) or 26 (aiding unlawful acts) to be treated as having committed against the complainant such an act;

may be presented to an employment tribunal.

(2) This regulation applies to any act of discrimination or harassment which is unlawful by virtue of any provision of Part 2 other than—

    (a) where the act is one in respect of which an appeal or proceedings in the nature of an appeal may be brought under any enactment, regulation 19 (qualifications bodies);

    (b) regulation 23 (institutions of further and higher education); or

    (c) where the act arises out of and is closely connected to a relationship between the complainant and the respondent which has come to an end but during the course of which an act of discrimination against, or harassment of, the complainant by the respondent would have been unlawful by virtue of regulation 23, regulation 24 (relationships which have come to an end).

(3) In paragraph (2)(c), reference to an act of discrimination or harassment which would have been unlawful includes, in the case of a relationship which has come to an end before the coming into force of these Regulations, reference to an act of discrimination or harassment which would, after the coming into force of these Regulations, have been unlawful.

(4) In this regulation, 'enactment' includes an enactment comprised in, or in an instrument made under, an Act of the Scottish Parliament.

37 Burden of proof: employment tribunals

(1) This regulation applies to any complaint presented under regulation 36 to an employment tribunal.

(2) Where, on the hearing of the complaint, the complainant proves facts from which the tribunal could, apart from this regulation, conclude in the absence of an adequate explanation that the respondent—

    (a) has committed against the complainant an act to which regulation 36 applies; or

171

(b)   is by virtue of regulation 25 (liability of employers and principals) or 26 (aiding unlawful acts) to be treated as having committed against the complainant such an act,

the tribunal shall uphold the complaint unless the respondent proves that he did not commit, or as the case may be, is not to be treated as having committed, that act.

38   Remedies on complaints in employment tribunals

(1)   Where an employment tribunal finds that a complaint presented to it under regulation 36 is well-founded, the tribunal shall make such of the following as it considers just and equitable—

(a)   an order declaring the rights of the complainant and the respondent in relation to the act to which the complaint relates;

(b)   an order requiring the respondent to pay to the complainant compensation of an amount corresponding to any damages he could have been ordered by a county court or by a sheriff court to pay to the complainant if the complaint had fallen to be dealt with under regulation 39 (jurisdiction of county and sheriff courts);

(c)   a recommendation that the respondent take within a specified period action appearing to the tribunal to be practicable for the purpose of obviating or reducing the adverse effect on the complainant of any act of discrimination or harassment to which the complaint relates.

(2)   As respects an unlawful act of discrimination falling within regulation 3(1)(b) (discrimination on the grounds of age), if the respondent proves that the provision, criterion or practice was not applied with the intention of treating the complainant unfavourably on grounds of age, an order may be made under paragraph (1)(b) only if the employment tribunal—

(a)   makes such order under paragraph (1)(a) (if any) and such recommendation under paragraph (1)(c) (if any) as it would have made if it had no power to make an order under paragraph (1)(b); and

(b)   (where it makes an order under paragraph (1)(a) or a recommendation under paragraph (1)(c) or both) considers that it is just and equitable to make an order under paragraph (1)(b) as well.

(3)   If without reasonable justification the respondent to a complaint fails to comply with a recommendation made by an employment tribunal under paragraph (1)(c), then, if it thinks it just and equitable to do so—

(a)   the tribunal may increase the amount of compensation required to be paid to the complainant in respect of the complaint by an order made under paragraph (1)(b); or

(b)   if an order under paragraph (1)(b) was not made, the tribunal may make such an order.

(4)   Where an amount of compensation falls to be awarded under paragraph (1)(b), the tribunal may include in the award interest on that amount subject to, and in accordance with, the provisions of the Employment Tribunals (Interest on Awards in Discrimination Cases) Regulations 1996.

(5)   This regulation has effect subject to paragraph 6 of Schedule 2 (pension schemes).

39 Jurisdiction of county and sheriff courts

(1)   A claim by any person ('the claimant') that another person ('the respondent')—

(a)   has committed against the claimant an act to which this regulation applies; or

(b)   is by virtue of regulation 25 (liability of employers and principals) or 26 (aiding unlawful acts) to be treated as having committed against the claimant such an act,

may be made the subject of civil proceedings in like manner as any other claim in tort or (in Scotland) in reparation for breach of statutory duty.

(2)   Proceedings brought under paragraph (1) shall—

(a)   in England and Wales, be brought only in a county court; and

(b)   in Scotland, be brought only in a sheriff court.

(3)   For the avoidance of doubt it is hereby declared that damages in respect of an unlawful act to which this regulation applies may include compensation for injury to feelings whether or not they include compensation under any other head.

(4)   This regulation applies to any act of discrimination or harassment which is unlawful by virtue of—

(a)   regulation 23 (institutions of further and higher education); or

(b)   where the act arises out of and is closely connected to a relationship between the claimant and the respondent which has come to an end but during the course of which an act of discrimination against, or harassment of, the claimant by the respondent would have been unlawful by virtue of regulation 23, regulation 24 (relationships which have come to an end).

(5)   In paragraph (4)(b), reference to an act of discrimination or harassment which would have been unlawful includes, in the case of a relationship which has come to an end before the coming into force of these Regulations, reference to an act of discrimination or harassment which would, after the coming into force of these Regulations, have been unlawful.

40 Burden of proof: county and sheriff courts

(1)   This regulation applies to any claim brought under regulation 39 in a county court in England and Wales or a sheriff court in Scotland.

(2)   Where, on the hearing of the claim, the claimant proves facts from which the court could, apart from this regulation, conclude in the absence of an adequate explanation that the respondent—

(a)   has committed against the claimant an act to which regulation 39 applies; or

(b)   is by virtue of regulation 25 (liability of employers and principals) or 26 (aiding unlawful acts) to be treated as having committed against the claimant such an act,

the court shall uphold the claim unless the respondent proves that he did not commit, or as the case may be, is not to be treated as having committed, that act.

41   Help for persons in obtaining information etc

(1)   In accordance with this regulation, a person ('the person aggrieved') who considers he may have been discriminated against, or subjected to harassment, in contravention of these Regulations may serve on the respondent to a complaint presented under regulation 36 (jurisdiction of employment tribunals) or a claim brought under regulation 39 (jurisdiction of county and sheriff courts) questions in the form set out in Schedule 3 or forms to the like effect with such variation as the circumstances require; and the respondent may if he so wishes reply to such questions by way of the form set out in Schedule 4 or forms to the like effect with such variation as the circumstances require.

(2)   Where the person aggrieved questions the respondent (whether in accordance with paragraph (1) or not)—

(a)   the questions, and any reply by the respondent (whether in accordance with paragraph (1) or not) shall, subject to the following provisions of this regulation, be admissible as evidence in the proceedings;

(b)   if it appears to the court or tribunal that the respondent deliberately, and without reasonable excuse, omitted to reply within eight weeks of service of the questions or that his reply is evasive or equivocal, the court or tribunal may draw any inference from that fact that it considers it just and equitable to draw, including an inference that he committed an unlawful act.

(3)   In proceedings before a county court in England or Wales or a sheriff court in Scotland, a question shall only be admissible as evidence in pursuance of paragraph (2)(a)—

(a)   where it was served before those proceedings had been instituted, if it was so served within the period of six months beginning when the act complained of was done;

(b)   where it was served when those proceedings had been instituted, if it was served with the leave of, and within a period specified by, the court in question.

(4)   In proceedings before an employment tribunal, a question shall only be admissible as evidence in pursuance of paragraph (2)(a)—

(a)   where it was served before a complaint had been presented to the tribunal, if it was so served within the period of three months beginning when the act complained of was done;

(b)   where it was so served when a complaint had been presented to the tribunal, either—

        (i)   if it was served within the period of twenty-one days beginning with the day on which the complaint was presented, or

        (ii)   if it was so served later with leave given, and within a period specified, by a direction of the tribunal.

(5)   A question and any reply thereto may be served on the respondent or, as the case may be, on the person aggrieved—

    (a)   by delivering it to him;

    (b)   by sending it by post to him at his usual or last-known residence or place of business;

    (c)   where the person to be served is a body corporate or is a trade union or employers' association within the meaning of the Trade Union and Labour Relations (Consolidation) Act 1992, by delivering it to the secretary or clerk of the body, union or association at its registered or principal office or by sending it by post to the secretary or clerk at that office;

    (d)   where the person to be served is acting by a solicitor, by delivering it at, or by sending it by post to, the solicitor's address for service; or

    (e)   where the person to be served is the person aggrieved, by delivering the reply, or sending it by post, to him at his address for reply as stated by him in the document containing the questions.

(6)   This regulation is without prejudice to any other enactment or rule of law regulating interlocutory and preliminary matters in proceedings before a county court, sheriff court or employment tribunal, and has effect subject to any enactment or rule of law regulating the admissibility of evidence in such proceedings.

(7)   In this regulation 'respondent' includes a prospective respondent.

42   Period within which proceedings to be brought

(1)   An employment tribunal shall not consider a complaint under regulation 36 unless it is presented to the tribunal before the end of the period of three months beginning when the act complained of was done.

(2)   A county court or a sheriff court shall not consider a claim brought under regulation 39 unless proceedings in respect of the claim are instituted before the end of the period of six months beginning when the act complained of was done.

(3)   A court or tribunal may nevertheless consider any such complaint or claim which is out of time if, in all the circumstances of the case, it considers that it is just and equitable to do so.

(4)   For the purposes of this regulation and regulation 41 (help for persons in obtaining information etc)—

    (a)   when the making of a contract is, by reason of the inclusion of any term, an unlawful act, that act shall be treated as extending throughout the duration of the contract; and

(b)   any act extending over a period shall be treated as done at the end of that period; and

(c)   a deliberate omission shall be treated as done when the person in question decided upon it,

and in the absence of evidence establishing the contrary a person shall be taken for the purposes of this regulation to decide upon an omission when he does an act inconsistent with doing the omitted act or, if he has done no such inconsistent act, when the period expires within which he might reasonably have been expected to do the omitted act if it was to be done.

Part 6
Supplemental

43   Validity of contracts, collective agreements and rules of undertakings

Schedule 5 (validity of contracts, collective agreements and rules of undertakings) shall have effect.

44   Application to the Crown etc

(1)   These Regulations apply—

(a)   to an act done by or for purposes of a Minister of the Crown or government department; or

(b)   to an act done on behalf of the Crown by a statutory body, or a person holding a statutory office,

as they apply to an act done by a private person.

(2)   These Regulations apply to Crown employment as they apply to employment by a private person, and shall so apply as if references to a contract of employment included references to the terms of service and references to dismissal included references to termination of Crown employment.

(3)   Paragraphs (1) and (2) have effect subject to paragraph (4) and regulations 13 (police) and 14 (Serious Organised Crime Agency).

(4)   These regulations do not apply to service in any of the naval, military or air forces of the Crown.

(5)   Regulation 10(3) (meaning of employment and contract work at establishment in Great Britain) shall have effect in relation to any ship, aircraft or hovercraft belonging to or possessed by Her Majesty in right of the government of the United Kingdom as it has effect in relation to a ship, aircraft or hovercraft specified in regulation 10(3)(a) or (b).

(6)   The provisions of Parts 2 to 4 of the Crown Proceedings Act 1947 shall apply to proceedings against the Crown under these Regulations as they apply to proceedings in England and Wales which by virtue of section 23 of that Act are treated for the purposes of Part 2 of that Act as civil proceedings by or against the Crown, except that in their application to proceedings under these Regulations section 20 of that Act (removal and transfer of proceedings) shall not apply.

(7)   The provisions of Part 5 of the Crown Proceedings Act 1947 shall apply to proceedings against the Crown under these Regulations as they apply to proceedings in Scotland which by virtue of the said Part are treated as civil proceedings by or against the Crown, except that in their application to proceedings under these Regulations the proviso to section 44 of that Act (proceedings against the Crown in the Sheriff Court) shall not apply.

45   Application to House of Commons staff

(1)   Subject to paragraphs (2) and (3), these Regulations apply in relation to employment as a relevant member of the House of Commons staff as they apply in relation to other employment.

(2)   These Regulations apply to employment as such a member as they apply to employment by a private person, and shall so apply as if references to a contract of employment included references to the terms of employment of such a member and references to dismissal included references to termination of such employment.

(3)   In relation to employment as such a member, subsections (6) to (12) of section 195 of the 1996 Act (person to be treated as employer of House of Commons staff) apply, with any necessary modifications, for the purposes of these Regulations.

46   Application to House of Lords staff

(1)   These Regulations apply in relation to employment as a relevant member of the House of Lords staff as they apply in relation to other employment.

(2)   Section 194(7) of the 1996 Act (continuity of employment) applies for the purposes of this regulation.

47   Duty to consider working beyond retirement

Schedule 6, which sets out the procedure to be followed if an employee (within the meaning of that Schedule) is to be retired, shall have effect.

48   Duty to consider working beyond retirement—transitional provisions

Schedule 7, which sets out transitional provisions in relation to the duty to consider working beyond retirement, shall have effect.

49   Amendments, transitionals, repeals and revocations

(1)   Schedule 8, which contains amendments to and repeals of legislation and related transitional provisions, shall have effect.

(2)   Schedule 9, which contains repeals and revocations, shall have effect.

SCHEDULE 1
NORWEGIAN PART OF THE FRIGG GAS FIELD

Regulation 10(4)

1

The part of the Norwegian sector of the Continental Shelf described in this Schedule is the area defined by—

(a)   the sets of lines of latitude and longitude joining the following surface co-ordinates—

Longitude	Latitude
02 degrees 05 minutes 30 seconds E	60 degrees 00 minutes 45 seconds N
02 degrees 05 minutes 30 seconds E	59 degrees 58 minutes 45 seconds N
02 degrees 06 minutes 00 seconds E	59 degrees 58 minutes 45 seconds N
02 degrees 06 minutes 00 seconds E	59 degrees 57 minutes 45 seconds N
02 degrees 07 minutes 00 seconds E	59 degrees 57 minutes 45 seconds N
02 degrees 07 minutes 00 seconds E	59 degrees 57 minutes 30 seconds N
02 degrees 07 minutes 30 seconds E	59 degrees 57 minutes 30 seconds N
02 degrees 07 minutes 30 seconds E	59 degrees 55 minutes 30 seconds N
02 degrees 10 minutes 30 seconds E	59 degrees 55 minutes 30 seconds N
02 degrees 10 minutes 30 seconds E	59 degrees 54 minutes 45 seconds N
02 degrees 11 minutes 00 seconds E	59 degrees 54 minutes 45 seconds N
02 degrees 11 minutes 00 seconds E	59 degrees 54 minutes 15 seconds N
02 degrees 12 minutes 30 seconds E	59 degrees 54 minutes 15 seconds N
02 degrees 12 minutes 30 seconds E	59 degrees 54 minutes 00 seconds N
02 degrees 13 minutes 30 seconds E	59 degrees 54 minutes 00 seconds N
02 degrees 13 minutes 30 seconds E	59 degrees 54 minutes 30 seconds N
02 degrees 15 minutes 30 seconds E	59 degrees 54 minutes 30 seconds N
02 degrees 15 minutes 30 seconds E	59 degrees 53 minutes 15 seconds N
02 degrees 10 minutes 30 seconds E	59 degrees 53 minutes 15 seconds N
02 degrees 10 minutes 30 seconds E	59 degrees 52 minutes 45 seconds N
02 degrees 09 minutes 30 seconds E	59 degrees 52 minutes 45 seconds N
02 degrees 09 minutes 30 seconds E	59 degrees 52 minutes 15 seconds N
02 degrees 08 minutes 30 seconds E	59 degrees 52 minutes 15 seconds N
02 degrees 08 minutes 30 seconds E	59 degrees 52 minutes 00 seconds N
02 degrees 07 minutes 30 seconds E	59 degrees 52 minutes 00 seconds N
02 degrees 07 minutes 30 seconds E	59 degrees 51 minutes 30 seconds N
02 degrees 05 minutes 30 seconds E	59 degrees 51 minutes 30 seconds N
02 degrees 05 minutes 30 seconds E	59 degrees 51 minutes 00 seconds N
02 degrees 04 minutes 00 seconds E	59 degrees 51 minutes 00 seconds N
02 degrees 04 minutes 00 seconds E	59 degrees 50 minutes 30 seconds N
02 degrees 03 minutes 00 seconds E	59 degrees 50 minutes 30 seconds N
02 degrees 03 minutes 00 seconds E	59 degrees 50 minutes 00 seconds N

(b)   a line from the point 02 degrees 03 minutes 00 seconds E 59 degrees 50 minutes 00 seconds N west along the parallel of latitude 59 degrees 50 minutes 00 seconds N until its intersection with the Dividing Line;

(c)   a line from the point of intersection specified in sub-paragraph (b) along the Dividing Line until its intersection with the parallel of latitude 60 degrees 00 minutes 45 seconds N;

(d)   a line from the point of intersection specified in sub-paragraph (c) east along the parallel of latitude 60 degrees 00 minutes 45 degrees N until its intersection with the meridian 02 degrees 05 minutes 30 seconds E.

2

In this Schedule, the 'Dividing Line' means the dividing line as defined in an Agreement dated 10th March 1965 and made between the government of the

United Kingdom of Great Britain and Northern Ireland and the government of the Kingdom of Norway as supplemented by a Protocol dated 22nd December 1978.

SCHEDULE 2
PENSION SCHEMES

Regulation 11(3)

Part 1
Pension Schemes—General

Interpretation

1

(1) In this Schedule, subject to sub-paragraphs (2) and (3), 'occupational pension scheme' means an occupational pension scheme within the meaning of section 1(1) of the Pension Schemes Act 1993.

(2) In relation to rules, practices, actions and decisions identified at paragraph 7(a), 'occupational pension scheme' means an occupational pension scheme within the meaning of section 1(1) of the Pension Schemes Act 1993 under which only retirement-benefit activities within the meaning of section 255(4) of the Pensions Act 2004 are carried out.

(3) In relation to rules, practices, actions and decisions identified at paragraphs 12, 13 and 30, 'occupational pension scheme' means an occupational pension scheme within the meaning of either section 1(1) of the Pension Schemes Act 1993 or section 150(5) of the Finance Act 2004.

(4) In this Schedule, 'scheme' means an occupational pension scheme, construed in accordance with sub-paragraphs (1) to (3).

(5) In this Schedule, in relation to a scheme—

'active member' has the meaning given by section 124(1) of the Pensions Act 1995, but in paragraph 13 also includes an active member within the meaning of section 151(2) of the Finance Act 2004;

'age related benefit' means benefit provided from a scheme to a member—

(a) on or following his retirement (including early retirement on grounds of ill health or otherwise),

(b) on his reaching a particular age, or

(c) on termination of his service in an employment;

'death benefit' means benefit payable from a pension scheme, in respect of a member, in consequence of his death;

'deferred member' has the meaning given by section 124(1) of the Pensions Act 1995;

'defined benefits arrangement' has the meaning given by section 152(6) of the Finance Act 2004, but the reference in that section to an arrangement shall be read as referring to an arrangement in respect of a member under a

179

scheme as defined in section 1(1) of the Pension Schemes Act 1993 rather than in respect of a member under a pension scheme as defined in section 150(1) of the Finance Act 2004;

'dependant' means dependant as defined in the scheme rules;

'early retirement pivot age' means an age specified in the scheme rules as the earliest age at which age related benefit becomes payable without actuarial reduction (disregarding any special provision as to early payment on grounds of ill health or otherwise);

'employer' has the meaning given by section 318(1) of the Pensions Act 2004;

'employer contribution' means any contribution to a scheme by an employer in respect of a member;

'employment' includes any trade, business, profession, office or vocation, whether or not a person is employed in it under a contract of employment or is self employed;

'late retirement pivot age' means an age specified in the scheme rules above which benefit becomes payable with actuarial enhancement;

'managers' has the meaning given by section 124(1) of the Pensions Act 1995;

'member' means any active member, deferred member or pensioner member, but in paragraph 12 includes any active, deferred or pensioner member within the meaning of section 151(2) to (4) of the Finance Act 2004;

'member contribution' means any contribution to a scheme by a member;

'money purchase arrangement' has the meaning given by section 152(2) of the Finance Act 2004, but the reference in that section to an arrangement shall be read as referring to an arrangement in respect of a member under a scheme as defined in section 1(1) of the Pension Schemes Act 1993 rather than in respect of a member under a pension scheme as defined in section 150(1) of the Finance Act 2004;

'non-discrimination rule' means the rule in paragraph 2(1);

'normal pension age' has the meaning given by section 180 of the Pension Schemes Act 1993;

'normal retirement age', in relation to a member, means the age at which workers in the undertaking for which the member worked at the time of his retirement, and who held the same kind of position as the member held at his retirement, were normally required to retire;

'pensionable age' has the meaning given by section 122(1) of the Social Security Contributions and Benefits Act 1992;

'pensionable pay' means that part of a member's pay which counts as pensionable pay under the scheme rules;

'pensionable service' has the meaning given by section 124(1) of the Pensions Act 1995;

'pensioner member' has the meaning given by section 124(1) of the Pensions Act 1995; and

'prospective member' means any person who, under the terms of his employment or the scheme rules or both—

(a)   is able, at his own option, to become a member of the scheme,

(b)   shall become so able if he continues in the same employment for a sufficient period of time,

(c)   shall be so admitted to it automatically unless he makes an election not to become a member, or

(d)   may be admitted to it subject to the consent of any person.

(6)   In their application to a scheme which is divided into two or more sections, the provisions of this Schedule shall apply as if each section of the scheme was a separate scheme.

(7)   In this Schedule—

'personal pension scheme' has the meaning given by section 1(1) of the Pension Schemes Act 1993;

'registered pension scheme' has the meaning given by section 150(2) of the Finance Act 2004; and

references to contributions under a money purchase arrangement shall be construed as including amounts credited to a member's account whether or not they reflect payments actually made under the scheme.

(8)   Any term used in regulation 11 (pension schemes) shall have the same meaning in that regulation as it has in this Schedule.

Non-discrimination rule

2

(1)   Every scheme shall be treated as including a provision ('the non-discrimination rule') containing a requirement that the trustees or managers of the scheme refrain from doing any act which is unlawful by virtue of regulation 11.

(2)   The other provisions of the scheme are to have effect subject to the non-discrimination rule.

(3)   The trustees or managers of a scheme may—

(a)   if they do not (apart from this sub-paragraph) have power to make such alterations to the scheme as may be required to secure conformity with the non-discrimination rule, or

(b)   if they have such power but the procedure for doing so—

(i)   is liable to be unduly complex or protracted, or

(ii)   involves the obtaining of consents which cannot be obtained, or can only be obtained with undue delay or difficulty,

by resolution make such alterations to the scheme.

(4)   Alterations made by a resolution such as is referred to in sub-paragraph (3)—

   (a)   may have effect in relation to a period before the alterations are made (but may not have effect in relation to any time before the coming into force of these Regulations), and

   (b)   shall be subject to the consent of any employer in relation to the scheme whose consent would be required for such a modification if it were to be made under the scheme rules.

Exception for rules, practices, actions and decisions relating to occupational pension schemes

3

Nothing in Part 2 or 3 of these Regulations shall render it unlawful for an employer, or for trustees or managers, to maintain or use, in relation to a scheme, any of the rules, practices, actions or decisions set out in Part 2 of this Schedule.

Exception for rules, practices, actions and decisions relating to contributions by employers to personal pension schemes

4

Nothing in Part 2 or 3 of these Regulations shall render it unlawful for an employer, in relation to the payment of contributions to any personal pension scheme in respect of a worker, to maintain or use any of the rules, practices, actions or decisions set out in Part 3 of this Schedule.

Procedure in employment tribunals

5

Where under regulation 36 (jurisdiction of employment tribunals) a member or prospective member of a scheme presents to an employment tribunal a complaint that the trustees or managers of the scheme—

   (a)   have committed against him an act which is unlawful by virtue of regulation 11 (pension schemes) or 24 (relationships which have come to an end); or

   (b)   are by virtue of regulation 25 (liability of employers and principals) or 26 (aiding unlawful acts) to be treated as having committed against him such an act,

   the employer in relation to the scheme shall, for the purposes of the rules governing procedure, be treated as a party and be entitled to appear and be heard in accordance with those rules.

Remedies in employment tribunals

6

(1)   This paragraph applies where—

(a) under regulation 36 (jurisdiction of employment tribunals) a member or prospective member of a scheme ('the complainant') presents to an employment tribunal a complaint against the trustees or managers of the scheme or an employer;

(b) the complainant is not a pensioner member of the scheme;

(c) the complaint relates to the terms on which persons become members of the scheme, or the terms on which members of the scheme are treated; and

(d) the tribunal finds the complaint to be well-founded.

(2) Where this paragraph applies, the employment tribunal may, without prejudice to the generality of its power under regulation 38(1)(a) (power to make order declaring rights of complainant and respondent), make an order declaring that the complainant has a right—

(a) where the complaint relates to the terms on which persons become members of the scheme, to be admitted to the scheme;

(b) where the complaint relates to the terms on which members of the scheme are treated, to membership of the scheme without discrimination.

(3) An order under sub-paragraph (2)—

(a) may be made in respect of such period as is specified in the order (but may not be made in respect of any time before the coming into force of these Regulations);

(b) may make such provision as the employment tribunal considers appropriate as to the terms on which, or the capacity in which, the complainant is to enjoy such admission or membership.

(4) Where this paragraph applies, the employment tribunal may not make an order for compensation under regulation 38(1)(b), whether in relation to arrears of benefits or otherwise, except—

(a) for injury to feelings;

(b) by virtue of regulation 38(3).

Part 2
Excepted Rules, Practices, Actions and Decisions Relating to Occupational Pension Schemes

Admission to schemes

7

In relation to admission to a scheme—

(a) a minimum or maximum age for admission, including different ages for admission for different groups or categories of worker;

(b) a minimum level of pensionable pay for admission, provided that such a minimum is not above the lower earnings limit referred to in section 5(1) of the Social Security Contributions and Benefits Act 1992.

The use of age criteria in actuarial calculations

8

The use of age criteria in actuarial calculations, for example in the actuarial calculation of—

(a) any age related benefit commencing before any early retirement pivot age or enhancement of such benefit commencing after any late retirement pivot age;

(b) member or employer contributions to a scheme; or

(c) any age related benefit commuted in exchange for the payment of any lump sum.

Contributions

9

Any difference in the rate of member or employer contributions by or in respect of different members to the extent that this is attributable to any differences in the pensionable pay of those members.

Contributions under money purchase arrangements

10

Under a money purchase arrangement—

(a) different rates of member or employer contributions according to the age of the members by or in respect of whom contributions are made where the aim in setting the different rates is—

(i) to equalise the amount of benefit to which members of different ages who are otherwise in a comparable situation will become entitled under the arrangement, or

(ii) to make the amount of benefit to which such members will become entitled under the arrangement more nearly equal;

(b) equal rates of member or employer contributions irrespective of the age of the members by or in respect of whom contributions are made.

Contributions under defined benefits arrangements

11

Under a defined benefits arrangement, different rates of member or employer contributions according to the age of the members by or in respect of whom contributions are made, to the extent that—

(a)   each year of pensionable service entitles members in a comparable situation to accrue a right to defined benefits based on the same fraction of pensionable pay, and

(b)   the aim in setting the different rates is to reflect the increasing cost of providing the defined benefits in respect of members as they get older.

Age related rules, practices, actions and decisions relating to benefit

12

A minimum age for entitlement to or payment of any age related benefit to a member, provided that, in the case of any age related benefit paid under a defined benefits arrangement before any early retirement pivot age—

(a)   such benefit is subject to actuarial reduction for early receipt, and

(b)   the member is not credited with additional periods of pensionable service.

13

In relation to workers who are active or prospective members of a scheme on the date on which these Regulations come into force, a minimum age for entitlement to or payment of any age related benefit to such members under defined benefit arrangements before any early retirement pivot age, where such benefit is calculated in one or both of the following ways—

(a)   it is not made subject to actuarial reduction for early receipt;

(b)   it results from crediting the member with additional periods of pensionable service.

14

An early retirement pivot age or a late retirement pivot age, including different such ages for different groups or categories of member.

15

The enhancement of any age related benefit in the event of a member's retirement before any early retirement pivot age on ill health grounds, where that enhancement is calculated by reference to the years of pensionable service which that member would have completed if he had continued in pensionable service up to the age specified for that purpose in the scheme rules.

16

Any rule, practice, action or decision whereby a male member who reaches pensionable age is not entitled or is no longer entitled to any additional amount of pension which would have been payable to such a member before pensionable age in the circumstances prescribed for the purposes of section 64(2) of the Pensions Act 1995 by regulation 13 of the Occupational Pension Schemes (Equal Treatment) Regulations 1995.

17

The reduction of any pension payable in consequence of a member's death to any dependant of the member where that dependant is more than a specified number of years younger than the member.

18

In relation to pensioner members who have retired on ill health grounds before any early retirement pivot age, discontinuation of any life assurance cover once any such members reach the normal retirement age which applied to them at the time they retired, or in relation to members to whom no such normal retirement age applied, once such members reach the age of 65.

Other rules, practices, actions and decisions relating to benefit

19

Any difference in the amount of any age related benefit or death benefit payable under a defined benefits arrangement to or in respect of members with different lengths of pensionable service to the extent that the difference in amount is attributable to their differing lengths of service, provided that, for each year of pensionable service, members in a comparable situation are entitled to accrue a right to benefit based upon the same fraction of pensionable pay.

20

Any difference in the amount of any age related benefit or death benefit payable from a scheme to or in respect of different members to the extent that the difference in amount is attributable to differences over time in the pensionable pay of those members.

21

Any limitation of the amount of any age related benefit or death benefit payable from a scheme where the limitation results from imposing a maximum number of years of service by reference to which such benefit may be calculated.

22

Any rule, practice, action or decision whereby any age related benefit or death benefit is only payable to or in respect of members who have completed a minimum period of service, provided that such a minimum period is not longer than 2 years qualifying service within the meaning of section 71(7) of the Pension Schemes Act 1993.

23

Any limitation on the amount of any age related benefit or death benefit payable from a scheme where the limitation results from imposing a minimum level of pensionable pay by reference to which any such benefit may be calculated, provided that such a minimum is not above the lower earnings limit referred to in section 5(1) of the Social Security Contributions and Benefits Act 1992.

24

Any limitation on the amount of any age related benefit or death benefit payable from a scheme where the limitation results from imposing a maximum level of pensionable pay by reference to which such benefit may be calculated.

Closure of schemes

25

The closure of a scheme, from a particular date, to workers who have not already joined it.

Other rules, practices, actions and decisions

26

Increases of pensions in payment which are made to members over 55 but not to members below that age.

27

Any difference in the rate of increase of pensions in payment for members of different ages to the extent that the aim in setting the different rates is to maintain the relative value of members' pensions.

28

Any difference in the rate of increase of pensions in payment for members whose pensions have been in payment for different lengths of time to the extent that the aim in setting the different rates is to maintain the relative value of members' pensions.

29

The application of an age limit for transfer of the value of a member's accrued rights into or out of a scheme, provided that any such age limit is not more than one year before the member's normal pension age.

Registered pension schemes

30

(1)   Subject to sub-paragraph (2), any rules, practices, actions or decisions relating to entitlement to or payment of benefits under a registered pension scheme insofar as compliance is necessary to secure any tax relief or

exemption available under Part 4 of the Finance Act 2004 or to prevent any charge to tax arising under that Part of that Act, whoever is liable in relation to such charge.

(2)   Sub-paragraph (1) does not apply to any rules, practices, actions or decisions setting a minimum age for entitlement to or payment of any age related benefit.

Part 3

Excepted Rules, Practices, Actions and Decisions Relating to Contributions by Employers to Personal Pension Schemes

Contributions by employers

31

Different rates of contributions by an employer according to the age of the workers in respect of whom the contributions are made where the aim in setting the different rates is—

(a)   to equalise the amount of benefit to which workers of different ages who are otherwise in a comparable situation will become entitled under their personal pension schemes, or

(b)   to make the amount of benefit to which such workers will become entitled under their personal pension schemes more nearly equal.

32

Any difference in the rate of contributions by an employer in respect of different workers to the extent that this is attributable to any differences in remuneration payable to those workers.

SCHEDULE 3
QUESTIONNAIRE OF PERSON AGGRIEVED

Regulation 41(1)

To ... ... (*name of person to be questioned*)

of ... ...

... ... (*address*)

1(1) I ... ... (*name of questioner*)

of ... ...

... ... (*address*)

consider that you may have discriminated against me [subjected me to harrass-ment] contrary to the Employment Equality (Age) Regulations 2006.

(2)   (*Give date, approximate time and a factual description of the treatment received and of the circumstances leading up to the treatment.*)

(3)   I consider that this treatment may have been unlawful because ... ...
       ... ...

... ...

... ...

... ... (*complete if you wish to give reasons, otherwise delete*).

2 Do you agree that the statement in paragraph 1(2) above is an accurate description of what happened? If not, in what respect do you disagree or what is your version of what happened?

3 Do you accept that your treatment of me was unlawful discrimination [harrassment]? If not—

(a) why not,

(b) for what reason did I receive the treatment accorded to me, and

(c) how far did considerations of age affect your treatment of me?

4 (*Any other questions you wish to ask.*)

5 My address for any reply you may wish to give to the questions raised above is [that set out in paragraph 1(1) above] [the following address ... ...

... ...]

... ... (*signature of questioner*)

... ... (*date*)

NB—By virtue of regulation 41 of the Employment Equality (Age) Regulations 2006 this questionnaire and any reply are (subject to the provisions of that regulation) admissible in proceedings under the Regulations. A court or tribunal may draw any such inference as is just and equitable from a failure without reasonable excuse to reply within eight weeks of service of this questionnaire, or from an evasive or equivocal reply, including an inference that the person questioned has committed an unlawful act.

SCHEDULE 4
REPLY BY RESPONDENT

Regulation 41(1)

To ... ... (*name of questioner*)

of ... ...

... ... (*address*)

1 I ... ... (*name of person questioned*)

of ... ...

... ... (*address*)

hereby acknowledge receipt of the questionnaire signed by you and dated ... ...

which was served on me on ... ... (*date*).

2 [I agree that the statement in paragraph 1(2) of the questionnaire is an accurate description of what happened.]

[I disagree with the statement in paragraph 1(2) of the questionnaire in that ... ...

…]

3   I accept/dispute that my treatment of you was unlawful discrimination [harrassment].

[My reasons for so disputing are … … … … … … … … … … … … … … … … .

… ..

The reason why you received the treatment accorded to you and the answers to the other questions in paragraph 3 of the questionnaire are … … … … … … … … … …

… … … … … ..

… ..]

4   *(Replies to questions in paragraph 4 of the questionnaire.)*

5   [I have deleted (in whole or in part) the paragraph(s) numbered … … … …
… above, since

I am unable/unwilling to reply to the relevant questions in the correspondingly numbered paragraph(s) of the questionnaire for the following reasons … … … …

… … … … … … … … … … … ..

…]

… … … … … … … … … … … … … … … … . *(signature of questioner)*

… … … … … … … … … … *(date)*

SCHEDULE 5
VALIDITY OF CONTRACTS, COLLECTIVE AGREEMENTS AND RULES OF UNDERTAKINGS

Regulation 43

Part 1
Validity and Revision of Contracts

1

(1)   A term of a contract is void where—

(a)   the making of the contract is, by reason of the inclusion of the term, unlawful by virtue of these Regulations;

(b)   it is included in furtherance of an act which is unlawful by virtue of these Regulations; or

(c)   it provides for the doing of an act which is unlawful by virtue of these Regulations.

(2)   Sub-paragraph (1) does not apply to a term the inclusion of which constitutes, or is in furtherance of, or provides for, unlawful discrimination against, or harassment of, a party to the contract, but the term shall be unenforceable against that party.

(3)   A term in a contract which purports to exclude or limit any provision of these Regulations is unenforceable by any person in whose favour the term would operate apart from this paragraph.

(4)   Sub-paragraphs (1), (2) and (3) shall apply whether the contract was entered into before or after the date on which these Regulations come into force, but

in the case of a contract made before that date, those sub-paragraphs do not apply in relation to any period before that date.

2

(1)   Paragraph 1(3) does not apply—

(a)   to a contract settling a complaint to which regulation 36(1) (jurisdiction of employment tribunals) applies where the contract is made with the assistance of a conciliation officer within the meaning of section 211 of the Trade Union and Labour Relations (Consolidation) Act 1992;

(b)   to a contract settling a complaint to which regulation 36(1) applies if the conditions regulating compromise contracts under this Schedule are satisfied in relation to the contract; or

(c)   to a contract settling a claim to which regulation 39 (jurisdiction of county or sheriff courts) applies.

(2)   The conditions regulating compromise contracts under this Schedule are that—

(a)   the contract must be in writing;

(b)   the contract must relate to the particular complaint;

(c)   the complainant must have received advice from a relevant independent adviser as to the terms and effect of the proposed contract and in particular its effect on his ability to pursue a complaint before an employment tribunal;

(d)   there must be in force, when the adviser gives the advice, a contract of insurance, or an indemnity provided for members of a profession or professional body, covering the risk of a claim by the complainant in respect of loss arising in consequence of the advice;

(e)   the contract must identify the adviser; and

(f)   the contract must state that the conditions regulating compromise contracts under this Schedule are satisfied.

(3)   A person is a relevant independent adviser for the purposes of sub-paragraph (2)(c)—

(a)   if he is a qualified lawyer;

(b)   if he is an officer, official, employee or member of an independent trade union who has been certified in writing by the trade union as competent to give advice and as authorised to do so on behalf of the trade union; or

(c)   if he works at an advice centre (whether as an employee or a volunteer) and has been certified in writing by the centre as competent to give advice and as authorised to do so on behalf of the centre.

(4)   But a person is not a relevant independent adviser for the purposes of sub-paragraph (2)(c) in relation to the complainant—

(a) if he is employed by, or is acting in the matter for the other party, or is a person who is connected with the other party;

(b) in the case of a person within sub-paragraph (3)(b) or (c), if the trade union or advice centre is the other party or a person who is connected with the other party; or

(c) in the case of a person within sub-paragraph (3)(c), if the complainant makes a payment for the advice received from him.

(5) In sub-paragraph (3)(a) 'qualified lawyer' means—

(a) as respects England and Wales, a barrister (whether in practice as such or employed to give legal advice), a solicitor who holds a practising certificate, or a person other than a barrister or solicitor who is an authorised advocate or authorised litigator (within the meaning of the Courts and Legal Services Act 1990; and

(b) as respects Scotland, an advocate (whether in practice as such or employed to give legal advice), or a solicitor who holds a practising certificate.

(6) A person shall be treated as being a qualified lawyer within sub-paragraph (5)(a) if he is a Fellow of the Institute of Legal Executives employed by a solicitors' practice.

(7) In sub-paragraph (3)(b) 'independent trade union' has the same meaning as in the Trade Union and Labour Relations (Consolidation) Act 1992.

(8) For the purposes of sub-paragraph (4)(a) any two persons are to be treated as connected—

(a) if one is a company of which the other (directly or indirectly) has control; or

(b) if both are companies of which a third person (directly or indirectly) has control.

(9) An agreement under which the parties agree to submit a dispute to arbitration—

(a) shall be regarded for the purposes of sub-paragraphs (1)(a) and (b) as being a contract settling a complaint if—

(i) the dispute is covered by a scheme having effect by virtue of an order under section 212A of the Trade Union and Labour Relations (Consolidation) Act 1992, and

(ii) the agreement is to submit it to arbitration in accordance with the scheme, but

(b) shall be regarded as neither being nor including such a contract in any other case.

3

(1) On the application of a person interested in a contract to which paragraph 1(1) or (2) applies, a county court or a sheriff court may make such order as it thinks fit for—

(a)   removing or modifying any term rendered void by paragraph 1(1), or

(b)   removing or modifying any term made unenforceable by paragraph 1(2);

but such an order shall not be made unless all persons affected have been
given notice in writing of the application (except where under rules of court
notice may be dispensed with) and have been afforded an opportunity to
make representations to the court.

(2)   An order under sub-paragraph (1) may include provision as respects any
period before the making of the order (but after the coming into force of
these Regulations).

Part 2
Collective Agreements and Rules of Undertakings

4

(1)   This Part of this Schedule applies to—

(a)   any term of a collective agreement, including an agreement which was
not intended, or is presumed not to have been intended, to be a legally
enforceable contract;

(b)   any rule made by an employer for application to all or any of the
persons who are employed by him or who apply to be, or are,
considered by him for employment;

(c)   any rule made by a trade organisation (within the meaning of regulation 18) or a qualifications body (within the meaning of regulation 19)
for application to—

(i)   all or any of its members or prospective members; or

(ii)   all or any of the persons on whom it has conferred professional
or trade qualifications (within the meaning of regulation 19) or
who are seeking the professional or trade qualifications which it
has power to confer.

(2)   Any term or rule to which this Part of this Schedule applies is void where—

(a)   the making of the collective agreement is, by reason of the inclusion of
the term, unlawful by virtue of these Regulations;

(b)   the term or rule is included or made in furtherance of an act which is
unlawful by virtue of these Regulations; or

(c)   the term or rule provides for the doing of an act which is unlawful by
virtue of these Regulations.

(3)   Sub-paragraph (2) shall apply whether the agreement was entered into, or the
rule made, before or after the date on which these Regulations come into
force; but in the case of an agreement entered into, or a rule made, before the
date on which these Regulations come into force, that sub-paragraph does not
apply in relation to any period before that date.

5

A person to whom this paragraph applies may present a complaint to an employment tribunal that a term or rule is void by virtue of paragraph 4 if he has reason to believe—

(a)   that the term or rule may at some future time have effect in relation to him; and

(b)   where he alleges that it is void by virtue of paragraph 4(2)(c), that—

      (i)   an act for the doing of which it provides, may at some such time be done in relation to him, and

      (ii)   the act would be unlawful by virtue of these Regulations if done in relation to him in present circumstances.

6

In the case of a complaint about—

(a)   a term of a collective agreement made by or on behalf of—

      (i)   an employer,

      (ii)   an organisation of employers of which an employer is a member, or

      (iii)   an association of such organisations of one of which an employer is a member, or

(b)   a rule made by an employer within the meaning of paragraph 4(1)(b),

paragraph 5 applies to any person who is, or is genuinely and actively seeking to become, one of his employees.

7

In the case of a complaint about a rule made by an organisation or body to which paragraph 4(1)(c) applies, paragraph 5 applies to any person—

(a)   who is, or is genuinely and actively seeking to become, a member of the organisation or body;

(b)   on whom the organisation or body has conferred a professional or trade qualification (within the meaning of regulation 19) which the organisation or body has power to confer; or

(c)   who is genuinely and actively seeking such a professional or trade qualification which the organisation or body has power to confer.

8

(1)   When an employment tribunal finds that a complaint presented to it under paragraph 5 is well-founded the tribunal shall make an order declaring that the term or rule is void.

(2)   An order under sub-paragraph (1) may include provision as respects any period before the making of the order (but after the coming into force of these Regulations).

9

The avoidance by virtue of paragraph 4(2) of any term or rule which provides for any person to be discriminated against shall be without prejudice to the following rights (except in so far as they enable any person to require another person to be treated less favourably than himself), namely—

(a)   such of the rights of the person to be discriminated against; and

(b)   such of the rights of any person who will be treated more favourably in direct or indirect consequence of the discrimination,

as are conferred by or in respect of a contract made or modified wholly or partly in pursuance of, or by reference to, that term or rule.

10

In this Schedule 'collective agreement' means any agreement relating to one or more of the matters mentioned in section 178(2) of the Trade Union and Labour Relations (Consolidation) Act 1992 (collective agreements and collective bargaining), being an agreement made by or on behalf of one or more employers or one or more organisations of employers or associations of such organisations with one or more organisations of workers or associations of such organisations.

SCHEDULE 6
DUTY TO CONSIDER WORKING BEYOND RETIREMENT

Regulation 47

Interpretation

1

(1)   In this Schedule—

'dismissal' means a dismissal within the meaning of section 95 of the 1996 Act;

'employee' means a person to whom regulation 30 (exception for retirement) applies and references to 'employer' shall be construed accordingly;

'intended date of retirement' has the meaning given by sub-paragraph (2);

'operative date of termination' means (subject to paragraph 10(3))—

(a)   where the employer terminates the employee's contract of employment by notice, the date on which the notice expires, or

(b)   where the employer terminates the contract of employment without notice, the date on which the termination takes effect;

'request' means a request made under paragraph 5; and

'worker' has the same meaning as in section 230(3) of the 1996 Act.

(2)   In this Schedule 'intended date of retirement' means—

(a)   where the employer notifies a date in accordance with paragraph 2, that date;

(b)   where the employer notifies a date in accordance with paragraph 4 and either no request is made or a request is made after the notification, that date;

(c)   where,

        (i)   the employer has not notified a date in accordance with paragraph 2,

        (ii)   a request is made before the employer has notified a date in accordance with paragraph 4 (including where no notification in accordance with that paragraph is given),

        (iii)   the request is made by an employee who has reasonable grounds for believing that the employer intends to retire him on a certain date, and,

        (iv)   the request identifies that date,
the date so identified;

(d)   in a case to which paragraph 3 has applied, any earlier or later date that has superseded the date mentioned in paragraph (a), (b) or (c) as the intended date of retirement by virtue of paragraph 3(3);

(e)   in a case to which paragraph 10 has applied, the later date that has superseded the date mentioned in paragraph (a), (b) or (c) as the intended date of retirement by virtue of paragraph 10(3)(b).

Duty of employer to inform employee

2

(1)   An employer who intends to retire an employee has a duty to notify the employee in writing of—

(a)   the employee's right to make a request; and

(b)   the date on which he intends the employee to retire,

not more than one year and not less than six months before that date.

(2)   The duty to notify applies regardless of—

(a)   whether there is any term in the employee's contract of employment indicating when his retirement is expected to take place,

(b)   any other notification of, or information about, the employee's date of retirement given to him by the employer at any time, and

(c)   any other information about the employee's right to make a request given to him by the employer at any time.

3

(1)   This paragraph applies if the employer has notified the employee in accordance with paragraph 2 or 4 or the employee has made a request before being notified in accordance with paragraph 4 (including where no notification in accordance with that paragraph is given), and—

    (a)   the employer and employee agree, in accordance with paragraph 7(3)(b) or 8(5)(b), that the dismissal is to take effect on a date later than the relevant date;

    (b)   the employer gives notice to the employee, in accordance with paragraph 7(7)(a)(ii) or, where the employee appeals, paragraph 8(9)(a)(ii), that the dismissal is to take effect on a date later than the relevant date; or

    (c)   the employer and employee agree that the dismissal is to take effect on a date earlier than the relevant date.

(2)   This Schedule does not require the employer to give the employee a further notification in respect of dismissal taking effect on a date—

    (a)   agreed as mentioned in sub-paragraph (1)(a) or notified as mentioned in sub-paragraph (1)(b) that is later than the relevant date and falls six months or less after the relevant date; or

    (b)   agreed as mentioned in sub-paragraph (1)(c) that is earlier than the relevant date.

(3)   If—

    (a)   a date later than the relevant date is agreed as mentioned in sub-paragraph (1)(a) or notified as mentioned in sub-paragraph (1)(b) and falls six months or less after the relevant date, or

    (b)   a date earlier than the relevant date is agreed as mentioned in sub-paragraph (1)(c),

the earlier or later date shall supersede the relevant date as the intended date of retirement.

(4)   In this paragraph, 'the relevant date' means the date that is defined as the intended date of retirement in paragraph (a), (b) or (c) of paragraph 1(2).

Continuing duty to inform employee

4

Where the employer has failed to comply with paragraph 2, he has a continuing duty to notify the employee in writing as described in paragraph 2(1) until the fourteenth day before the operative date of termination.

Statutory right to request not to retire

5

(1)   An employee may make a request to his employer not to retire on the intended date of retirement.

(2)   In his request the employee must propose that his employment should continue, following the intended date of retirement—

    (a)   indefinitely,

    (b)   for a stated period, or

    (c)   until a stated date;

and, if the request is made at a time when it is no longer possible for the employer to notify in accordance with paragraph 2 and the employer has not yet notified in accordance with paragraph 4, must identify the date on which he believes that the employer intends to retire him.

(3)   A request must be in writing and state that it is made under this paragraph.

(4)   An employee may only make one request under this paragraph in relation to any one intended date of retirement and may not make a request in relation to a date that supersedes a different date as the intended date of retirement by virtue of paragraph 3(3) or 10(3)(b).

(5)   A request is only a request made under this paragraph if it is made—

    (a)   in a case where the employer has complied with paragraph 2, more than three months but not more than six months before the intended date of retirement, or

    (b)   in a case where the employer has not complied with paragraph 2, before, but not more than six months before, the intended date of retirement.

An employer's duty to consider a request

6

An employer to whom a request is made is under a duty to consider the request in accordance with paragraphs 7 to 9.

Meeting to consider request

7

(1)   An employer having a duty under paragraph 6 to consider a request shall hold a meeting to discuss the request with the employee within a reasonable period after receiving it.

(2)   The employer and employee must take all reasonable steps to attend the meeting.

(3)   The duty to hold a meeting does not apply if, before the end of the period that is reasonable—

    (a)   the employer and employee agree that the employee's employment will continue indefinitely and the employer gives notice to the employee to that effect; or

    (b)   the employer and employee agree that the employee's employment will continue for an agreed period and the employer gives notice to the employee of the length of that period or of the date on which it will end.

(4)   The duty to hold a meeting does not apply if—

    (a)   it is not practicable to hold a meeting within the period that is reasonable, and

    (b)   the employer complies with sub-paragraph (5).

(5)   Where sub-paragraph (4)(a) applies, the employer may consider the request without holding a meeting provided he considers any representations made by the employee.

(6)   The employer shall give the employee notice of his decision on the request as soon as is reasonably practicable after the date of the meeting or, if sub-paragraphs (4) and (5) apply, his consideration of the request.

(7)   A notice given under sub-paragraph (6) shall—

    (a)   where the decision is to accept the request, state that it is accepted and—

        (i)   where the decision is that the employee's employment will continue indefinitely, state that fact, or

        (ii)   where the decision is that the employee's employment will continue for a further period, state that fact and specify the length of the period or the date on which it will end,

    (b)   where the decision is to refuse the request, confirm that the employer wishes to retire the employee and the date on which the dismissal is to take effect,

and, in the case of a notice falling within paragraph (b), and of a notice referred to in paragraph (a) that specifies a period shorter than the period proposed by the employee in the request, shall inform the employee of his right to appeal.

(8)   All notices given under this paragraph shall be in writing and be dated.

Appeals

8

(1)   An employee is entitled to appeal against—

    (a)   a decision of his employer to refuse the request, or

    (b)   a decision of his employer to accept the request where the notice given under paragraph 7(6) states as mentioned in paragraph 7(7)(a)(ii) and specifies a period shorter than the period proposed by the employee in the request,

by giving notice in accordance with sub-paragraph (2) as soon as is reasonably practicable after the date of the notice given under paragraph 7(6).

(2)   A notice of appeal under sub-paragraph (1) shall set out the grounds of appeal.

(3)   The employer shall hold a meeting with the employee to discuss an appeal within a reasonable period after the date of the notice of appeal.

(4)   The employer and employee must take all reasonable steps to attend the meeting.

(5)   The duty to hold a meeting does not apply if, before the end of the period that is reasonable—

    (a)   the employer and employee agree that the employee's employment will continue indefinitely and the employer gives notice to the employee to that effect; or

    (b)   the employer and employee agree that the employee's employment will continue for an agreed period and the employer gives notice to the employee of the length of that period or of the date on which it will end.

(6)   The duty to hold a meeting does not apply if—

    (a)   it is not practicable to hold a meeting within the period that is reasonable, and

    (b)   the employer complies with sub-paragraph (7).

(7)   Where sub-paragraph (6)(a) applies, the employer may consider the appeal without holding a meeting provided he considers any representations made by the employee.

(8)   The employer shall give the employee notice of his decision on the appeal as soon as is reasonably practicable after the date of the meeting or, if sub-paragraphs (6) and (7) apply, his consideration of the appeal.

(9)   A notice under sub-paragraph (8) shall—

    (a)   where the decision is to accept the appeal, state that it is accepted and—

        (i)   where the decision is that the employee's employment will continue indefinitely, state that fact, or

        (ii)   where the decision is that the employee's employment will continue for a further period, state that fact and specify the length of the period or the date on which it will end,

    (b)   where the decision is to refuse the appeal, confirm that the employer wishes to retire the employee and the date on which the dismissal is to take effect.

(10)   All notices given under this paragraph shall be in writing and be dated.

Right to be accompanied

9

(1)   This paragraph applies where—

    (a)   a meeting is held under paragraph 7 or 8, and

    (b)   the employee reasonably requests to be accompanied at the meeting.

(2)   Where this paragraph applies the employer must permit the employee to be accompanied at the meeting by one companion who—

    (a)   is chosen by the employee;

    (b)   is a worker employed by the same employer as the employee;

    (c)   is to be permitted to address the meeting (but not to answer questions on behalf of the employee); and

(d)   is to be permitted to confer with the employee during the meeting.

(3)   If—

(a)   an employee has a right under this paragraph to be accompanied at a meeting,

(b)   his chosen companion will not be available at the time proposed for the meeting by the employer, and

(c)   the employee proposes an alternative time which satisfies sub-paragraph (4),

the employer must postpone the meeting to the time proposed by the employee.

(4)   An alternative time must—

(a)   be convenient for employer, employee and companion, and

(b)   fall before the end of the period of seven days beginning with the first day after the day proposed by the employer.

(5)   An employer shall permit a worker to take time off during working hours for the purpose of accompanying an employee in accordance with a request under sub-paragraph (1)(b).

(6)   Sections 168(3) and (4), 169 and 171 to 173 of the Trade Union and Labour Relations (Consolidation) Act 1992 (time off for carrying out trade union duties) shall apply in relation to sub-paragraph (5) above as they apply in relation to section 168(1) of that Act.

Dismissal before request considered

10

(1)   This paragraph applies where—

(a)   by virtue of paragraph 6 an employer is under a duty to consider a request;

(b)   the employer dismisses the employee;

(c)   that dismissal is the contemplated dismissal to which the request relates; and

(d)   the operative date of termination would, but for sub-paragraph (3), fall on or before the day on which the employer gives notice in accordance with paragraph 7(6).

(2)   Subject to sub-paragraph (4), the contract of employment shall continue in force for all purposes, including the purpose of determining for any purpose the period for which the employee has been continuously employed, until the day following that on which the notice under paragraph 7(6) is given.

(3)   The day following the day on which that notice is given shall supersede—

(a)   the date mentioned in sub-paragraph (1)(d) as the operative date of termination; and

(b)   the date defined as the intended date of retirement in paragraph (a), (b) or (c) of paragraph 1(2) as the intended date of retirement.

(4)   Any continuation of the contract of employment under sub-paragraph (2) shall be disregarded when determining the operative date of termination for the purposes of sections 98ZA to 98ZH of the 1996 Act.

Complaint to employment tribunal: failure to comply with paragraph 2

11

(1)   An employee may present a complaint to an employment tribunal that his employer has failed to comply with the duty to notify him in paragraph 2.

(2)   A tribunal shall not consider a complaint under this paragraph unless the complaint is presented—

    (a)   before the end of the period of three months beginning with—

        (i)   the last day permitted to the employer by paragraph 2 for complying with the duty to notify, or

        (ii)   if the employee did not then know the date that would be the intended date of retirement, the first day on which he knew or should have known that date; or

    (b)   within such further period as the tribunal considers reasonable in a case where it is satisfied that it was not reasonably practicable for the complaint to be presented before the end of that period of three months.

(3)   Where a tribunal finds that a complaint under this paragraph is well-founded it shall order the employer to pay compensation to the employee of such amount, not exceeding 8 weeks' pay, as the tribunal considers just and equitable in all the circumstances.

(4)   Chapter 2 of Part 14 of the 1996 Act (calculation of a week's pay) shall apply for the purposes of sub-paragraph (3); and in applying that Chapter the calculation date shall be taken to be the date on which the complaint was presented or, if earlier, the operative date of termination.

(5)   The limit in section 227(1) of the 1996 Act (maximum amount of a week's pay) shall apply for the purposes of sub-paragraph (3).

Complaint to employment tribunal: denial of right to be accompanied

12

(1)   An employee may present a complaint to an employment tribunal that his employer has failed, or threatened to fail, to comply with paragraph 9(2) or (3).

(2)   A tribunal shall not consider a complaint under this paragraph in relation to a failure or threat unless the complaint is presented—

    (a)   before the end of the period of three months beginning with the date of the failure or threat; or

(b)   within such further period as the tribunal considers reasonable in a case where it is satisfied that it was not reasonably practicable for the complaint to be presented before the end of that period of three months.

(3)   Where a tribunal finds that a complaint under this paragraph is well-founded it shall order the employer to pay compensation to the worker of an amount not exceeding two weeks' pay.

(4)   Chapter 2 of Part 14 of the 1996 Act (calculation of a week's pay) shall apply for the purposes of sub-paragraph (3); and in applying that Chapter the calculation date shall be taken to be the date on which the relevant meeting took place (or was to have taken place).

(5)   The limit in section 227(1) of the 1996 Act (maximum amount of a week's pay) shall apply for the purposes of sub-paragraph (3).

Detriment and dismissal

13

(1)   An employee has the right not to be subjected to any detriment by any act by his employer done on the ground that he exercised or sought to exercise his right to be accompanied in accordance with paragraph 9.

(2)   A worker has the right not to be subjected to any detriment by any act, or any deliberate failure to act, by his employer done on the ground that he accompanied or sought to accompany an employee pursuant to a request under paragraph 9.

(3)   Section 48 of the 1996 Act shall apply in relation to contraventions of sub-paragraph (1) or (2) above as it applies in relation to contraventions of certain sections of that Act.

(4)   Sub-paragraph (2) does not apply where the worker is an employee and the detriment in question amounts to dismissal (within the meaning of Part 10 of the 1996 Act).

(5)   An employee who is dismissed shall be regarded for the purposes of Part 10 of the 1996 Act as unfairly dismissed if the reason (or, if more than one, the principal reason) for the dismissal is that he—

(a)   exercised or sought to exercise his right to be accompanied in accordance with paragraph 9, or

(b)   accompanied or sought to accompany an employee pursuant to a request under that paragraph.

(6)   Sections 128 to 132 of the 1996 Act (interim relief) shall apply in relation to dismissal for the reason specified in sub-paragraph (5)(a) or (b) above as they apply in relation to dismissal for a reason specified in section 128(1)(b) of that Act.

SCHEDULE 7
Duty to Consider Working Beyond Retirement—Transitional Provisions

Regulation 48

1
In paragraphs 2 to 6—

    (a)   'the expiry date' means the date on which notice of dismissal given by an employer expires; and

    (b)   words and expressions shall have the same meanings as they do in Schedule 6.

2

(1)   This paragraph applies in a case where—

    (a)   an employer has given notice of dismissal to the employee before the commencement date of—

        (i)   at least the period required by the contract of employment; or

        (ii)   where the period required by the contract exceeds four weeks, at least four weeks;

    (b)   the expiry date falls before 1st April 2007; and

    (c)   the employer has made the employee aware, before the commencement date, that the employer considers that the employee is being retired on the expiry date.

(2)   Where this paragraph applies and the employer on or as soon as is practicable after the commencement date notifies the employee in writing of the employee's right to make a request under paragraph 5 of Schedule 6—

    (a)   the employer shall be treated as complying with the duty in paragraph 2 of Schedule 6;

    (b)   a request shall be treated as being a request made under paragraph 5 of Schedule 6 provided it—

        (i)   is made after the employer notified the employee of his right to make a request;

        (ii)   satisfies the requirements of sub-paragraphs (2) and (3) of paragraph 5 of Schedule 6; and

        (iii)   is made—
        (aa)   where practicable, at least four weeks before the expiry date; or
        (bb)   where that is not practicable, as soon as reasonably practicable (whether before or after the expiry date) after the employer notified the employee of his right to make a request, but not more than four weeks after the expiry date.

(3)   Where this paragraph applies and the employer does not, on or as soon as is practicable after the commencement date, notify the employee in writing of the employee's right to make a request under paragraph 5 of Schedule 6—

    (a)   the duty to notify in accordance with paragraph 2 of Schedule 6 does not apply;

    (b)   the duty to notify in accordance with paragraph 4 of Schedule 6 applies as if—

        (i)   the employer had failed to notify in accordance with paragraph 2 of that Schedule; and

    (ii)   the duty was one to notify at any time before the expiry date;

(c)   a request shall be treated as being a request made under paragraph 5 of Schedule 6 if it satisfies the requirements of sub-paragraphs (2) and (3) of that paragraph and is made—

    (i)   before any notification given in accordance with paragraph 4 of Schedule 6; or

    (ii)   after such notification and—

    (aa)   where practicable, at least four weeks before the expiry date; or

    (bb)   where that is not practicable, as soon as reasonably practicable (whether before or after the expiry date) after the employer notified the employee of his right to make a request, but not more than four weeks after the expiry date.

3

(1)   This paragraph applies in a case where the employer has given notice of dismissal to the employee before the commencement date and—

(a)   the expiry date falls before 1st April 2007, but

(b)   the period of notice given is shorter than the minimum period of notice required by paragraph 2(1)(a) or the employer has not complied with paragraph 2(1)(c).

(2)   Where this paragraph applies—

(a)   the duty to notify in accordance with paragraph 2 of Schedule 6 does not apply;

(b)   the duty to notify in accordance with paragraph 4 of Schedule 6 applies as if—

    (i)   the employer had failed to notify in accordance with paragraph 2 of that Schedule; and

    (ii)   the duty was one to notify at any time before the expiry date;

(c)   a request shall be treated as being a request made under paragraph 5 of Schedule 6 if it satisfies the requirements of sub-paragraphs (2) and (3) of that paragraph and is made—

    (i)   before any notification given in accordance with paragraph 4 of Schedule 6; or

    (ii)   after such notification and—

    (aa)   where practicable, at least four weeks before the expiry date; or

    (bb)   where that is not practicable, as soon as reasonably practicable (whether before or after the expiry date) after the employer notified the employee of his right to make a request, but not more than four weeks after the expiry date.

4

(1)   This paragraph applies in a case where—

(a)   notice of dismissal is given on or after the commencement date of at least—

    (i)   the period required by the contract of employment; or

    (ii)   if longer, the period required by section 86 of the 1996 Act; and

(b)   the expiry date falls before 1st April 2007.

(2)   Where this paragraph applies and the employer notifies the employee in writing of the employee's right to make a request under paragraph 5 of Schedule 6 before, or on the same day as, the day on which notice of dismissal is given—

(a)   the employer shall be treated as complying with the duty in paragraph 2 of Schedule 6;

(b)   a request shall be treated as being a request made under paragraph 5 of Schedule 6 provided it—

    (i)   is made after the employer notified the employee of his right to make a request;

    (ii)   satisfies the requirements of sub-paragraphs (2) and (3) of paragraph 5 of Schedule 6; and

    (iii)   is made—
    (aa)   where practicable, at least four weeks before the expiry date; or
    (bb)   where that is not practicable, as soon as reasonably practicable (whether before or after the expiry date) after the employer notified the employee of his right to make a request, but not more than four weeks after the expiry date.

(3)   Where this paragraph applies but the employer does not notify the employee in writing of the employee's right to make a request under paragraph 5 of Schedule 6 before, or on the same day as, the day on which notice of dismissal is given—

(a)   the duty to notify in accordance with paragraph 2 of Schedule 6 does not apply;

(b)   the duty to notify in accordance with paragraph 4 of Schedule 6 applies as if—

    (i)   the employer had failed to notify in accordance with paragraph 2 of that Schedule; and

    (ii)   the duty was one to notify at any time before the expiry date;

(c)   a request shall be treated as being a request made under paragraph 5 of Schedule 6 if it satisfies the requirements of sub-paragraphs (2) and (3) of that paragraph and is made—

    (i)   before any notification given in accordance with paragraph 4 of Schedule 6; or

    (ii)   after such notification and—
    (aa)   where practicable, at least four weeks before the expiry date; or

(bb) where that is not practicable, as soon as reasonably practicable (whether before or after the expiry date) after the employer notified the employee of his right to make a request, but not more than four weeks after the expiry date.

5

(1) This paragraph applies in a case where—

(a) notice of dismissal is given on or after the commencement date and is for a period shorter than—

(i) the period required by the contract of employment; or

(ii) if longer, the period required by section 86 of the 1996 Act; and

(b) the period of notice expires on a date falling before 1st April 2007.

(2) Where this paragraph applies—

(a) the duty to notify in accordance with paragraph 2 of Schedule 6 does not apply;

(b) the duty to notify in accordance with paragraph 4 of Schedule 6 applies as if—

(i) the employer had failed to notify in accordance with paragraph 2 of that Schedule; and

(ii) the duty was one to notify at any time before the expiry date;

(c) a request shall be treated as being a request made under paragraph 5 of Schedule 6 if it satisfies the requirements of sub-paragraphs (2) and (3) of that paragraph and is made—

(i) before any notification given in accordance with paragraph 4 of Schedule 6; or

(ii) after such notification and—

(aa) where practicable, at least four weeks before the expiry date; or

(bb) where that is not practicable, as soon as reasonably practicable (whether before or after the expiry date) after the employer notified the employee of his right to make a request, but not more than four weeks after the expiry date.

6

In every case to which paragraph 2, 3, 4 or 5 applies—

(a) paragraph 10 of Schedule 6 does not apply; and

(b) the employer is under a duty to consider any request which complies with the requirements of paragraph 2(2)(b), 2(3)(c), 3(2)(c), 4(2)(b), 4(3)(c) or 5(2)(c) in accordance with paragraphs 7 to 9 of Schedule 6.

Appendix 1

AMENDMENTS TO LEGISLATION AND RELATED TRANSITIONAL PROVISIONS

Regulation 49(1)

Part 1
Primary Legislation

The Mines and Quarries Act 1954

1

The Mines and Quarries Act 1954 is amended as follows.

2

(1)   In section 42(1) (charge of winding and rope haulage apparatus when persons are carried) omit the words 'who has attained the age of twenty-two years'.

(2)   In section 43(2) (charge of winding and rope haulage apparatus when persons are not carried) omit the words 'who has attained the age of eighteen years'.

(3)   In section 44 (charge of conveyors at working faces) omit the words 'who has attained the age of eighteen years'.

The Parliamentary Commissioner Act 1967

3

The Parliamentary Commissioner Act 1967 is amended as follows—

4

(1)   Section 1 (appointment and tenure of office) is amended in accordance with this paragraph.

(2)   In subsection (2) omit the words from ', and any person' to 'during good behaviour'.

(3)   After subsection (2) insert—

'(2A)   A person appointed to be the Commissioner shall hold office until the end of the period for which he is appointed.

(2B)   That period must be not more than seven years.

(2C)   Subsection (2A) is subject to subsections (3) and (3A).'.

(4)   For subsection (3) substitute—

'(3)   A person appointed to be the Commissioner may be—

(a)   relieved of office by Her Majesty at his own request, or

(b)   removed from office by Her Majesty, on the ground of misbehaviour, in consequence of Addresses from both Houses of Parliament.'.

(5)   After subsection (3A) insert—

'(3B) A person appointed to be the Commissioner is not eligible for re-appointment.'.

5

(1) Section 3A (appointment of acting Commissioner) is amended in accordance with this paragraph.

(2) After subsection (1) insert—

'(1A) A person appointed to act as the Commissioner ('an acting Commissioner') may have held office as the Commissioner.

(1B) A person appointed as an acting Commissioner is eligible for appointment as the Commissioner unless he has already held office as the Commissioner.'.

(3) In subsection (2) for the words 'under this section' substitute 'as an acting Commissioner'.

(4) For subsection (3) substitute—

'(3) A person appointed as an acting Commissioner shall, while he holds office, be treated for all purposes, except for the purposes of section 1 and 2, and this section of this Act, as the Commissioner.'.

6

The amendments made to the Parliamentary Commissioner Act 1967 apply in relation to appointments made on or after the commencement date.

The Pilotage Act 1987

7

(1) The Pilotage Act 1987 is amended in accordance with this paragraph.

(2) In section 3(2) (authorisation of pilots) omit the word 'age,'.

The Social Security Contributions and Benefits Act 1992

8

The Social Security Contributions and Benefits Act 1992 is amended as follows.

9

(1) Section 163(1) (interpretation of Part 11 and supplementary provisions) is amended in accordance with this paragraph.

(2) In the definition of 'employee' omit paragraph (b) and the word 'and' preceding it.

(3) For the definition of 'employer' substitute—

"employer', in relation to an employee and a contract of service of his, means a person who—

(a) under section 6 above is liable to pay secondary Class 1 contributions in relation to any earnings of the employee under the contract, or

(b)   would be liable to pay such contributions but for—
(i)   the condition in section 6(1)(b), or
(ii) the employee being under the age of 16:'.

10

(1)   Section 171(1) (interpretation of Part 12 and supplementary provisions) is amended in accordance with this paragraph.

(2)   In the definition of 'employee' omit paragraph (b) and the word 'and' preceding it.

(3)   For the definition of 'employer' substitute—

"employer', in relation to a woman who is an employee, means a person who—

(a)   under section 6 above is liable to pay secondary Class 1 contributions in relation to any of her earnings; or

(b)   would be liable to pay such contributions but for—
(i)   the condition in section 6(1)(b), or
(ii) the employee being under the age of 16;'.

(4)   This paragraph applies in relation to any case where the expected week of confinement begins on or after 14th January 2007.

11

(1)   Section 171ZJ (Part 12ZA: supplementary) is amended in accordance with this paragraph.

(2)   In subsection (1) for the definition of 'employer' substitute—

"employer', in relation to a person who is an employee, means a person who—

(a)   under section 6 above is, liable to pay secondary Class 1 contributions in relation to any of the earnings of the person who is an employee; or

(b)   would be liable to pay such contributions but for—
(i)   the condition in section 6(1)(b), or
(ii) the employee being under the age of 16;'.

(3)   In subsection (2) omit paragraph (b) and the word 'and' preceding it.

(4)   This paragraph applies in relation to an entitlement to—

(a)   statutory paternity pay (birth) in respect of children whose expected week of birth begins on or after 14th January 2007;

(b)   statutory paternity pay (adoption) in respect of children—

(i)   matched with a person who is notified of having been matched on or after the commencement date; or

(ii) placed for adoption on or after the commencement date.

12

(1) Section 171ZS (Part 12ZB: supplementary) is amended in accordance with this paragraph.

(2) In subsection (1) for the definition of 'employer' substitute—

"employer', in relation to a person who is an employee, means a person who—

(a) under section 6 above is liable to pay secondary Class 1 contributions in relation to any of the earnings of the person who is an employee; or

(b) would be liable to pay such contributions but for—

(ii) the condition in section 6(1)(b), or

(ii) the employee being under the age of 16;'.

(3) In subsection (2) omit paragraph (b) and the word 'and' preceding it.

(4) This paragraph applies in relation to an entitlement to statutory adoption pay in respect of children—

(a) matched with a person who is notified of having been matched on or after the commencement date; or

(b) placed for adoption on or after that commencement.

13

(1) In Schedule 11 omit paragraph 2(a) (period of entitlement not to arise if at the relevant date the employee is over 65).

(2) Sub-paragraph (1) applies in relation to a period of incapacity for work which—

(a) begins on or after the commencement date, or

(b) begins before and continues on or after the commencement date.

(3) But in a case falling within sub-paragraph (2)(b), sub-paragraph (1) does not affect the application of paragraph 1 of Schedule 11 to the 1992 Act in relation to the part of the period of incapacity for work that falls before the commencement date.

The Health Service Commissioners Act 1993

14

The Health Service Commissioners Act 1993 is amended as follows.

15

(1) Schedule 1 (the English Commissioner) is amended in accordance with this paragraph.

(2) For paragraph 1 (appointment of Commissioners) substitute the following new paragraphs—

'1

Her Majesty may by Letters Patent appoint a person to be the Commissioner.

1A

Subject to paragraphs 1C and 1D a person appointed to be the Commissioner shall hold office until the end of the period for which he is appointed.

1B

That period must be not more than seven years.

1C

A person appointed to be the Commissioner may be relieved of office by Her Majesty at his own request.

1D

A person appointed to be the Commissioner may be removed from office by Her Majesty, on the ground of misbehaviour, in consequence of Addresses from both Houses of Parliament.

1E

A person appointed to be the Commissioner is not eligible for re-appointment.'.

    (3)   In paragraph 2 (appointment of acting Commissioners)—

        (a)   after sub-paragraph (1) insert—

    '(1A) A person appointed to act as the Commissioner ('an acting Commissioner') may have held office as the Commissioner.

(1B) A person appointed as an acting Commissioner is eligible for appointment as the Commissioner unless he has already held office as the Commissioner.';

        (b)   in sub-paragraph (2) for the words 'under this paragraph' substitute 'as acting Commissioner,'; and

        (c)   for sub-paragraph (3), substitute—

    '(3)   A person appointed as an acting Commissioner shall, while he holds office, be treated for all purposes, except for the purposes of paragraphs 1, 4 to 10 and this paragraph, as the Commissioner.'.

16

The amendments made to the Health Service Commissioners Act 1993 apply in relation to appointments made on or after the commencement date.

The Statutory Sick Pay Act 1994

17

(1)   The Statutory Sick Pay Act 1994 is amended in accordance with this paragraph.

(2)   In section 1(2) omit the words after paragraph (b).

The Employment Tribunals Act 1996

18

The Employment Tribunals Act 1996 is amended as follows.

19

(1) Section 18(1) (conciliation) is amended in accordance with this paragraph.

(2) At the end of paragraph (p), omit 'or'.

(3) After paragraph (q), insert

'or

(r) under regulation 36 of the Employment Equality (Age) Regulations 2006.'.

20

(1) Section 21(1) (jurisdiction of Appeal Tribunal) is amended in accordance with this paragraph.

(2) At the end of paragraph (q), omit 'or'.

(3) After paragraph (r) insert—

'or

(s) the Employment Equality (Age) Regulations 2006.'.

The Employment Rights Act 1996

21

The 1996 Act is amended as follows.

22

(1) Section 98 (fairness of dismissal: general) is amended as follows.

(2) In subsection (2), after paragraph (b) insert—

'(ba) is retirement of the employee,'.

(3) After subsection (2) insert—

'(2A) Subsections (1) and (2) are subject to sections 98ZA to 98ZF.'.

(4) After subsection (3) insert—

'(3A) In any case where the employer has fulfilled the requirements of subsection (1) by showing that the reason (or the principal reason) for the dismissal is retirement of the employee, the question whether the dismissal is fair or unfair shall be determined in accordance with section 98ZG.'.

(5) In subsection (4) for 'Where' substitute 'In any other case where'.

Appendix 1

23

After section 98 insert—

'Retirement

98ZA   No normal retirement age: dismissal before 65

(1)   This section applies to the dismissal of an employee if—

    (a)   the employee has no normal retirement age, and

    (b)   the operative date of termination falls before the date when the employee reaches the age of 65.

(2)   Retirement of the employee shall not be taken to be the reason (or a reason) for the dismissal.

98ZB   No normal retirement age: dismissal at or after 65

(1)   This section applies to the dismissal of an employee if—

    (a)   the employee has no normal retirement age, and

    (b)   the operative date of termination falls on or after the date when the employee reaches the age of 65.

(2)   In a case where—

    (a)   the employer has notified the employee in accordance with paragraph 2 of Schedule 6 to the 2006 Regulations, and

    (b)   the contract of employment terminates on the intended date of retirement,

retirement of the employee shall be taken to be the only reason for the dismissal by the employer and any other reason shall be disregarded.

(3)   In a case where—

    (a)   the employer has notified the employee in accordance with paragraph 2 of Schedule 6 to the 2006 Regulations, but

    (b)   the contract of employment terminates before the intended date of retirement,

retirement of the employee shall not be taken to be the reason (or a reason) for dismissal.

(4)   In a case where—

    (a)   the employer has not notified the employee in accordance with paragraph 2 of Schedule 6 to the 2006 Regulations, and

    (b)   there is an intended date of retirement in relation to the dismissal, but

    (c)   the contract of employment terminates before the intended date of retirement,

retirement of the employee shall not be taken to be the reason (or a reason) for dismissal.

(5)   In all other cases where the employer has not notified the employee in accordance with paragraph 2 of Schedule 6 to the 2006 Regulations, particular regard shall be had to the matters in section 98ZF when determining the reason (or principal reason) for dismissal.

98ZC   Normal retirement age: dismissal before retirement age

(1)   This section applies to the dismissal of an employee if—

    (a)   the employee has a normal retirement age, and

    (b)   the operative date of termination falls before the date when the employee reaches the normal retirement age.

(2)   Retirement of the employee shall not be taken to be the reason (or a reason) for the dismissal.

98ZD   Normal retirement age 65 or higher: dismissal at or after retirement age

(1)   This section applies to the dismissal of an employee if—

    (a)   the employee has a normal retirement age,

    (b)   the normal retirement age is 65 or higher, and

    (c)   the operative date of termination falls on or after the date when the employee reaches the normal retirement age.

(2)   In a case where—

    (a)   the employer has notified the employee in accordance with paragraph 2 of Schedule 6 to the 2006 Regulations, and

    (b)   the contract of employment terminates on the intended date of retirement,

retirement of the employee shall be taken to be the only reason for the dismissal by the employer and any other reason shall be disregarded.

(3)   In a case where—

    (a)   the employer has notified the employee in accordance with paragraph 2 of Schedule 6 to the 2006 Regulations, but

    (b)   the contract of employment terminates before the intended date of retirement,

retirement of the employee shall not be taken to be the reason (or a reason) for dismissal.

(4)   In a case where—

    (a)   the employer has not notified the employee in accordance with paragraph 2 of Schedule 6 to the 2006 Regulations, and

    (b)   there is an intended date of retirement in relation to the dismissal, but

    (c)   the contract of employment terminates before the intended date of retirement,

retirement of the employee shall not be taken to be the reason (or a reason) for dismissal.

(5)   In all other cases where the employer has not notified the employee in accordance with paragraph 2 of Schedule 6 to the 2006 Regulations, particular regard shall be had to the matters in section 98ZF when determining the reason (or principal reason) for dismissal.

98ZE   Normal retirement age below 65: dismissal at or after retirement age

(1)   This section applies to the dismissal of an employee if—

(a)   the employee has a normal retirement age,

(b)   the normal retirement age is below 65, and

(c)   the operative date of termination falls on or after the date when the employee reaches the normal retirement age.

(2)   If it is unlawful discrimination under the 2006 Regulations for the employee to have that normal retirement age, retirement of the employee shall not be taken to be the reason (or a reason) for dismissal.

(3)   Subsections (4) to (7) apply if it is not unlawful discrimination under the 2006 Regulations for the employee to have that normal retirement age.

(4)   In a case where—

(a)   the employer has notified the employee in accordance with paragraph 2 of Schedule 6 to the 2006 Regulations, and

(b)   the contract of employment terminates on the intended date of retirement,

retirement of the employee shall be taken to be the only reason for dismissal by the employer and any other reason shall be disregarded.

(5)   In a case where—

(a)   the employer has notified the employee in accordance with paragraph 2 of Schedule 6 to the 2006 Regulations, but

(b)   the contract of employment terminates before the intended date of retirement,

retirement of the employee shall not be taken to be the reason (or a reason) for dismissal.

(6)   In a case where—

(a)   the employer has not notified the employee in accordance with paragraph 2 of Schedule 6 to the 2006 Regulations, and

(b)   there is an intended date of retirement in relation to the dismissal, but

(c)   the contract of employment terminates before the intended date of retirement,

retirement of the employee shall not be taken to be the reason (or a reason) for dismissal.

(7)   In all other cases where the employer has not notified the employee in accordance with paragraph 2 of Schedule 6 to the 2006 Regulations, particular regard shall be had to the matters in section 98ZF when determining the reason (or principal reason) for dismissal

98ZF   Reason for dismissal: particular matters

(1)   These are the matters to which particular regard is to be had in accordance with section 98ZB(5), 98ZD(5) or 98ZE(7)—

    (a)   whether or not the employer has notified the employee in accordance with paragraph 4 of Schedule 6 to the 2006 Regulations;

    (b)   if the employer has notified the employee in accordance with that paragraph, how long before the notified retirement date the notification was given;

    (c)   whether or not the employer has followed, or sought to follow, the procedures in paragraph 7 of Schedule 6 to the 2006 Regulations.

(2)   In subsection (1)(b) 'notified retirement date' means the date notified to the employee in accordance with paragraph 4 of Schedule 6 to the 2006 Regulations as the date on which the employer intends to retire the employee.

98ZG   Retirement dismissals: fairness

(1)   This section applies if the reason (or principal reason) for a dismissal is retirement of the employee.

(2)   The employee shall be regarded as unfairly dismissed if, and only if, there has been a failure on the part of the employer to comply with an obligation imposed on him by any of the following provisions of Schedule 6 to the 2006 Regulations—

    (a)   paragraph 4 (notification of retirement, if not already given under paragraph 2),

    (b)   paragraphs 6 and 7 (duty to consider employee's request not to be retired),

    (c)   paragraph 8 (duty to consider appeal against decision to refuse request not to be retired).

98ZH   Interpretation

In sections 98ZA to 98ZG—

'2006 Regulations' means the Employment Equality (Age) Regulations 2006;

'intended date of retirement' means the date which, by virtue of paragraph 1(2) of Schedule 6 to the 2006 Regulations, is the intended date of retirement in relation to a particular dismissal;

'normal retirement age', in relation to an employee, means the age at which employees in the employer's undertaking who hold, or have held, the same kind of position as the employee are normally required to retire;

'operative date of termination' means—

    (a)   where the employer terminates the employee's contract of employment by notice, the date on which the notice expires, or

    (b)   where the employer terminates the contract of employment without notice, the date on which the termination takes effect.

Other Dismissals'.

24

In section 108 (qualifying period of employment) in subsection (3) (cases where no qualifying period of employment is required)—

    (a)   at the end of paragraph (l) omit 'or'; and

    (b)   after paragraph (m) insert—

'or

    (n)   paragraph (a) or (b) of paragraph 13(5) of Schedule 6 to the Employment Equality (Age) Regulations 2006 applies.'.

25

Omit section 109 (upper age limit on unfair dismissal right).

26

(1)   Section 112 (remedies for unfair dismissal: orders and compensation) is amended as follows.

(2)   In subsection (5)(a) after 'section' insert '98ZG or'.

27

(1)   Section 119 (basic award) is amended as follows.

(2)   Omit subsections (4) and (5).

28

(1)   Section 120 (basic award: minimum in certain cases) is amended as follows.

(2)   In subsection (1A) after 'section' insert '98ZG or'.

29

In section 126(1) (acts which are both unfair dismissal and discrimination), for paragraph (b) substitute—

    '(b)   any one or more of the following—

        (i)   the Sex Discrimination Act 1975;

        (ii)   the Race Relations Act 1976;

        (iii)   the Disability Discrimination Act 1995;

        (iv)   the Employment Equality (Sexual Orientation) Regulations 2003;

        (v)   the Employment Equality (Religion or Belief) Regulations 2003;

        (vi)   the Employment Equality (Age) Regulations 2006.'.

30

Section 156 (upper age limit) is repealed.

31

Section 158 (pension rights) is repealed.

32

(1) Section 162 (amount of a redundancy payment) is amended in accordance with this paragraph.

(2) Subsections (4), (5) and (8) are repealed.

(3) In subsection (6), for the words 'Subsections (1) to (5)' substitute 'Subsections (1) to (3)'.

33

In relation to any case where the date that is the relevant date by virtue of section 153 of the 1996 Act falls before the commencement date, paragraphs 30 to 32 do not apply.

34

(1) Section 209 (powers to amend Act) is amended as follows.

(2) In subsection (5) omit '109(1),'.

35

(1) Section 211 (period of continuous employment) is amended in accordance with this paragraph.

(2) In paragraph (a) of subsection (1) for the words 'subsections (2) and' substitute 'subsection'.

(3) Subsection (2) is repealed.

The Employment Act 2002

36

(1) The Employment Act 2002 is amended in accordance with this paragraph.

(2) At the end of each of the following Schedules—

(a) Schedule 3 (tribunal jurisdictions to which section 31 applies for adjustment of awards for non-completion of statutory procedure);

(b) Schedule 4 (tribunal jurisdictions to which section 32 applies for complaints where the employee must first submit a statement of grievance to employer); and

(c) Schedule 5 (tribunal jurisdictions to which section 38 applies in relation to proceedings where the employer has failed to give a statement of employment particulars),

insert—

'Regulation 36 of the Employment Equality (Age) Regulations 2006 (discrimination in the employment field)'.

Appendix 1

The Equality Act 2006

37

The Equality Act 2006 is amended as follows.

38

(1) Section 14(1) (codes of practice) is amended in accordance with this paragraph.

(2) At the end of paragraph (g) omit 'and'.

(3) After paragraph (h) insert—

'and

    (i) Parts 2 and 3 of the Employment Equality (Age) Regulations 2006.'.

39

(1) Section 27(1) (conciliation) is amended in accordance with this paragraph.

(2) At the end of paragraph (f) omit 'or'.

(3) After paragraph (g) insert—

'or

    (h) regulation 39 of the Employment Equality (Age) Regulations 2006 (Jurisdiction of County and Sheriff Courts).'.

40

(1) Section 33(1) (equality and human rights enactments) is amended in accordance with this paragraph.

(2) At the end of paragraph (g) omit 'and'.

(3) After paragraph (h) insert—

'and

    (i) the Employment Equality (Age) Regulations 2006.'.

Part 2
Other Legislation

41

(1) The Coal and Other Mines (Locomotives) Regulations 1956, Schedule 1 to the Coal and Other Mines (Locomotives) Order 1956 is amended in accordance with this paragraph.

(2) In regulation 17(1) (drivers of locomotives) omit the words 'and no appointed driver shall operate a locomotive hauling persons in vehicles unless he has attained the age of—

    (a) in the case of a mine of shale, eighteen years;

    (b) in the case of any other mine, twenty-one years'.

42

(1)   The Stratified Ironstone, Shale and Fireclay Mines (Explosives) Regulations 1956 are amended in accordance with this paragraph.

(2)   In regulation 3 (qualification of shot firers) omit the words 'he has attained the age of twenty-one years; and'.

43

(1)   The Miscellaneous Mines (Explosives) Regulations 1959 are amended in accordance with this paragraph.

(2)   Omit regulation 6(2).

(3)   In regulation 8(2) (control of issue of detonators) omit the words 'has attained the age of eighteen years and'.

44

(1)   The Lynemouth Mine (Diesel Vehicles and Storage Battery Vehicles) Special Regulations 1961 are amended in accordance with this paragraph.

(2)   In regulation 15 after the words 'Regulations 17' insert 'as amended by the Employment Equality (Age) Regulations 2006'.

45

(1)   The South Crofty Mine (Locomotive) Special Regulations 1965 are amended in accordance with this paragraph.

(2)   In regulation 11(2) omit the words 'has attained the age of twenty-one years and'.

46

(1)   The Glebe Mine (Locomotives and Diesel Vehicles) Special Regulations 1967 are amended in accordance with this paragraph.

(2)   In regulation 15(2) omit the words 'has attained the age of eighteen years and'.

47

(1)   The Winsford Rock Salt Mine (Diesel Vehicles and Storage Battery Vehicles) Special Regulations 1971 are amended in accordance with this paragraph.

(2)   In regulation 14(2) omit the words 'is under the age of twenty-one years and'.

48

(1)   The Thoresby Mine (Cable Reel Load-Haul-Dump Vehicles) Special Regulations 1978 are amended in accordance with this paragraph.

(2)   In regulation 17 after the words 'Regulations 17' insert 'as amended by the Employment Equality (Age) Regulations 2006'.

49

The Statutory Sick Pay (General) Regulations 1982 are amended as follows.

50

(1)   Regulation 16 (meaning of 'employee') is amended in accordance with this paragraph.

(2)   In paragraph (1)—

    (a)   at the beginning insert the words 'Subject to paragraph (1ZA),', and

    (b)   omit the words 'over the age of 16'.

(3)   After paragraph (1) insert—

'(1ZA) Any person under the age of 16 who would have been treated as an employed earner or, as the case may be, would have been treated otherwise than as an employed earner by virtue of the Social Security (Categorisation of Earners) Regulations 1978 had he been aged 16 or over, shall be treated as if he is aged 16 or over for the purposes of paragraph (1).'.

51

(1)   Regulation 17(2) (meaning of 'earnings') is amended in accordance with this paragraph.

(2)   At the end of sub-paragraph (a) insert ' (or would have been so excluded had he not been under the age of 16)'.

(3)   At the end of sub-paragraph (b) insert ' (or where such a payment or amount would have been so excluded and in consequence he would not have been entitled to statutory sick pay had he not been under the age of 16)'.

52

The Statutory Maternity Pay (General) Regulations 1986 are amended as follows.

53

(1)   Regulation 17 (meaning of 'employee') is amended in accordance with this paragraph.

(2)   In paragraph (1)—

    (a)   at the beginning insert the words 'Subject to paragraph (1A),', and

    (b)   omit the words 'over the age of 16'.

(3)   After paragraph (1) insert—

'(1A) Any woman under the age of 16 who would have been treated as an employed earner or, as the case may be, would have been treated otherwise than as an employed earner by virtue of the Social Security (Categorisation of Earners) Regulations 1978 had she been aged 16 or over, shall be treated as if she is aged 16 or over for the purposes of paragraph (1).'.

54

(1)   Regulation 20(2) (Meaning of 'earnings') is amended in accordance with this paragraph.

(2)   At the end of sub-paragraph (a) insert ' (or would have been so excluded had she not been under the age of 16)'.

(3)   At the end of sub-paragraph (b) insert ' (or where such a payment or amount would have been so excluded and in consequence she would not have been entitled to statutory maternity pay had she not been under the age of 16)'.

(4)   This paragraph applies in relation to any case where the expected week of confinement begins on or after 14th January 2007.

55

(1)   The Coal and Other Safety-Lamp Mines (Explosives) Regulations 1993 are amended in accordance with this paragraph.

(2)   In regulation 4(4) (appointment of shotfirers and trainee shotfirers) omit the words 'he is at least 21 years of age and'.

56

(1)   The Employment Tribunals (Interest on Awards In Discrimination Cases) Regulations 1996 are amended in accordance with this paragraph.

(2)   In sub-paragraph (b) of the definition of 'an award under the relevant legislation' in regulation 1(2) (interpretation)—

(a)   after 'regulation 30(1)(b) of the Employment Equality (Sexual Orientation) Regulations 2003' omit 'or'; and

(b)   after 'regulation 30(1)(b) of the Employment Equality (Religion or Belief) Regulations 2003' insert—

'or regulation 38(1)(b) of the Employment Equality (Age) Regulations 2006'.

57

(1)   The Employment Protection (Continuity of Employment) Regulations 1996 are amended in accordance with this paragraph.

(2)   In regulation 2 (application)—

(a)   omit the word 'or' at the end of paragraph (e); and

(b)   after paragraph (f) insert—

', or

(g)   a decision taken arising out of the use of the statutory duty to consider procedure contained in Schedule 6 to the Employment Equality (Age) Regulations 2006.'.

58

(1)   The National Minimum Wage Regulations 1999 are amended in accordance with this paragraph.

(2)   Omit regulation 12(2)(a).

(3)   Omit paragraphs (2) to (6) of regulation 13.

(4)   In regulation 13(7) for the words 'Paragraphs (1) and (2) do' substitute 'Paragraph (1) does'.

(5)   In relation to any case where, before the commencement date, a worker within the meaning of regulation 12(2) has attained the age of 26, sub-paragraph (2) does not apply.

59

The Statutory Paternity Pay and Statutory Adoption Pay (General) Regulations 2002 are amended as follows.

60

(1)   Regulation 32 (Treatment of persons as employees) is amended in accordance with this paragraph.

(2)   In paragraph (1)—

    (a)   at the beginning insert the words 'Subject to paragraph (1A),', and

    (b)   omit the words 'over the age of 16'.

(3)   After paragraph (1) insert—

'(1A)   Any person under the age of 16 who would have been treated as an employed earner or, as the case may be, would have been treated otherwise than as an employed earner by virtue of the Social Security (Categorisation of Earners) Regulations 1978 had he been aged 16 or over, shall be treated as if he is aged 16 or over for the purposes of paragraph (1).'.

61

(1)   Regulation 39(2) (Meaning of 'earnings') is amended in accordance with this paragraph.

(2)   At the end of sub-paragraph (a) insert ' (or would have been so excluded had he not been under the age of 16)'.

(3)   At the end of sub-paragraph (b) insert ' (or where such a payment or amount would have been so excluded and in consequence he would not have been entitled to statutory paternity pay or, as the case may be, statutory adoption pay had he not been under the age of 16)'.

62

(1)   Schedule 1A (occupational pension schemes) to the Employment Equality (Religion or Belief) Regulations 2003 is amended in accordance with this paragraph.

(2)   In paragraph 1(1)—

    (a)   in the definition of 'active member', 'deferred member', 'managers', 'pensioner member' and 'trustees or managers', omit the words 'as at the date of the coming into force of these Regulations', and

    (b)   in the definition of 'occupational pension scheme' omit the words 'as at the date of the coming into force of these Regulations'.

(3)   In paragraph 1(2) omit the words 'as at the date of the coming into force of these Regulations'.

63

(1) Schedule 1A (occupational pension schemes) to the Employment Equality (Sexual Orientation) Regulations 2003 is amended in accordance with this paragraph.

(2) In paragraph 1(1)—

(a) in the definition of 'active member', 'deferred member', 'managers', 'pensioner member' and 'trustees or managers', omit the words 'as at the date of the coming into force of these Regulations', and

(b) in the definition of 'occupational pension scheme' omit the words 'as at the date of the coming into force of these Regulations'.

(3) In paragraph 1(2) omit the words 'as at the date of the coming into force of these Regulations'.

64

(1) The Employment Act 2002 (Dispute Resolution) Regulations 2004 are amended in accordance with this paragraph.

(2) In regulation 4(1) (dismissals to which the dismissal and disciplinary procedures do not apply)—

(a) omit the word 'or' at the end of sub-paragraph (f); and

(b) after sub-paragraph (g) insert—

', or

(h) the reason (or, if more than one, the principal reason) for the dismissal is retirement of the employee (to be determined in accordance with section 98ZA to 98ZF of the 1996 Act)'.

SCHEDULE 9
REPEALS AND REVOCATIONS

Regulation 49(2)

(1) Repeals	
Short title and chapter	Extent of repeal
Marriage (Scotland) Act 1977 (c 15)	In section 9(1) the proviso, In section 12 the proviso, and In section 17 the proviso
Education (Scotland) Act 1980 (c 44)	Section 89
Solicitors (Scotland) Act 1980 (c 46)	Section 6(1)(a)
Weights and Measures Act 1985 (c 72)	Section 73(3)
Electricity Act 1989 (c 29)	In Schedule 10, paragraph 9(3)
Judicial Pensions and Retirement Act 1993 (c 8)	In Schedule 6, paragraph 66
Scottish Public Services Ombudsman Act 2002 (asp 11)	In Schedule 1, paragraph 4(1)(c) In Schedule 1, in paragraph 4(3), the words in brackets
Freedom of Information (Scotland) Act 2002 (asp 13)	Section 42(4)(b) In section 42(5), the words in brackets

(2) Revocations	
Title and reference	Extent of revocation
Coal and Other Mines (Sidings) Regulations 1956, Schedule to the Coal and Other Mines (Sidings) Order 1956 (SI 1956/1773)	Regulation 21 In regulation 22, the definition of locomotive
The Management and Administration of Safety and Health in Mines Regulations 1993 (SI 1993/1897)	Regulation 17(2)

APPENDIX 2
Council Directive 2000/78/EC

of 27 November 2000

establishing a general framework for equal treatment in employment and occupation

THE COUNCIL OF THE EUROPEAN UNION,

Having regard to the Treaty establishing the European Community, and in particular Article 13 thereof,

Having regard to the proposal from the Commission[1],

Having regard to the Opinion of the European Parliament[2],

Having regard to the Opinion of the Economic and Social Committee[3],

Having regard to the Opinion of the Committee of the Regions[4],

Whereas:

(1) In accordance with Article 6 of the Treaty on European Union, the European Union is founded on the principles of liberty, democracy, respect for human rights and fundamental freedoms, and the rule of law, principles which are common to all Member States and it respects fundamental rights, as guaranteed by the European Convention for the Protection of Human Rights and Fundamental Freedoms and as they result from the constitutional traditions common to the Member States, as general principles of Community law.

(2) The principle of equal treatment between women and men is well established by an important body of Community law, in particular in Council Directive 76/207/EEC of 9 February 1976 on the implementation of the principle of equal treatment for men and women as regards access to employment, vocational training and promotion, and working conditions[5].

(3) In implementing the principle of equal treatment, the Community should, in accordance with Article 3(2) of the EC Treaty, aim to eliminate inequalities, and to promote equality between men and women, especially since women are often the victims of multiple discrimination.

(4) The right of all persons to equality before the law and protection against discrimination constitutes a universal right recognised by the Universal Declaration of Human Rights, the United Nations Convention on the Elimination of All Forms of Discrimination against Women, United Nations Covenants on Civil and Political Rights and on Economic, Social and Cultural Rights and by the European Convention for the Protection of Human Rights and Fundamental Freedoms, to which

all Member States are signatories. Convention No 111 of the International Labour Organisation (ILO) prohibits discrimination in the field of employment and occupation.

(5)   It is important to respect such fundamental rights and freedoms. This Directive does not prejudice freedom of association, including the right to establish unions with others and to join unions to defend one's interests.

(6)   The Community Charter of the Fundamental Social Rights of Workers recognises the importance of combating every form of discrimination, including the need to take appropriate action for the social and economic integration of elderly and disabled people.

(7)   The EC Treaty includes among its objectives the promotion of coordination between employment policies of the Member States. To this end, a new employment chapter was incorporated in the EC Treaty as a means of developing a coordinated European strategy for employment to promote a skilled, trained and adaptable workforce.

(8)   The Employment Guidelines for 2000 agreed by the European Council at Helsinki on 10 and 11 December 1999 stress the need to foster a labour market favourable to social integration by formulating a coherent set of policies aimed at combating discrimination against groups such as persons with disability. They also emphasise the need to pay particular attention to supporting older workers, in order to increase their participation in the labour force.

(9)   Employment and occupation are key elements in guaranteeing equal opportunities for all and contribute strongly to the full participation of citizens in economic, cultural and social life and to realising their potential.

(10)   On 29 June 2000 the Council adopted Directive 2000/43/EC[6] implementing the principle of equal treatment between persons irrespective of racial or ethnic origin. That Directive already provides protection against such discrimination in the field of employment and occupation.

(11)   Discrimination based on religion or belief, disability, age or sexual orientation may undermine the achievement of the objectives of the EC Treaty, in particular the attainment of a high level of employment and social protection, raising the standard of living and the quality of life, economic and social cohesion and solidarity, and the free movement of persons.

(12)   To this end, any direct or indirect discrimination based on religion or belief, disability, age or sexual orientation as regards the areas covered by this Directive should be prohibited throughout the Community. This prohibition of discrimination should also apply to nationals of third countries but does not cover differences of treatment based on nationality and is without prejudice to provisions governing the entry and residence of third-country nationals and their access to employment and occupation.

(13) This Directive does not apply to social security and social protection schemes whose benefits are not treated as income within the meaning given to that term for the purpose of applying Article 141 of the EC Treaty, nor to any kind of payment by the State aimed at providing access to employment or maintaining employment.

(14) This Directive shall be without prejudice to national provisions laying down retirement ages.

(15) The appreciation of the facts from which it may be inferred that there has been direct or indirect discrimination is a matter for national judicial or other competent bodies, in accordance with rules of national law or practice. Such rules may provide, in particular, for indirect discrimination to be established by any means including on the basis of statistical evidence.

(16) The provision of measures to accommodate the needs of disabled people at the workplace plays an important role in combating discrimination on grounds of disability.

(17) This Directive does not require the recruitment, promotion, maintenance in employment or training of an individual who is not competent, capable and available to perform the essential functions of the post concerned or to undergo the relevant training, without prejudice to the obligation to provide reasonable accommodation for people with disabilities.

(18) This Directive does not require, in particular, the armed forces and the police, prison or emergency services to recruit or maintain in employment persons who do not have the required capacity to carry out the range of functions that they may be called upon to perform with regard to the legitimate objective of preserving the operational capacity of those services.

(19) Moreover, in order that the Member States may continue to safeguard the combat effectiveness of their armed forces, they may choose not to apply the provisions of this Directive concerning disability and age to all or part of their armed forces. The Member States which make that choice must define the scope of that derogation.

(20) Appropriate measures should be provided, i.e. effective and practical measures to adapt the workplace to the disability, for example adapting premises and equipment, patterns of working time, the distribution of tasks or the provision of training or integration resources.

(21) To determine whether the measures in question give rise to a disproportionate burden, account should be taken in particular of the financial and other costs entailed, the scale and financial resources of the organisation or undertaking and the possibility of obtaining public funding or any other assistance.

(22) This Directive is without prejudice to national laws on marital status and the benefits dependent thereon.

(23) In very limited circumstances, a difference of treatment may be justified where a characteristic related to religion or belief, disability, age or sexual orientation constitutes a genuine and determining occupational requirement, when the objective is legitimate and the requirement is proportionate. Such circumstances should be included in the information provided by the Member States to the Commission.

(24) The European Union in its Declaration No 11 on the status of churches and non-confessional organisations, annexed to the Final Act of the Amsterdam Treaty, has explicitly recognised that it respects and does not prejudice the status under national law of churches and religious associations or communities in the Member States and that it equally respects the status of philosophical and non-confessional organisations. With this in view, Member States may maintain or lay down specific provisions on genuine, legitimate and justified occupational requirements which might be required for carrying out an occupational activity.

(25) The prohibition of age discrimination is an essential part of meeting the aims set out in the Employment Guidelines and encouraging diversity in the workforce. However, differences in treatment in connection with age may be justified under certain circumstances and therefore require specific provisions which may vary in accordance with the situation in Member States. It is therefore essential to distinguish between differences in treatment which are justified, in particular by legitimate employment policy, labour market and vocational training objectives, and discrimination which must be prohibited.

(26) The prohibition of discrimination should be without prejudice to the maintenance or adoption of measures intended to prevent or compensate for disadvantages suffered by a group of persons of a particular religion or belief, disability, age or sexual orientation, and such measures may permit organisations of persons of a particular religion or belief, disability, age or sexual orientation where their main object is the promotion of the special needs of those persons.

(27) In its Recommendation 86/379/EEC of 24 July 1986 on the employment of disabled people in the Community[7], the Council established a guideline framework setting out examples of positive action to promote the employment and training of disabled people, and in its Resolution of 17 June 1999 on equal employment opportunities for people with disabilities[8], affirmed the importance of giving specific attention *inter alia* to recruitment, retention, training and lifelong learning with regard to disabled persons.

(28) This Directive lays down minimum requirements, thus giving the Member States the option of introducing or maintaining more favourable provisions. The implementation of this Directive should not serve to justify any regression in relation to the situation which already prevails in each Member State.

(29) Persons who have been subject to discrimination based on religion or belief, disability, age or sexual orientation should have adequate means of legal protection. To provide a more effective level of protection, associations or legal entities should also be empowered to engage in proceedings, as the Member States so determine, either on behalf or in support of any victim, without prejudice to national rules of procedure concerning representation and defence before the courts.

(30) The effective implementation of the principle of equality requires adequate judicial protection against victimisation.

(31) The rules on the burden of proof must be adapted when there is a prima facie case of discrimination and, for the principle of equal treatment to be applied effectively, the burden of proof must shift back to the respondent when evidence of such discrimination is brought. However, it is not for the respondent to prove that the plaintiff adheres to a particular religion or belief, has a particular disability, is of a particular age or has a particular sexual orientation.

(32) Member States need not apply the rules on the burden of proof to proceedings in which it is for the court or other competent body to investigate the facts of the case. The procedures thus referred to are those in which the plaintiff is not required to prove the facts, which it is for the court or competent body to investigate.

(33) Member States should promote dialogue between the social partners and, within the framework of national practice, with non-governmental organisations to address different forms of discrimination at the workplace and to combat them.

(34) The need to promote peace and reconciliation between the major communities in Northern Ireland necessitates the incorporation of particular provisions into this Directive.

(35) Member States should provide for effective, proportionate and dissuasive sanctions in case of breaches of the obligations under this Directive.

(36) Member States may entrust the social partners, at their joint request, with the implementation of this Directive, as regards the provisions concerning collective agreements, provided they take any necessary steps to ensure that they are at all times able to guarantee the results required by this Directive.

(37) In accordance with the principle of subsidiarity set out in Article 5 of the EC Treaty, the objective of this Directive, namely the creation within the Community of a level playing-field as regards equality in employment and occupation, cannot be sufficiently achieved by the Member States and can therefore, by reason of the scale and impact of the action, be better achieved at Community level. In accordance with the principle of proportionality, as set out in that Article, this Directive does not go beyond what is necessary in order to achieve that objective,

HAS ADOPTED THIS DIRECTIVE:

CHAPTER I

GENERAL PROVISIONS

Article 1

Purpose

The purpose of this Directive is to lay down a general framework for combating discrimination on the grounds of religion or belief, disability, age or sexual orientation as regards employment and occupation, with a view to putting into effect in the Member States the principle of equal treatment.

Article 2

Concept of discrimination

1   For the purposes of this Directive, the 'principle of equal treatment' shall mean that there shall be no direct or indirect discrimination whatsoever on any of the grounds referred to in Article 1.

2   For the purposes of paragraph 1:

    (a)   direct discrimination shall be taken to occur where one person is treated less favourably than another is, has been or would be treated in a comparable situation, on any of the grounds referred to in Article 1;

    (b)   indirect discrimination shall be taken to occur where an apparently neutral provision, criterion or practice would put persons having a particular religion or belief, a particular disability, a particular age, or a particular sexual orientation at a particular disadvantage compared with other persons unless:

        (i)   that provision, criterion or practice is objectively justified by a legitimate aim and the means of achieving that aim are appropriate and necessary, or

        (ii)   as regards persons with a particular disability, the employer or any person or organisation to whom this Directive applies, is obliged, under national legislation, to take appropriate measures in line with the principles contained in Article 5 in order to eliminate disadvantages entailed by such provision, criterion or practice.

3   Harassment shall be deemed to be a form of discrimination within the meaning of paragraph 1, when unwanted conduct related to any of the grounds referred to in Article 1 takes place with the purpose or effect of violating the dignity of a person and of creating an intimidating, hostile, degrading, humiliating or offensive environment. In this context, the concept of harassment may be defined in accordance with the national laws and practice of the Member States.

4   An instruction to discriminate against persons on any of the grounds referred to in Article 1 shall be deemed to be discrimination within the meaning of paragraph 1.

5   This Directive shall be without prejudice to measures laid down by national law which, in a democratic society, are necessary for public security, for the maintenance of public order and the prevention of criminal offences, for the protection of health and for the protection of the rights and freedoms of others.

Article 3

Scope

1   Within the limits of the areas of competence conferred on the Community, this Directive shall apply to all persons, as regards both the public and private sectors, including public bodies, in relation to:

   (a)   conditions for access to employment, to self-employment or to occupation, including selection criteria and recruitment conditions, whatever the branch of activity and at all levels of the professional hierarchy, including promotion;

   (b)   access to all types and to all levels of vocational guidance, vocational training, advanced vocational training and retraining, including practical work experience;

   (c)   employment and working conditions, including dismissals and pay;

   (d)   membership of, and involvement in, an organisation of workers or employers, or any organisation whose members carry on a particular profession, including the benefits provided for by such organisations.

2   This Directive does not cover differences of treatment based on nationality and is without prejudice to provisions and conditions relating to the entry into and residence of third-country nationals and stateless persons in the territory of Member States, and to any treatment which arises from the legal status of the third-country nationals and stateless persons concerned.

3   This Directive does not apply to payments of any kind made by state schemes or similar, including state social security or social protection schemes.

4   Member States may provide that this Directive, in so far as it relates to discrimination on the grounds of disability and age, shall not apply to the armed forces.

Article 4

Occupational requirements

1   Notwithstanding Article 2(1) and (2), Member States may provide that a difference of treatment which is based on a characteristic related to any of the grounds referred to in Article 1 shall not constitute discrimination where, by reason of the nature of the particular occupational activities concerned or of the context in which they are carried out, such a characteristic constitutes a

genuine and determining occupational requirement, provided that the objective is legitimate and the requirement is proportionate.

2   Member States may maintain national legislation in force at the date of adoption of this Directive or provide for future legislation incorporating national practices existing at the date of adoption of this Directive pursuant to which, in the case of occupational activities within churches and other public or private organisations the ethos of which is based on religion or belief, a difference of treatment based on a person's religion or belief shall not constitute discrimination where, by reason of the nature of these activities or of the context in which they are carried out, a person's religion or belief constitute a genuine, legitimate and justified occupational requirement, having regard to the organisation's ethos. This difference of treatment shall be implemented taking account of Member States' constitutional provisions and principles, as well as the general principles of Community law, and should not justify discrimination on another ground.

Provided that its provisions are otherwise complied with, this Directive shall thus not prejudice the right of churches and other public or private organisations, the ethos of which is based on religion or belief, acting in conformity with national constitutions and laws, to require individuals working for them to act in good faith and with loyalty to the organisation's ethos.

Article 5

Reasonable accommodation for disabled persons

In order to guarantee compliance with the principle of equal treatment in relation to persons with disabilities, reasonable accommodation shall be provided. This means that employers shall take appropriate measures, where needed in a particular case, to enable a person with a disability to have access to, participate in, or advance in employment, or to undergo training, unless such measures would impose a disproportionate burden on the employer. This burden shall not be disproportionate when it is sufficiently remedied by measures existing within the framework of the disability policy of the Member State concerned.

Article 6

Justification of differences of treatment on grounds of age

1   Notwithstanding Article 2(2), Member States may provide that differences of treatment on grounds of age shall not constitute discrimination, if, within the context of national law, they are objectively and reasonably justified by a legitimate aim, including legitimate employment policy, labour market and vocational training objectives, and if the means of achieving that aim are appropriate and necessary.

Such differences of treatment may include, among others:

(a)   the setting of special conditions on access to employment and vocational training, employment and occupation, including dismissal and remuneration conditions, for young people, older workers and persons with caring responsibilities in order to promote their vocational integration or ensure their protection;

(b)   the fixing of minimum conditions of age, professional experience or seniority in service for access to employment or to certain advantages linked to employment;

(c)   the fixing of a maximum age for recruitment which is based on the training requirements of the post in question or the need for a reasonable period of employment before retirement.

2   Notwithstanding Article 2(2), Member States may provide that the fixing for occupational social security schemes of ages for admission or entitlement to retirement or invalidity benefits, including the fixing under those schemes of different ages for employees or groups or categories of employees, and the use, in the context of such schemes, of age criteria in actuarial calculations, does not constitute discrimination on the grounds of age, provided this does not result in discrimination on the grounds of sex.

Article 7

Positive action

1   With a view to ensuring full equality in practice, the principle of equal treatment shall not prevent any Member State from maintaining or adopting specific measures to prevent or compensate for disadvantages linked to any of the grounds referred to in Article 1.

2   With regard to disabled persons, the principle of equal treatment shall be without prejudice to the right of Member States to maintain or adopt provisions on the protection of health and safety at work or to measures aimed at creating or maintaining provisions or facilities for safeguarding or promoting their integration into the working environment.

Article 8

Minimum requirements

1   Member States may introduce or maintain provisions which are more favourable to the protection of the principle of equal treatment than those laid down in this Directive.

2   The implementation of this Directive shall under no circumstances constitute grounds for a reduction in the level of protection against discrimination already afforded by Member States in the fields covered by this Directive.

CHAPTER II

REMEDIES AND ENFORCEMENT

Article 9

Defence of rights

1   Member States shall ensure that judicial and/or administrative procedures, including where they deem it appropriate conciliation procedures, for the enforcement of obligations under this Directive are available to all persons

who consider themselves wronged by failure to apply the principle of equal treatment to them, even after the relationship in which the discrimination is alleged to have occurred has ended.

2   Member States shall ensure that associations, organisations or other legal entities which have, in accordance with the criteria laid down by their national law, a legitimate interest in ensuring that the provisions of this Directive are complied with, may engage, either on behalf or in support of the complainant, with his or her approval, in any judicial and/or administrative procedure provided for the enforcement of obligations under this Directive.

3   Paragraphs 1 and 2 are without prejudice to national rules relating to time limits for bringing actions as regards the principle of equality of treatment.

Article 10

Burden of proof

1   Member States shall take such measures as are necessary, in accordance with their national judicial systems, to ensure that, when persons who consider themselves wronged because the principle of equal treatment has not been applied to them establish, before a court or other competent authority, facts from which it may be presumed that there has been direct or indirect discrimination, it shall be for the respondent to prove that there has been no breach of the principle of equal treatment.

2   Paragraph 1 shall not prevent Member States from introducing rules of evidence which are more favourable to plaintiffs.

3   Paragraph 1 shall not apply to criminal procedures.

4   Paragraphs 1, 2 and 3 shall also apply to any legal proceedings commenced in accordance with Article 9(2).

5   Member States need not apply paragraph 1 to proceedings in which it is for the court or competent body to investigate the facts of the case.

Article 11

Victimisation

Member States shall introduce into their national legal systems such measures as are necessary to protect employees against dismissal or other adverse treatment by the employer as a reaction to a complaint within the undertaking or to any legal proceedings aimed at enforcing compliance with the principle of equal treatment.

Article 12

Dissemination of information

Member States shall take care that the provisions adopted pursuant to this Directive, together with the relevant provisions already in force in this field, are brought to the attention of the persons concerned by all appropriate means, for example at the workplace, throughout their territory.

Article 13

Social dialogue

1   Member States shall, in accordance with their national traditions and practice, take adequate measures to promote dialogue between the social partners with a view to fostering equal treatment, including through the monitoring of workplace practices, collective agreements, codes of conduct and through research or exchange of experiences and good practices.

2   Where consistent with their national traditions and practice, Member States shall encourage the social partners, without prejudice to their autonomy, to conclude at the appropriate level agreements laying down anti-discrimination rules in the fields referred to in Article 3 which fall within the scope of collective bargaining. These agreements shall respect the minimum requirements laid down by this Directive and by the relevant national implementing measures.

Article 14

Dialogue with non-governmental organisations

Member States shall encourage dialogue with appropriate non-governmental organisations which have, in accordance with their national law and practice, a legitimate interest in contributing to the fight against discrimination on any of the grounds referred to in Article 1 with a view to promoting the principle of equal treatment.

CHAPTER III

PARTICULAR PROVISIONS

Article 15

Northern Ireland

1   In order to tackle the under-representation of one of the major religious communities in the police service of Northern Ireland, differences in treatment regarding recruitment into that service, including its support staff, shall not constitute discrimination insofar as those differences in treatment are expressly authorised by national legislation.

2   In order to maintain a balance of opportunity in employment for teachers in Northern Ireland while furthering the reconciliation of historical divisions between the major religious communities there, the provisions on religion or belief in this Directive shall not apply to the recruitment of teachers in schools in Northern Ireland in so far as this is expressly authorised by national legislation.

CHAPTER IV

FINAL PROVISIONS

Article 16

Compliance

Member States shall take the necessary measures to ensure that:

    (a)   any laws, regulations and administrative provisions contrary to the principle of equal treatment are abolished;

    (b)   any provisions contrary to the principle of equal treatment which are included in contracts or collective agreements, internal rules of undertakings or rules governing the independent occupations and professions and workers' and employers' organisations are, or may be, declared null and void or are amended.

Article 17

Sanctions

Member States shall lay down the rules on sanctions applicable to infringements of the national provisions adopted pursuant to this Directive and shall take all measures necessary to ensure that they are applied. The sanctions, which may comprise the payment of compensation to the victim, must be effective, proportionate and dissuasive. Member States shall notify those provisions to the Commission by 2 December 2003 at the latest and shall notify it without delay of any subsequent amendment affecting them.

Article 18

Implementation

Member States shall adopt the laws, regulations and administrative provisions necessary to comply with this Directive by 2 December 2003 at the latest or may entrust the social partners, at their joint request, with the implementation of this Directive as regards provisions concerning collective agreements. In such cases, Member States shall ensure that, no later than 2 December 2003, the social partners introduce the necessary measures by agreement, the Member States concerned being required to take any necessary measures to enable them at any time to be in a position to guarantee the results imposed by this Directive. They shall forthwith inform the Commission thereof.

In order to take account of particular conditions, Member States may, if necessary, have an additional period of 3 years from 2 December 2003, that is to say a total of 6 years, to implement the provisions of this Directive on age and disability discrimination. In that event they shall inform the Commission forthwith. Any Member State which chooses to use this additional period shall report annually to the Commission on the steps it is taking to tackle age and disability discrimination and on the progress it is making towards implementation. The Commission shall report annually to the Council.

When Member States adopt these measures, they shall contain a reference to this Directive or be accompanied by such reference on the occasion of their official publication. The methods of making such reference shall be laid down by Member States.

Article 19

Report

1 Member States shall communicate to the Commission, by 2 December 2005 at the latest and every five years thereafter, all the information necessary for the Commission to draw up a report to the European Parliament and the Council on the application of this Directive.

2 The Commission's report shall take into account, as appropriate, the viewpoints of the social partners and relevant non-governmental organisations. In accordance with the principle of gender mainstreaming, this report shall, inter alia, provide an assessment of the impact of the measures taken on women and men. In the light of the information received, this report shall include, if necessary, proposals to revise and update this Directive.

Article 20

Entry into force

This Directive shall enter into force on the day of its publication in the *Official Journal of the European Communities*.

Article 21

Addressees

This Directive is addressed to the Member States.

Done at Brussels, 27 November 2000.

1　OJ C 177E, 27.6.2000, p 42.
2　Opinion delivered on 12 October 2000 (not yet published in the Official Journal).
3　OJ C 204, 18.7.2000, p 82.
4　OJ C 226, 8.8.2000, p 1.
5　OJ L 39, 14.2.1976, p 40.
6　OJ L 180, 19.7.2000, p 22.
7　OJ L 225, 12.8.1986, p 43.
8　OJ C 186, 2.7.199, p 3.

APPENDIX 3
ACAS Age and the Workplace

From 1 October 2006 the Employment Equality (Age) Regulations make it unlawful to discriminate against workers, employees, job seekers and trainees because of their age. This booklet describes the regulations and gives you guidance on how to implement them.

Terms in this guide – workers and employees
Workers are covered in the regulations and in this guidance.
Workers often undertake roles similar to employees but do not have contracts of employment like employees, these include office holders, police, barristers and partners in a business.

Our Guidance uses the term 'employee' throughout to cover all workers except under length of service issues, retirement, and right to request which are for a narrower range of employees.

Fairness at work and good job performance go hand in hand. Tackling discrimination helps to attract, motivate and retain staff and enhances your reputation as an employer. Eliminating discrimination helps everyone to have an equal opportunity to work and to develop their skills.

Employees who are subjected to discrimination, harassment or victimisation may:

- be unhappy, less productive and less motivated
- resign
- make a complaint to an employment tribunal.

In addition employers may find:

- their reputation as a business and as an employer may be damaged
- the cost of recruitment and training will increase because of higher employee turnover

they may be liable to pay compensation following a claim to an employment tribunal – there is no upper limit to the amount of this compensation.

There is already legislation to protect people against discrimination on the grounds of sex, race, disability, gender reassignment, sexual orientation and religion or belief.

The new regulations should pose few difficulties in organisations where people are treated fairly and with consideration.

This guidance aims to:

- help employers and vocational training providers fulfil their obligations under the Employment Equality (Age) Regulations 2006

- make employees, job seekers and trainees aware of how they will be affected by the regulations.

What the regulations say – in summary

These regulations apply to all employers, private and public sector vocational training providers, trade unions, professional organisations, employer organisations and trustees and managers of occupational pension schemes. In this context an employer is anyone who has employees or who enters into a contract with a person for them to do work. The regulations cover recruitment, terms and conditions, promotions, transfers, dismissals and training. They do not cover the provision of goods and services.

The regulations make it unlawful on the grounds of age to:

- discriminate directly against anyone – that is, to treat them less favourably than others because of their age – unless objectively justified

- discriminate indirectly against anyone – that is, to apply a criterion, provision or practice which disadvantages people of a particular age unless it can be objectively justified

- subject someone to harassment. Harassment is unwanted conduct that violates a person's dignity or creates an intimidating, hostile, degrading, humiliating or offensive environment for them having regard to all the circumstances including the perception of the victim

- victimise someone because they have made or intend to make a complaint or allegation or have given or intend to give evidence in relation to a complaint of discrimination on grounds of age

- discriminate against someone, in certain circumstances, after the working relationship has ended.

Employers could be responsible for the acts of employees who discriminate on grounds of age. This makes it important to train staff about the regulations.

Introduction

Upper age limits on unfair dismissal and redundancy will be removed.

There will be a national default retirement age of 65, making compulsory retirement below 65 unlawful unless objectively justified.

Employees will have the right to request to work beyond 65 or any other retirement age set by the company. The employer has a duty to consider such requests.

There are limited circumstances when discrimination may be lawful (see section on genuine occupational requirements, objective justifications, exceptions and exemptions).

This guide does not use the precise legal terms contained within the regulations – reference needs to be made to the regulations.

Guidance for employers

What do the regulations mean?

A brief explanation of the regulations

Direct discrimination

Direct discrimination is less favourable treatment because of someone's age.

For example it will be unlawful on the grounds of age to:

- decide not to employ someone
- dismiss them
- refuse to provide them with training
- deny them promotion
- give them adverse terms and conditions
- retire an employee before the employer's usual retirement age (if there is one) or retire an employee before the default retirement age of 65 without an objective justification (see page 30).

Example: Whilst being interviewed, a job applicant says that she took her professional qualification 30 years ago. Although she has all the skills and competences required of the job holder, the organisation decides not to offer her the job because of her age. This is direct discrimination.

NOTE: A job applicant can make a claim to an employment tribunal, it is not necessary for them to have been employed by the organisation to make a claim of discrimination.

Indirect discrimination

Indirect discrimination means selection criteria, policies, benefits, employment rules or any other practices which, although they are applied to all employees, have the effect of disadvantaging people of a particular age unless the practice can be justified. Indirect discrimination is unlawful whether it is intentional or not.

Lawful discrimination

There are limited circumstances when it is lawful to treat people differently because of their age.

It is not unlawful to discriminate on the grounds of age if:

- there is an objective justification for treating people differently – for example, it might be necessary to fix a maximum age for the recruitment or promotion of employees (this maximum age might reflect the training requirements of the post or the need for a reasonable period of employment before retirement)

- where a person is older than, or within six months of, the employer's normal retirement age, or 65 if the employer doesn't have one, there is a specific exemption allowing employers to refuse to recruit that person.

- the discrimination is covered by one of the exceptions or exemptions given in the regulations – for example pay related to the National Minimum Wage

- there is a genuine occupational requirement (GOR) that a person must be of a certain age – for example, if you are producing a play which has parts for older or younger characters.

For more details see the section on genuine occupational requirements, objective justifications, exceptions and exemptions on page 30.

Harassment

Harassment includes behaviour that is offensive, frightening or in any way distressing. It may be intentional bullying which is obvious or violent, but it can also be unintentional, subtle and insidious. It may involve nicknames, teasing, name calling or other behaviour which is not with malicious intent but which is upsetting. It may be about the individual's age or it may be about the age of those with whom the individual associates. It may not be targeted at an individual(s) but consist of a general culture which, for instance, appears to tolerate the telling of ageist jokes.

You may be held responsible for the actions of your employees – as well as the employees being individually responsible. If harassment takes place in the workplace or at a time and place associated with the workplace, for example a work-related social gathering, you may be liable. You may be ordered to pay compensation unless it can be shown that you took reasonable steps to prevent harassment. Individuals who harass may also be ordered to pay compensation.

It is good practice to protect your workers from harassment by third parties, such as service users and customers.

When you are investigating claims of harassment, consider all the circumstances before reaching a conclusion. Harassment is often subjective so think carefully about the complainant's perception of what has happened to them. Ask yourself if what has taken place could 'be reasonably considered to have caused offence?'

Example: A young employee is continually told he is 'wet behind the ears' and 'straight out of the pram' which he finds humiliating and distressing. This is harassment.

Example: An employee has a father working in the same workplace. People in the workplace often tell jokes about 'old fogies' and tease the employee about teaching 'old dogs new tricks'. This may be harassment on the grounds of age, even though it is not the victim's own age that is the subject of the teasing.

Victimisation

Victimisation is when an individual is treated detrimentally because they have made a complaint or intend to make a complaint about discrimination or harassment or have given evidence or intend to give evidence relating to a complaint about discrimination or harassment.

They may become labelled 'troublemaker', denied promotion or training, or be 'sent to Coventry' by their colleagues. If this happens or if you fail to take reasonable steps to prevent it from happening, you may be ordered to pay compensation. Individuals who victimise may also be ordered to pay compensation.

> **Example:** An employee claims discrimination against their employer on the grounds of age. A work colleague gives evidence on their behalf at the employment tribunal. When the work colleague applies for promotion her application is rejected even though she is able to show she has all the necessary skills and experience. Her manager maintains she is a 'troublemaker' because she had given evidence at the tribunal and should not be promoted. This is victimisation.

Discrimination, harassment or victimisation following the end of a working relationship covers issues such as references either written or verbal.

> **Example:** A manager is approached by someone from another organisation. He says that Ms 'A' has applied for a job and asks for a reference. The manager says that he cannot recommend her as she was not accepted by other staff because she was 'too young and inexperienced'. This is direct discrimination because of age.

An equality policy and action plan

You can start to address fairness at work by writing an equality policy or updating an existing one – with an action plan to back it up. You may already have equal opportunity or diversity policies which cover age but, if not, age should now be included. It is good practice in drawing up a policy to consult with your workforce or their representatives.

To make sure age discrimination is eliminated in your workforce draw up an action plan to review your policies for:

- recruitment, selection and promotion
- training
- pay, benefits and other conditions
- bullying and harassment
- retirement.

Also consider the make up of your workforce and whether positive action is required to tackle any age imbalance (guidance on positive action can be found on page 29).

Introduction

Ensure that all employees know about your equality policy and what is expected of them; a communications strategy should be a key part of your action plan.

Employees are often attracted to an organisation if it has a robust equality policy. Although not a legal necessity, such a policy makes applicants feel confident and discourages those who do not embrace equality of opportunity.

Acas can help you to draw up and implement an equality policy and to train you and your employees to use it. For further information see the Acas booklet *Tackling discrimination and promoting equality – good practice guidance for employers*.

Recruitment

See comment about specific recruitment exemption – on page 7.

Base your decisions about recruitment on the skills required to do the job. Provide training to help those making judgements to be objective and avoid stereotyping people because of their age.

Application form

Remove age/date of birth from the main application form and include it in a diversity monitoring form to be retained by HR/Personnel. In addition review your application form to ensure that you are not asking for unnecessary information about periods and dates. Asking for age-related information on an application form could allow discrimination to take place.

Monitor your decisions for any evidence of age bias, particularly after shortlisting (see page 14).

Job description and person specification

A job description outlines the duties required of a particular post holder. A person specification gives the skills, knowledge and experience required to carry out these duties.

Avoid references, however oblique, to age in both the job description and the person specification. For example, avoid asking for 'so many years' experience. This may rule out younger people who have the skills required but have not had the opportunity to demonstrate them over an extended period. A jobseeker could challenge any time requirement and you may have to justify it in objective terms.

Example: Scrape and Co, a local driving school have been advertising for instructors who must be qualified and have a minimum of 10 years driving experience. Effectively this would prevent people under 28 applying for this job and could therefore be discriminatory. Scrape would need to justify this 10 year experience criterion if challenged by a jobseeker under 28 especially as only four years experience is formally required to qualify as a driving instructor.

Educational and vocational qualifications have changed and developed over the years. Make sure that the qualifications you specify are not disadvantaging people at different ages.

Ask yourself:

● are the qualifications really necessary?

● are they still current?

● are there other ways of specifying the skill level you require?

If you are going to be specific about qualifications be sure you can justify their need in objective terms and make it clear you will consider equivalent or similar level alternative qualifications.

Advertising

It makes sound business sense to attract a wide field of applicants – if you rely on the friends or family of current staff you will miss the opportunity to tap into the diverse skills of your local community.

Advertise in a way that will be accessible to a large audience. For instance, avoid using a publication or employment agency that is focused on a niche market. This may limit the diversity of applicants and may constitute indirect discrimination.

Example: An advertisement placed only in a magazine aimed at young people may indirectly discriminate against older people because they are less likely to subscribe to the magazine and therefore less likely to find out about the vacancy and apply.

Write your job advert using the information in the job description and person specification. Avoid using language that might imply that you would prefer someone of a certain age, such as 'mature', 'young' or 'energetic'.

Example: Try to avoid stereotyping. For example, which vacancy is asking for an older person and which a younger person?

1   'We require an enthusiastic person, flexible enough to fit in with our fast moving market place, not afraid of challenging the status quo and in touch with latest thinking'

2   'Our ideal candidate will need to manage competing demands. He or she should be reflective, and have boardroom presence and gravitas'.

Be clear about what skills you actually need for the post – and what skills are merely desirable or reflect the personal preferences of the selector. Recruit and/or promote for these essential skills and aptitudes

– you can always decide not to recruit or promote someone if the applicant does not have these necessary skills or abilities.

As well as considering the language you use in adverts think also about the hidden messages that may be present in any promotional literature that you have, particularly the pictures.

Graduates

If you ask for graduates, remember that the term can be interpreted as code for someone in their early twenties. Graduates can be almost any age. Make it clear that you are interested in the qualification and not the age of the applicant.

A local engineering company is looking for a new Personnel Officer and asks for applicants to be graduates and hold the IPD qualification. As many more people attend university today than say 25 years ago, there is a lower chance that older Personnel Officers will be university graduates even though holding the IPD qualification and having considerable practical experience. This graduate requirement might thus be indirect age discrimination if the employer is unable to justify it. Remember also that the IPD qualification was formerly the IPM qualification.

If you limit your recruitment to university 'milk rounds' only, you may find that this is indirect age discrimination as this practice would severely restrict the chances of someone over say, 25 applying for your vacancies. If challenged you would need to objectively justify this practice (see section on genuine occupational requirements, objective justifications, exceptions and exemptions).

Consider enhancing any 'milk round' programme with a broader recruitment strategy, using other avenues to capture a wider pool of applicants of differing ages.

Shortlisting

If you have removed age-related material from your application form then you will generally not know a person's age although applicants may make reference to their age on the form so this is not always the case.

Whether or not you know someone's age, it is important that those doing the shortlisting, ideally more than one person, base their decisions on skills and ability alone. They should be trained, reminded of their responsibility not to discriminate on age grounds and use the requirements of the person specification to judge applicants.

Before moving on to the next stage of the recruitment process, check that no bias, deliberate or unintentional, has influenced decisions. In all organisations this check should be carried out by someone who has not been involved in the shortlisting. In all instances, you should record your decisions and retain these records, ideally for 12 months.

Interviewing

Interviews should preferably not be carried out by one person on their own. When interviewing, try to avoid:

Asking questions related to age, for example, 'how would you feel about managing older/younger people?'

Throwaway comments such as 'you're a bit young for a post of this responsibility' or 'don't you think someone like you should be looking for something with more responsibility'.

Focus on the applicant's competence and where more than one demonstrates the required competence the one who is more competent or offers the best skill mix should be appointed.

Check decisions for any bias and make sure interviewers have received training in the skills required and equal opportunities/ diversity.

Again, in all instances, record your decisions and retain these records, ideally for 12 months from the date of the interviews.

Working with employment agencies

Introduction

If you use a recruitment agency you need to be sure the agency acts appropriately and in accordance with your company's equality and diversity policies.

If you tell an employment agency to discriminate on age grounds because you consider you have objective justification for doing so, then the regulations enable the agency to rely on this justification if challenged. In such circumstances the agency should obtain this justification in writing from the employer and if at all unhappy to raise that with the employer.

Vocational training

As well as training provided by employers for their own employees, the regulations also cover organisations providing vocational education and training to the wider community. For the purpose of anti-discrimination law, all forms of vocational training including general educational provision at further, higher and other adult education institutions will be covered.

This means that vocational training providers will not be able to set age limits or age related criteria:

- for entry to training; or

- in the terms under which they provide training, for example when offering help with costs to encourage participation among under represented groups of people.

As an employer, training provider, college or university you will need to consider the following questions:

- do you set a minimum or maximum age for entry generally or in relation to admission or access to particular courses? If so, what are the justifications for these?

- even if you do not have formal minimum or maximum ages, is age taken into account when you consider applications for admission or access, eg do you offer preferential fee discount arrangements based on age?

In either case, you need to consider:

- can you objectively justify any age-related criterion, eg what evidence have you in support of restricting such financial help to a particular age group?

- what legitimate aim does any age-related criterion help you achieve, eg have you clear evidence that demonstrates particular age groups would be excluded from your learning provision if they had to pay full fees?

- are your age-related criteria a proportionate means of achieving that aim?

- is there another way of achieving that aim without resorting to discrimination?

The EU Employment Directive allows for the setting of age requirements relating to institutions of further and higher education and in respect of access to vocational training if they can be objectively justified, for example on the grounds of vocational integration.

Retaining good staff

Many factors motivate employees and make them want to stay with an organisation. People are more likely to feel positive about an organisation if they are treated fairly and with consideration regardless of their age.

Promotion and training

Opportunities for promotion and training should be made known to all employees and be available to everyone on a fair and equal basis.

Where employees apply for internal transfers take care with informal and verbal references between departmental heads, supervisors, etc. These references are covered by the regulations and should be fair and non-discriminatory.

Job-related training or development opportunities should be available to all employees regardless of age – monitor the training to make sure no particular age group is missing out.

Review the style and location of training to ensure:

- there are no barriers to any particular age group participating

- it is suitable for people of all ages

- everyone is encouraged to participate.

For example, if you are using computer-based training, do not assume everyone will be fully competent using a PC.

Age discrimination awareness

However large or small an organisation, it is good practice for them to have an Equality Policy and to train all employees and update them on a regular basis. This will help to reduce the likelihood of discrimination, harassment and victimisation taking place and may help to limit liability if a complaint is made.

All employees should understand:

- what the terms 'discrimination' and 'harassment' mean
- why discrimination and harassment are hurtful, unlawful and totally unacceptable.

Tell all employees about your company policy on age discrimination and train those who make decisions that affect others. Training should apply not only to those who recruit and select but also to those involved in day-to-day decisions about work allocation, performance appraisal, etc. Supervisors and managers also need training in recognising and dealing with bullying and harassment.

Performance appraisal

Check any performance appraisal system you have to ensure that it is working fairly and without bias. Many people have preconceptions about age and these can influence the judgements we make about people. If these preconceptions appear in performance appraisals through use of inappropriate comments – such as 'does well despite their age' or 'shows remarkable maturity for their age' – they will undermine the whole basis of a fair appraisal system. Such comments could also lead to further discrimination when decisions about promotion or work allocation are being made.

A fair and transparent appraisal system will become increasingly important when the changes to the retirement age are introduced. However, young people in the early stages of their career also need to be assessed on their actual performance unclouded by any preconceptions about their age.

Example: Two candidates have done equally well for the post on offer, so the selectors decide to review previous assessments to try and draw a fair distinction between them. On one they read: 'Despite his many years with the company John remains capable and enthusiastic' and 'John does very well at work considering his age'.

There are no such comments on Mark's assessments.

Which candidate now has a question mark against them?

Treat all employees the same when setting objectives or measuring performance. Ignoring shortfalls in performance because an employee is nearing retirement may be discriminatory – particularly if the same short-falls are addressed in younger employees.

Redundancy selection

Check that your selection processes for redundancy are free of age discrimination. This means that practices such as last in first out (LIFO), and using length of service in any selection criteria are likely to be age discriminatory.

Policies and procedures

Review policies and procedures for age bias, including those covering:

- sick absence
- leave and holidays
- discipline and grievances
- staff transfers
- flexible working
- use of computers
- individual space requirements (ergonomic policies).

Annex 3 shows you how to use an age impact assessment to carry out these kinds of reviews.

Bullying and harassment

Every individual member of staff has the right to be treated fairly and with dignity and respect. Harassment occurs when someone engages in unwanted conduct which has the purpose or effect of violating someone else's dignity or creating an intimidating, hostile, degrading, humiliating or offensive environment.

It is not the intention of the perpetrator which defines whether a particular type of conduct is harassment but the effect it has on the recipient.

Bullying is just as unacceptable as any other form of harassment.

People can become targets of harassment because of their age. Harassment could take the form of:

- inappropriate comments – for example, by suggesting someone is

- too old ('over the hill') or too young ('wet behind the ears') •
  offensive jokes

- exclusion from informal groups such as social events.

Example: George is in his 60s and works in an office with a team of younger colleagues in their 20s and 30s. The team, including the manager, often go out socialising. They do not ask George because they feel that he wouldn't like the venues they choose for such events. However, George finds out that many workplace issues and problems are discussed and resolved during these informal meetings. George feels undervalued and disengaged by this unintended action. This is a form of harassment, even though unintended, as George is being excluded from the team. To prevent this, the manager ought to consider office-based meetings to consult more fully with all staff in decision-making to prevent George feeling excluded because of his age.

Dealing with harassment

Make sure your anti-harassment policy covers age. You may have a stand alone policy or one that is part of a wider equal opportunities policy (for more detailed information see the Acas booklet *Tackling discrimination and promoting equality*).

If managers see unacceptable behaviour whether or not a complaint is made they need to treat the matter seriously and take action to eliminate the behaviour in question. This may involve just pointing out to someone the effect that their behaviour has on others and getting them to stop. If this informal approach fails, or in more serious cases, or where the person being harassed prefers it will be necessary to take formal action within the normal disciplinary procedures of the company or within the guidelines laid down by a specific anti-harassment policy.

For further information see the Acas leaflet *Bullying and harassment at work: a guide for managers and employers*.

Retirement

Pension age is when an employee can draw down their pension; for many, but not all, it is also the time when they can retire if they wish.

> **Retirement age** in this guidance is either the employer's normal retirement age (if there is one) or the default retirement age of 65.
>
> **Normal retirement age** means the age at which the employer requires employees in the same kind of position as the employee to retire.

The regulations set a default retirement age of 65 (to be reviewed in 2011). This means you can retire employees or set retirement ages within your company at or above 65. Retirements or retirement ages below the default retirement age will need to satisfy the test of objective justification (see page 30).

However, you do not have to have a fixed retirement age. Indeed, there are many business benefits to adopting a flexible approach to the employment and work patterns of older workers. Employees will have the right to request to continue working beyond their retirement date and you have a duty to give consideration to such requests.

Think about each request on an individual basis – taking into account opportunities to vary the employee's hours or the duties they perform. You are under no obligation to agree to such requests.

Fair retirement

A fair retirement is one that:

- takes effect on or after the default retirement age (or on or after the employer's normal retirement age – if there is one) and

- where the employer has given the employee written notice of the date of their intended retirement and told them about their right to request to continue working. (See below for the timing requirements of this notice).

If the employer's normal retirement age is below the age of 65, it must be objectively justified.

For the retirement to be classed as 'fair' you need to have informed the employee in writing of their intended retirement date and of their right to make a request to work beyond retirement age at least six months in advance (but no more than 12 months before the intended date). If they do make such a request, you must have followed the correct procedure for dealing with it. Annex 5 sets out a guidance flowchart for fair retirements.

Working beyond retirement date –
Notification of right to request to continue working

Introduction

You should notify the employee in writing of their right to request to go on working beyond their retirement date (at least six months in advance but no more than 12 months before the intended date).

When you write to the employee it is good practice to set out how you will manage the retirement process. Remind them of your obligation to give consideration to any request to work after the normal retirement age and in order not to raise the expectations of the employee, explain that you are entitled to refuse the request. You are not required to give a reason for your decision as – if you have followed the retirement procedure correctly (see Annex 5) – the reason for their dismissal will always be retirement.

However giving reasons and a more detailed explanation of your retirement policy may enable the employee to leave with dignity and respect and help you maintain good workplace relationships with other employees. This would be in line with normal good practice recommended by Acas.

If you choose to give reasons, take the time to consider what you are going to say and how you are going to say it. You must be careful not to suggest that you might be discriminating against the employee on the grounds of race, gender, disability, sexual orientation or religion or belief.

If the employee has been properly notified (as above) and wishes to continue working, they must request to do so more than three months before the intended retirement date.

If you fail to notify the employee six months in advance of retirement, you may be liable for compensation and you have an ongoing duty (up until two weeks before the retirement dismissal) to inform the employee of both the intended date and their right to request working longer. Failure to do this will make the dismissal automatically unfair.

If you fail to inform the employee of their intended retirement date and of their right to request to continue working, the employee will still be able to make a request not to retire at any stage until dismissal. If the employee does make a request the employment must continue until the day after the employer notifies the employee of their decision on the request.

Employees should be able to retire with dignity so try and use as much tact and sensitivity as possible.

Dealing with the request

If the employee requests in writing not to be retired this request must be considered before the employee is retired. Failure to do so will make the dismissal automatically unfair. You must meet the employee to discuss their request within a reasonable period of receiving it (unless agreeing to the request or it is not practicable to hold a meeting) and inform them in writing of your decision as soon as is reasonably practicable. The employee's employment continues until you have informed them of your decision on the request.

As preparation for this meeting, it would be good practice for you to reflect on the positive reasons why you should grant an extension, in particular:

- savings to the organisation in recruitment and training costs

- retaining the valuable experience and knowledge of the employee

Try to avoid making stereotypical assumptions about the capabilities of the employee. At the meeting the employee has a right to be accompanied by a colleague. There is the same right in relation to any subsequent appeal meeting.

The individual accompanying the employee must be:

- chosen by the employee

- a worker or trade union representative employed by the same employer as the employee

- permitted to address the meeting but not answer questions on behalf of the employee; and

- permitted to confer with the employee during the meeting.

The employee may appeal against your decision as soon as is reasonably practicable after receiving notification of your decision. If the employee does appeal, the appeal meeting should be held as soon as is reasonable. The employee may appeal the decision if you refuse the request in its entirety or if you accept it but decide to continue employing the employee for a shorter period than the employee requested. The appeal meeting can be held after the retirement has taken effect.

This procedure must be repeated each time an individual nears an extended point for retirement. Annex 6 sets out a guidance framework for retirement and the duty to consider.

As long as employers follow this procedure correctly they may rely on their normal retirement age (if they have one) or the default retirement age without the dismissal being regarded as unfair or age discriminatory. Where a dismissal is for reasons of retirement, the statutory dismissals procedure does not apply.

Transitional arrangements

There are transitional arrangements produced by the Department for Trade and Industry (DTI) for employees who are retiring on or shortly after 1 October 2006. These arrangements are available at the DTI website and are summarised at Annex 12 of this guide (see page 59).

Know your employees

You will probably have information that shows the ages of your employees. It makes sense to analyse this information (probably in age bands – see Annex 4) to get an age profile of your workforce.

This profile will help you decide whether there is a need for any remedial action.

For example, do you need to:

- plan for a retirement peak?

- take positive action to rectify any obvious imbalance in the age bands?

You can also use this profile to check that your entire workforce is getting access to training and other facilities.

Staff attitude surveys and exit interviews can also give you valuable insights into how people view their work and you as an employer, and help you to create a positive working environment.

It is important to monitor in this way if you wish to claim an objective justification or, when reviewing service related benefits, 'conclude' a business benefit (see section on genuine occupational requirements, objective justifications, exceptions and exemptions). In considering these matters you should always use evidence in your decision-making rather than merely continuing old working practices or relying on 'gut feeling' as these may be based on unfounded assumptions.

Annex 4 sets out a framework for age monitoring.

Positive action

You can take positive action to prevent or compensate for disadvantages linked to age.

This might involve:

- giving people of a particular age access to vocational training; or

- encouraging people of a particular age to take up employment opportunities.

Where it reasonably appears to the person undertaking such positive action that it will prevent or compensate for disadvantages linked to age that they have or may suffer.

For example, you might place advertisements where they are more likely to be seen by people in a disadvantaged group. Or you might limit access to a computer training course to those over 60 because they may have had less exposure to such training in the past.

Positive action on age can help you to attract people from all age groups in your local community.

Example: Green and Co, a transport company, see from their internal monitoring processes that the company has a mature age profile with disproportionately few workers under 40. Not wanting to miss out on the talents of all the local community, they include a statement in their next adverts saying 'We welcome applications from everyone irrespective of age but, as we are under-represented by people under 40, would especially welcome applications from these jobseekers. Appointment will be on merit alone'.

Objective justifications, exceptions, exemptions and genuine occupational requirements

Treating people differently because of their age will only be justifiable in the following exceptional circumstances.

Objective justification

You may treat people differently on the grounds of their age if you have an objective justification.

An objective justification allows employers to set requirements that are directly age discriminatory. Remember that different treatment on grounds of age will only be possible exceptionally for good reasons (see below).

You will need to provide real evidence to support any claim of objective justification. Assertion alone will not be sufficient and each case must be considered on its individual merits.

Both direct and indirect discrimination will be justified if it is:

● a proportionate means (of)

● achieving a legitimate aim.

What is proportionate?

This means:

259

- what you are doing must actually contribute to a legitimate aim, eg if your aim is to encourage loyalty then you ought to have evidence that the provision or criterion you introduce is actually doing so

- the discriminatory effect should be significantly outweighed by the importance and benefits of the legitimate aim

- you should have no reasonable alternative to the action you are taking. If the legitimate aim can be achieved by less or nondiscriminatory means then these must take precedence.

What is a legitimate aim?

A legitimate aim might include:

- economic factors such as business needs and efficiency

- the health, welfare and safety of the individual (including protection of young people or older workers)

- the particular training requirements of the job.

A legitimate aim must correspond with a real need of the employer – economic efficiency may be a real aim but saving money because discrimination is cheaper than non-discrimination is not legitimate. The legitimate aim cannot be related to age discrimination itself.

The test of objective justification is not an easy one and it will be necessary to provide evidence if challenged; assertions alone will not be enough.

Jones and Company are unsure if they need an objective justification. To help make the decision they ask themselves:

- STOP – Why do we want to do this?

- Set out the reason clearly on paper

- Do we have evidence to support us in this reason?

- Are we certain this is real hard evidence and not just based on assumptions?

- Is there an alternative less or non-discriminatory way of achieving the same result?

The HR director seeks a second opinion from the Board and keeps all records of how the decision was made in case it is reviewed in the future.

In a smaller company, you could consult your partner or colleague.

Exceptions and exemptions

There are also exceptions to or exemptions from the age regulations in the following areas:

- pay and other employment benefits based on length of service

- pay related to the National Minimum Wage

- acts under statutory authority

- enhanced redundancy

- life assurance

- retirement (see separate section on page 23)

- occupational pension systems (not covered in this guidance).

Exemptions based on length of service

In many cases employers require a certain length of service before increasing or awarding a benefit such as holiday entitlement. Without the exemptions contained in the regulations this could often amount to indirect age discrimination because some age groups are more likely to have completed the length of service than others.

Any benefit earned by five years service or less will be exempt. Employers may use pay scales that reflect growing experience or limit the provision of non-pay benefits to those who have served a qualifying period, subject to the five-year limit.

The use of length of service of more than five years for all types of employment benefits is lawful if:

- awarding or increasing the benefit is meant to reflect a higher level of experience of the employee, or to reward loyalty, or to increase or maintain the motivation of the employee;

- the employer has reasonable grounds for concluding that using length of service in this way fulfils a business need of his undertaking.

In order to meet these requirements employers would need evidence from which they can conclude there is a benefit to the organisation. This could include information the employer might have gathered through monitoring, staff attitude surveys or focus groups for example.

Introduction

National Minimum wage

Nothing in the regulations will alter the provisions of the National Minimum Wage. The exemption linked to the National Minimum Wage will allow employers using exactly the same age bands, ie 16 and 17, 18 to 21 and 22 and over, to pay at or above the national minimum rates provided those in the lower age group(s) are paid less than the adult minimum wage.

This will allow an employer to pay those aged 22 and over more than those aged under 22 as long as those under 22 are paid less than the minimum adult rate; likewise an employer may pay those aged 18 to 21 more than those under 18 as long as those under 18 are paid less than the minimum adult rate. The exemption does not allow employers to pay different rates to those in the same age category. Apprentices not entitled to the National Minimum Wage may continue to be paid at a lower rate than those that are.

Acts under statutory authority

Age criteria are widely used in legislation, notably to qualify for various licences. Where this is the case the employer must follow the criteria laid down by statute and will not be contravening the age regulations by doing so.

Enhanced redundancy payments

The statutory redundancy scheme will not substantially change (except in respect of the years worked when an employee was below 18 or over 64). Both the statutory authority exemption and this regulation make it clear that, even though statutory redundancy payments are calculated using age-related criteria, such payments are lawful.

The exemption linked to statutory redundancy payments is for an employer who wants to make more generous redundancy payments than under the statutory scheme. It allows the employer to use one of the methods specified, based on the statutory redundancy scheme, to calculate the amount of redundancy payment. An employer can use a different method of their own to calculate the amount of redundancy payment, but if it is based on length of service and if an employee brings a discrimination claim under the regulations, the employer will have to objectively justify it in so far as age discrimination arises. (This is because the exception for pay and benefits based on length of service does not apply to redundancy payments).

The exemption allows the employer to either raise or remove the maximum amount of a week's pay so that a higher amount of pay is used in the calculation, or multiply the total amount calculated by a figure of more than one, or both. Having done this, the employer may again multiply the total by a figure of more that one.

The exemption also allows an employer to make a redundancy payment to an employee who has taken voluntary redundancy, and an employee with less than two years continuous employment. In such cases, where no statutory redundancy payment is required, an employer may make a payment equivalent to the statutory minimum payment, or if they so wish an enhanced payment as above.

Life assurance cover

Some employers provide life assurance cover for their workers. If a worker retires early due to ill health, the employer may continue to provide that life assurance cover for that worker. This exemption allows an employer to stop doing so when the worker reaches the age at which he would have retired had he not fallen ill. If there was no normal retirement age at which the worker would have retired, the employer can stop providing life assurance cover when the worker reaches 65.

Genuine occupational requirement (GOR)

In very limited circumstances, it will be lawful for an employer to treat people differently if it is a genuine occupational requirement that the job holder must be of a particular age. When deciding if this applies, it is necessary to consider the nature of the work and the context in which it is carried out. Jobs may change over time and you should review whether the requirement continues to apply, particularly when recruiting.

Example: An organisation advising on and promoting rights for older people may be able to show that it is essential that its chief executive – who will be the public face of the organisation – is of a certain age. The age of the holder of the post may be a genuine occupational requirement.

Guidance for the Individual

What do I do if I think I have suffered discrimination or harassment?

Expressing your concerns

If you think you are being harassed or discriminated against it is a good idea to make it clear to the person who is harassing you that their behaviour is unwelcome and that you want it to stop. However, you do not have to do this, particularly if you are feeling bullied or intimidated. If you do choose to address your concerns to the person, be clear and assertive but take care that you are not perceived to be bullying the individual. Some people may find it helpful to ask a friend, colleague, welfare officer or trade union representative to be with them in a support role.

If speaking to the person in question has failed to stop the problem, you should talk to your manager or your trade union representative. If it is your manager or supervisor who is harassing you, speak to someone higher up. Employers should deal with such complaints quickly, thoroughly and sympathetically.

It is usually best to try and sort things out quickly and as close to the problem as possible. If your organisation has a personnel or human resources department or an equality adviser you might find it helpful to talk to them. Discrimination can happen accidentally or through thoughtlessness. Harassment can be unintentional. Often, once a manager understands the problem, he or she will be willing to try and put things right.

Using the grievance procedure

If your manager is unable to help you, or refuses to help you, you must use your organisation's grievance procedure if you wish to proceed with your complaint. All organisations should have a grievance procedure by law. You also have a legal right to be accompanied by a trade union representative or a work colleague at any hearing into your grievance.

If you are not satisfied with the result of a grievance procedure, you have a right of appeal which should be heard, if the organisation's size allows it, by someone different from the person who conducted the original grievance hearing. You have a right to be accompanied by a trade union representative or a work colleague during the appeal hearing.

Making a claim to an employment tribunal

When you have tried all these things, or if your employer does not have a grievance procedure, or if you feel too intimidated to use the internal procedures, you may be able to bring a complaint to an employment tribunal under the age regulations. You do not have to hand in your notice to bring such a complaint. As part of your employment tribunal claim, you can require your employer to answer a set of questions about discrimination in your workplace. A questionnaire is available on the DTI website (www.dti.gov.uk) and from jobcentres and citizens advice bureaux.

You and any witnesses have a right not to be victimised for following up a grievance or complaining to an employment tribunal under these regulations provided the complaint was made in good faith.

If you have been dismissed because you objected to conduct towards you, you may be able to bring a complaint of unfair dismissal to an employment tribunal.

Complaints to an employment tribunal must normally be brought within three months of the act you are complaining about. Care should be taken to ensure that the three month point is not exceeded during any internal grievance/appeals process.

Retirement

You now have the right to request to continue working beyond your expected retirement date. If you do so your employer must give consideration to your request if you have made it in time and if they turn it down you have the right to appeal to the employer. If you do not make the request to continue working within three months of your expected date of retirement you may lose your opportunity to continue working.

You will not automatically be allowed to work beyond your expected retirement. Your employer does not have to agree to your request or give you a reason for turning it down.

If you want to continue working beyond your expected retirement date, but perhaps with alternative or variable working patterns take the initiative and discuss this with your employer at an early stage. Your employer does not have to agree to vary your job but early discussion could help highlight the mutual benefits of a different pattern of work or combination of duties.

Take advantage of training and development opportunities in the years approaching retirement. It will help you to make a stronger case for continuing to work.

Your employer should inform you of their intended retirement date for you and your right to request to continue working at least six months, but no more than twelve months, before the intended date. If your employer does not do this you may have the right to eight weeks pay as compensation.

If you ask to continue working, your employer should hold a meeting with you to consider your request. You have a right to be accompanied by a work colleague or trade union representative at the meeting. The trade union representative must also be a work colleague. You must be told the result of your request as soon as is reasonably practicable after the meeting. You can appeal against the decision if your request is not met. You will need to give your employer notice of the appeal as soon as is reasonably practicable after you have received his decision.

There will no longer be an upper age limit on unfair dismissal claims. The statutory redundancy payments scheme is also being adjusted to remove upper and lower age limits as is statutory sick pay and maternity pay.

Further Guidance for Employers

Some frequently asked questions

Q Do the regulations only cover older employees?

A No. The regulations cover workers of all ages – young and old.

Q Can I ask for a candidate's date of birth on the application form?

A Yes. But asking for age-related information on an application form could allow discrimination to take place. Remove the date of birth/age from the main application form and include it in a diversity monitoring form to be retained by HR/personnel. In addition review your application form to ensure that you are not asking for unnecessary information about periods and dates.

Q Am I responsible for what an employment agency does?

A Yes. If you use a recruitment agency you need to be sure the agency acts appropriately and in accordance with your company's equality and diversity policies.

Q Do I have to do anything new or different when the legislation comes in?

A Yes. Include age in your equality policy. Consider adding all forms of discrimination and harassment (sex, race, disability, gender reassignment, sexual orientation and religion or belief) to your disciplinary rules. These rules should also include bullying.

Make sure all employees are aware (through training, noticeboards, circulars, contracts of employment, etc) that it is not only unacceptable to discriminate, harass or victimise someone on the grounds of age, it is also unlawful. Make it clear that you will not tolerate such behaviour.

Individuals should know what to do if they believe they have been discriminated against or harassed, or if they believe someone else is being discriminated against or harassed. This should be included in the grievance procedure.

Reminder: The Employment Act 2002 requires all employers, however large or small, to have both a disciplinary and a grievance procedure.

Check your policies for retirement and redundancy. Upper age limits on unfair dismissal claims and redundancy payments will be removed. There will be a default retirement age of 65, making compulsory retirement below 65 unlawful unless objectively justified.

Give serious consideration to the benefits of flexible working. All employees will also have the right to request to work beyond 65 or any other retirement age set by the organisation. You have a duty to consider such requests.

Q Must I have an equality policy?

A No. However, an equality policy is the best way of demonstrating that you take discrimination seriously and have steps in place to tackle it. The policy should set the minimum standard of behaviour expected of all employees through recruitment right through to retirement. It also spells out what employees can expect from the organisation. It gives employees confidence that they will be treated with dignity and respect, and may be used as an integral part of a grievance or disciplinary process if necessary. If you would like help putting an equality policy in place Acas can help – call our helpline on 08457 47 47 47.

Q Do these regulations cover all workers?

A Yes. The regulations apply to all workers, including office holders, police, barristers and partners in a business. They also cover related areas such as membership of trade organisations, the award of qualifications, the services of careers guidance organisations, employment agencies and vocational training providers, including further and higher education institutions.

The regulations also cover anyone who applies to an organisation for work, or who already works for an organisation – whether they are directly employed, work under some other kind of contract, or are an agency worker. You will also be responsible for the behaviour of your employees towards an individual working for someone else but on their premises, for example someone from another organisation repairing a piece of your equipment.

Employees are sometimes harassed by third parties, such as customers or clients. Where possible you should protect your employees from such harassment and take steps to deal with actual or potential situations of this kind. This will enhance your reputation as a good employer and make the organisation a welcoming and safe place to work.

Many organisations provide visitors and visiting workers with guidance on health and safety matters. It may be appropriate to include some comments on your organisation's attitude to harassment.

However the default retirement age and the duty to consider procedure apply only to a narrower group of employees – this does not include office holders, partners, barristers etc. Refer to the regulations for the precise definition.

Q I am a partner, am I covered by the regulations?

A Yes, you are covered by the regulations except for the provisions covering retirement and the right to request. Partnerships will need to objectively justify their decisions on age issues and for retirement. It would be sensible for partners to have clear records of these decisions at partnership meetings to show they meet business objectives, are properly considered and regularly reviewed. Such records may help support any case for objective justification.

Q No one in my organisation has ever complained of discrimination or harassment so I don't need to do anything new, do I?

A People do not always feel able or confident enough to complain, particularly if the harasser is a manager or senior executive. Sometimes they will simply resign. One way to find out is to undertake exit interviews when people leave and to ask them if they have ever felt harassed, bullied or discriminated against in the workplace. If it is possible, exit interviews should be undertaken by someone out of the individual's line of management, for instance a personnel officer.

Discrimination includes harassment which can take place without management being aware of it. Make sure all your employees understand that harassment means any unwanted behaviour that makes someone feel intimidated, degraded, humiliated or offended.

This includes teasing, tormenting, name calling and gossip and it applies to whoever the perpetrator may be. The victim's perception of the effect of the behaviour is also important.

Take all possible steps to make sure employees understand that they and their management teams will not tolerate such behaviour and that they will deal with whoever is causing the problem.

Q Should I take positive action to promote age diversity?

A Your business could benefit from employing people of different ages. The law allows you to introduce positive action measures where you can demonstrate that employees of a particular age are at a career disadvantage or are under represented in the organisation (see page 29).

Annexes

Annex 1: An age healthcheck

Purpose

These questions are designed to kick start the planning and thinking process in your organisation. The answers to these questions should tell you if:

- any key personnel decisions are influenced by age

- your recruitment is attracting people from everyone in the local community.

The Checklist

1   Look at your records to establish your company age profile – insert 16–21, 22–30, 31–40, 41–50, 51–60, 60–65, 65+ (These age bands are for illustration only; you may wish to choose different ones to suit your company circumstances.) Compare this to census data available from websites, libraries, business and Chambers of Commerce. What do you find?

2   Look at your application forms for recent recruitments and compare with your age profile. Are you missing out on potential talent? **Yes/No**

3   Is your equality and diversity policy visibly supported by your board and chief executive? **Yes/No**

4   Do you train employees to recognise and tackle age discrimination? **Yes/No**

5   Is age ever used as a factor in staff recruitment/selection or training and development? **Yes/No**

     If yes, can it be justified? **Yes/No**

6   Do you offer variable and alternative working patterns to employees regardless of age? **Yes/No**

7   Are your managers aware of what behaviour could be perceived as harassment on the grounds of age? Yes/No/Not Sure

8   Do you have an action plan to ensure you are compliant with the age regulations in October 2006? **Yes/No**

Introduction

Annex 2: Age action plan – some potential quick wins

Purpose

To make your action plan successful:

- Agree who is responsible for the plan
- Launch it with the support of the head of your organisation
- Agree who should be involved and consulted, for example line managers, personnel staff, trade unions, other stakeholders
- Make sure your partners and suppliers support your action plan
- Agree and publish timescales for when you will do things and prioritise key objectives before October 2006
- Get feedback from employees and address their concerns/questions.

Some quick win areas for the action plan

1 Recruitment, promotion and selection

- Remove ageist language (see page 12) from job and promotion adverts and focus on the needs of the job. In the short-term make someone responsible for 'vetting' the wording
- In performance assessments challenge phrases that make assumptions about an individual and focus on actual performance
- Look at where you advertise and how you advertise to ensure you reach the whole labour market
- Train selectors in anti age discrimination
- Monitor and publish your results to show you mean business.

2 Hearts and minds

- Deliver a programme of age awareness training to all employees to focus on:

  – tackling deep seated stereotypes; and

  – bullying and harassment.

- Review company literature for age bias, look to how your organisation might be perceived by younger or older employees. If someone feels fully engaged with an organisation they are likely to be more productive.

3 Retirement and knowledge management

- Recognise that senior employees have a wealth of experiences that are valuable and can help the organisation. Set up a system to capture this knowledge.

- Make your retirement policy well known and treat requests to stay after retirement as an opportunity to retain knowledge.

Annex 3: Practical impact assessing for age bias in policies

Purpose

Impact assessments are designed to measure the impact of policies and processes on different groups of people. They can help to inform planning and decision-making.

Ask yourself:

- What is the purpose of a policy or practice?

- What is it achieving?

- Do any age groups benefit and, if so, do any not? And how?

What are the differences and adverse outcomes (if any) by age group.

To answer these questions you will need to look at:

- Your monitoring data (see section 'Know your staff' and Annex 4)

- Anecdotal views from managers and employee representatives about the way a policy is working locally

- Attitude surveys, focus groups, exit interviews and specific research and evaluation exercises you may wish to carry out

- What has worked elsewhere and why by comparing your data with that of other business groups/employer organisations.

This process will give you evidence of different outcomes by age groups. It is important to remember that not all differences are necessarily wrong and you need to ask the question 'is it justifiable for this to continue?' Our guidance on objective justification can give some pointers here.

Introduction

We would suggest that it would be good practice to undertake these assessments openly in the organisation as a sign of your commitment to tackle unwitting age discrimination.

Annex 4: Age monitoring – a framework

Monitoring the effect of the anti-age discrimination regulations can help you to:

- identify any problems
- gather evidence that might be needed by the courts for objective justification of any age discrimination (see page 30).

The following age bands might provide a useful starting point for gathering your information:

16–21, 22–30, 31–40, 41–50, 51–60, 60–65, 65+

Keep records on how all your employees fit into these age bands.

Also keep data on employees who:

- Apply for jobs (and those who are successful)
- Apply for training (and those who receive training)
- Apply for promotion (and those who are successful)
- Are being assessed to measure their performance
- Are involved in disciplinary and grievance processes (and the outcomes of these processes)
- Leave the organisation.

Another source of monitoring information are staff attitude surveys that can be used in concluding a business benefit when considering the exemptions surrounding service-related benefits.

Staff consultation groups and trade unions can also be valuable sources of information that can add to raw data figures.

Annex 5: Fair retirement flow chart

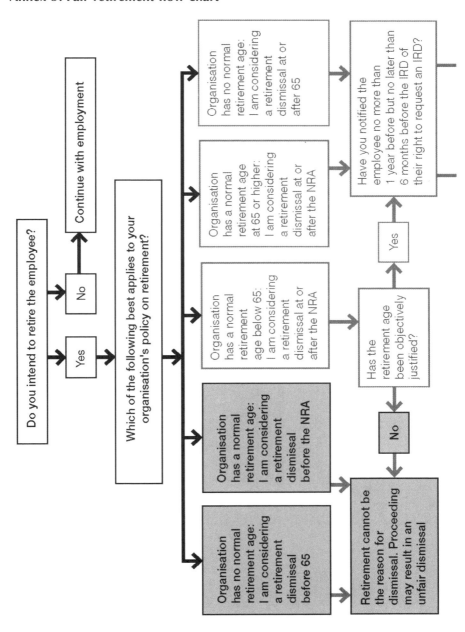

Notes: NRA means normal retirement age IRD means intended retirement date

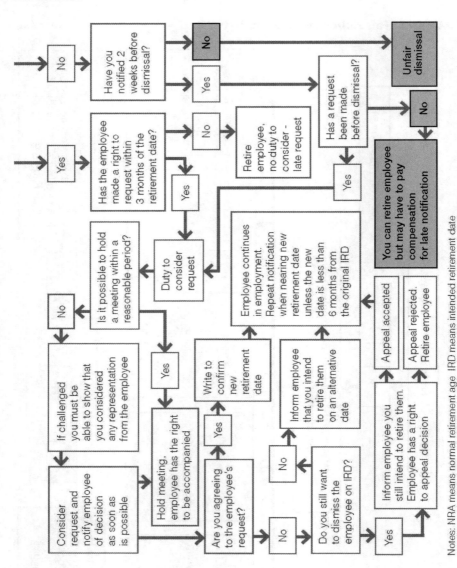

Notes: NRA means normal retirement age   IRD means intended retirement date

Annex 6: Request to work beyond retirement flow chart

Employer – Pre-Retirement
If you intend to retire the employee you must inform the employee of the retirement date, in writing, no more than one year but no later than six months before the intended retirement and that they have a right to request to work beyond the retirement age.

Employee – Responding to your employer's notification
When your employer has notified you of your intended retirement date and your right to request, if you want to request working beyond retirement age you must inform your employer no less than three months before the intended retirement date. Your request to your employer must be in writing and state whether you wish to continue work:

- indefinitely
- for a stated period
- or until a certain date.

You may only make one request in relation to each intended retirement date. If your employer has failed to notify you of your intended retirement date six months before that date, you may still make a request not to retire at any time before you retire.

Employer – Responding to your employee's request
When you receive your employee's request you must normally hold a meeting with your employee to discuss the request. If you accept there is no need to hold a meeting; simply amend the employee's contract of employment to reflect the new intended retirement date, and if required, the new employment pattern.

If after considering the request, you decide that you do wish to continue with the retirement you should hold a meeting with the employee. This will enable the employee to put their case to you. The employee has a right to be accompanied at the meeting.

The companion can be:

- chosen by the employee
- a worker or trade union representative employed by you or the organisation.

The companion can:

- address the meeting but not answer questions on behalf of the employee
- confer with the employee during the meeting.

The meeting must be held within a reasonable period after the request has been received from the employee. If the meeting cannot be held within a reasonable period, you may inform the employee of your decision in writing as long as you have considered any representation made by the employee.

Employee – The meeting to consider your request
If your employer does not accept your request, they must still offer you a meeting to discuss it. This is your opportunity to put your case before your employer. You have a right to be accompanied at the meeting.

The companion can be:

- chosen by you; but must be
- a worker or trade union representative employed by the same employer.

The companion can:

- address the meeting but not answer questions on your behalf
- confer with you during the meeting.

It is important to remember that your companion cannot answer questions on your behalf. You must take all reasonable steps to attend the meeting, although if it is not possible to hold the meeting within a reasonable period your employer may inform you of their decision in writing.

(continued)

The meeting
The meeting is an opportunity for the employee to put their case before the employer. At the end of the meeting the employer may decide that whilst they cannot accept the employee's stated request, there may be a compromise solution. It is perfectly acceptable for the employer to propose alternative working patterns and retirement dates, other than those proposed by the employee, if the employer is persuaded by the employee's case not to be retired.

Employer – Post-meeting action
If, after the meeting, you decide to accept the employee's request you should inform them that you have accepted the request and state the new employment pattern and when the new intended retirement date will be.

Where the decision is to refuse the request you should confirm with them that you still wish to retire them – either on the original intended retirement date or an alternative later date.

Any decision should be given in writing and should be dated. The employee has a right to appeal the employer's decision, or a decision on a new intended retirement date if it is shorter than the intended retirement proposed by the employee in the employee's initial request.

Employee – Post-meeting
The employer will inform you as soon as is reasonable after the meeting of their decision. If the employer rejects your request or proposes a new intended retirement date that is less than that in your original request, you may ask for an appeal meeting.

Appeal meeting
The appeal meeting is the final opportunity for the employee to put their case before the employer. At the end of the meeting the employer may decide that whilst they cannot accept the employee's stated request, there may be a compromise solution. It is perfectly acceptable for the employer to propose alternative working patterns and retirement dates, other than those proposed by the employee, if the employer is persuaded by the employee's case not to be retired.

Employer – Post-appeal meeting action
If, after the meeting you decide to accept the employee's request, you should inform them that you have accepted the appeal and state the new employment pattern and when the new intended retirement date will be.

Where the decision is to reject the appeal you should confirm with them that you still wish to retire them and the date that the dismissal is to take effect.

Any decision should be given in writing and should be dated.

Employee – Post-appeal meeting
The employer will inform you as soon as is reasonable after the appeal meeting of their decision. If your request is accepted, or a compromise solution is reached, the employer should inform you in writing of that decision.

If your appeal is rejected the employer is obliged to inform you of this in writing and of the date of your retirement. The employer does not need to give a reason why your application has been rejected.

Annex 7: Example of a letter informing employee of their retirement date

Letter to inform employee of their retirement date and of their right to make a request.

Note to employer: You must inform the employee no more than one year but no later than six months before their retirement date what the intended retirement date is and that they have a right to request not to be retired. Failure to inform the employee of the date and their right may mean that the dismissal is unfair. This letter should only be used if you are complying with the above time limits. If you do not, you are under an obligation to consider a request made by the employee at any time before retirement takes effect. You can get additional guidance on retirement from Acas.

Dear: Staff Number:

Date:

1   I am writing to inform you that your retirement date will be *[insert date]* and that you have a right to request not to be retired.

1a I will give careful consideration to any request you may make to work beyond this date and will inform you if I cannot let you. I am not required by law to give a reason.

2   Your request not to be retired must be returned to *[insert name]* no later than three months before the date stated in paragraph 1. Failure to do so will mean that you lose your statutory right to have your request considered and you will be retired on the retirement date above.

Name: | Signature:

Date:

Introduction

Annex 8: Example of a letter informing employee of a meeting to discuss a request not to retire

Note to employer: The meeting to discuss the request should be held within a reasonable period after the request has been received. The employee has a right to be accompanied at the meeting.

The companion can be:

- chosen by the employee
- a worker employed by you or the organisation.

The companion can:

- address the meeting but not answer questions on behalf of the employee
- confer with the employee during the meeting.

Dear: Staff Number:

Date:

I am writing to inform you that after receiving your request not to be retired that there will be a meeting to discuss your request.

The meeting will be held on *[insert date]* at *[insert time]* at *[insert location]*.

You have a right to be accompanied at the meeting by a fellow worker or a trade union representative. Your companion may be someone that you have chosen, but they must work for *[insert name of organisation]*. Your companion can address the meeting but not answer questions on your behalf although you may confer with your companion during the meeting.

After the meeting if it is decided to continue your employment beyond the intended retirement date of *[insert date]* you will receive written notification reflecting these agreed changes to your contract.

If no agreement is reached you will receive further notification confirming your intended retirement date and informing you of your right to appeal.

Name: Signature:

Date:

280

Annex 9: Example of a letter confirming retirement on the intended date

Note to employer: If after the meeting to discuss the employee's request not to be retired, you decided that you still wish to retire the employee, you must inform them as soon as is reasonably practicable. You must also inform them that they have a right to appeal

---

Dear: Staff Number:

Date:

I am writing to inform you that after our meeting held on *[insert date]* to discuss your request not to be retired, that *[insert organisation]* still intends to retire you on *[insert intended retirement date]*.

You have a right to appeal this decision. If you wish to appeal you must inform *[insert name]* as soon as is reasonable. Failure to do so may mean that you lose the right to an appeal meeting and *[insert organisation's name]* may consider your appeal without holding a meeting but they will consider any previous representations that you have made.

Name: Signature:

Date:

Introduction

Annex 10: Example of a letter to employee notifying the result of their appeal

Note to employer: You must hold the appeal meeting to discuss the employee's appeal not to be retired as soon as is reasonably practicable. If it is not reasonably practicable to hold an appeal meeting within a period that is reasonable you may consider the appeal without holding a meeting as long as you consider any representations that the employee has made.

Dear: Staff Number:

Date:

I am writing to inform you that after our meeting held on *[insert date]* to discuss your appeal not to be retired, that *[insert organisation]* still intends to retire you on *[insert intended retirement date]*.

Name: | Signature:

Date:

Annex 11: Example of a letter to employee confirming new retirement date

Note to employer: You should use this letter if you accept the employee's request or appeal.

Dear: Staff Number:

Date:

I am writing to inform you that following our meeting to consider your request not to be retired/appeal meeting *[delete as appropriate]* *[insert organisation]* has agreed that your new intended retirement date shall be *[insert date]*.

As agreed at the meeting to discuss your request not to be retired/ appeal meeting *[delete as appropriate]* your new working pattern will be as follows. *[Delete this paragraph if no new working pattern is agreed]*.

Name:	Signature:

Date:

Introduction

Annex 12: Retirement – transitional arrangements applicable up to 1 April 2007

Transitional arrangements apply to retirements from 1 October 2006 to 31 March 2007 because the DTI recognises that:

Where an employee is due to retire soon after 1 October 2006 the procedures for ensuring a retirement dismissal is fair are summarised below.

Notice given before 1 October 2006

If the employee is given notice before 1 October that they are to be retired after 1 October 2006 but before 1 April 2007:

notice must be at least the period required by the contract of employment;

or

where the employee is already serving a long period of notice required by the contract that exceeds four weeks, the employer must give at least four weeks notice before the 1 October 2006 to ensure the employee is aware and given the statutory minimum period of notice for retirement.

On 1 October, or as soon practicable afterwards, the employer must write to the employee telling them of their right to request working longer.

The employee can make such a request after their contract has been terminated but not more than four weeks afterwards.

A meeting to discuss the request, and any subsequent appeal meeting, must be held within a reasonable period. The employee can ask to be accompanied by a companion.

Notice given after 1 October 2006

If the employee is given notice after 1 October that they are to be retired before 1 April 2007 the employer must:

- write to the employee notifying them of the intended retirement date

- giving the longer of contractual or statutory notice; and

- tell them in writing that they have a right to request working longer.

An employee who wants to exercise this right should make a written request:

- where possible, four weeks before the intended retirement date; or

- as soon as reasonably practicable after being notified of the 'right to request'.

The request can be made after the employee's contract has been terminated but not more than four weeks after termination. A meeting to discuss the request, and any subsequent appeal meeting, must be held within a reasonable period. The employee can ask to be accompanied by a companion.

Anyone retiring on or after 1 April 2007 will be subject to the full retirement procedure set out in the Employment Equality (Age) Regulations 2006 and described in this guidance.

ACAS Age and the Workplace – Putting the Employment Equality (Age) Regulations 2006 into practice are reproduced by kind permission of ACAS.

Index

[all references are to page number]

A

ACAS Guidance
annexes
  age action plan, 270–271
  age health-check, 269
  age monitoring, 272
  example letters, 279–283
  fair retirement flow chart,
    273–274
  impact assessments, 271–272
  request to work beyond retire-
    ment flow chart, 275–278
  transitional arrangements,
    284–285
employees, for, 263–266
employers, for
  FAQ, 266–268
  generally, 242–258
  justification and exceptions,
    259–263
  know your employees, 258–259
example letters
  confirming new retirement date,
    283
  confirming retirement on
    intended date, 281
  informing employee of meeting
    to discuss request not to
    retire, 280
  informing employee of retire-
    ment date, 279
  notifying result of appeal, 282
generally, 3
introduction, 240–241
summary, 241–242
Actuarial calculations
occupational pension schemes,
  and, 110
Admissions
occupational pension schemes,
  and, 109–110
Advertising
ACAS Guidance, 247–248
checklist, 66

practical issues, 61–62
Advocates
scope of protection, and, 30
text of Regulations, 158–159
Age action plan
ACAS Guidance, 270–271
Age discrimination
introduction, 1–3
text of Regulations, 147
Age discrimination awareness
ACAS Guidance, 251–252
Age Discrimination Regulations
citation, 145
commencement date
  generally, 2
  text, 145
definitions, 145–146
discrimination in employment and
  vocational training, 148–165
enforcement, 170–176
exceptions, 166–170
general provisions, 147–148
interpretation, 145–146
introduction, 1–2
other unlawful acts, 165–166
Regulatory Impact Assessment, 1
schedules
  amendments to legislation,
    208–225
  collective agreements, 193–195
  'duty-to-consider', 195–207
  Frigg Gas Field, 177–179
  pension schemes, 179–188
  questionnaire of person
    aggrieved, 188–189
  repeals and revocations, 226
  reply by respondent, 189–190
  rules of undertakings, 193–195
  validity of contracts, 190–183
structure, 2–3
supplemental, 176–177
text, 145–226
Age health-check
ACAS Guidance, 269
Age limits
recruitment and selection, and, 53

287